America at the Polls
1996

America at the Polls
1996

General Editors:

Regina Dougherty
Everett C. Ladd
David Wilber
Lynn Zayachkiwsky

Roper Center•University of Connecticut

Occasional Papers and Monographs Series #5

ISBN 1-887415-02-5

Printed by Hall & Bill Printing Company, Willimantic, CT.

In Memory of
John W. Brennan, Jr.
and
Mary Komarnicki Yankelovich

CONTENTS

Preface

We are gratified by the reception *America at the Polls 1994* received. We believe that we learned from that publishing experience, and that *American at the Polls 1996* does an even better job of bringing together the essential election data and interpretation.

Many individuals contributed to this effort. The Roper Center staff and outside authors who worked on this volume are identified on the Contributors page at the end of this volume. Their fine (and prompt) efforts in compiling the data and in analyzing them are deeply appreciated.

We are especially pleased to acknowledge the generosity and the assistance of many polling organizations, who again made their data readily available to the Roper Center archive and to this volume. We can't list everyone—there were just too many national and state polling groups who helped us. Large and essential contributions were made by: ABC News, American Viewpoint, the Associated Press, CBS News, Chilton Research Services, CNN, the Field Poll, Fox News, the Gallup Organization, Gordon S. Black Corporation, Louis Harris & Associates, Peter D. Hart Research Associates, ICR Survey Research Group, Lake Research, the *Los Angeles Times*, the National Opinion Research Center, NBC News, *Newsweek*, *The New York Times*, Opinion Dynamics Corporation, The Pew Center for the People & the Press, Princeton Survey Research Associates, Reuters, The Tarrance Group, *Time*, *USA Today*, *US News and World Report*, *The Wall Street Journal*, *The Washington Post*, the Wirthlin Group, Yankelovich Partners, and the Zogby Group.

We want to extend special thanks to the *Los Angeles Times* for releasing the entire dataset from their national exit poll to us so soon after the November 5 balloting, and to Voter News Service for providing extensive top-line data from each state as well as the national exit poll.

Other individuals and research organizations contributed important data and assistance bearing on the election. The help extended by Rhodes Cook and other staff of *Congressional Quarterly*, the National Council of State Legislatures, Curtis Gans of the Committee for the Study of the American Electorate, Joan Ponessa of the Public Affairs Research Institute of New Jersey, Robert Biersack of the Federal Election Commission, and Karlyn Bowman of the American Enterprise Institute for Public Policy Research was especially important in completing this volume.

Closer to home, Karen Orfitelli—the newest member of our staff—took time during her first week of work to help in proofing this volume.

We estimate that *America at the Polls 1996* contains some 20,000 discrete items of information from the polls and actual elections tallies. We would hope that not one of them is incorrect. We know full well, however, that so complex a task of information compilation and display as we provide here cannot actually pass entirely error-free. We alone are responsible for any errors that might appear in the pages that follow.

—RMD
—ECL
—DW
—LAZ

Chapter 1

The 1996 Election and Postindustrial Realignment
By Everett C. Ladd

Two years ago, my colleagues and I at the Roper Center published *America at the Polls, 1994*, a comprehensive compilation of survey and aggregate vote data on this important off-year election. Now, we are pleased to bring forth the second volume in this biennial election series, *America at the Polls, 1996*. We call it a "databook." Its animating premise is that the essential data on who voted how, and why, properly assembled, are not only valuable as a convenient factual source of

> *If the dominant impulses of industrialization were centralizing and government-enhancing, those of the postindustrial years are the polar opposite. In the economic and technological spheres, dispersion and decentralization have proceeded apace. In this new setting, centering political power in national government bureaucracies has become increasingly anomalous.*

election information—"between two covers"—for researchers and students, but that to a large degree they speak for themselves. They tell the election's story.

In places, though, the numbers need some help, and we have interspersed interpretive essays among them. My purpose in this introductory essay is to locate the 1996 contest for control of the presidency and Congress in its broader context— the sociopolitical period in which it occurred.

A Status-Quo Election

In multiple understandings of the term, the 1996 vote was a status-quo election. It was obviously such in the sense it left control of the government essentially unchanged. The Republicans retained their majorities in both the House (where their margin dropped from the 32-seat edge they enjoyed following the 1994 balloting to 20 seats now) and the Senate (where they gained two seats, bringing their majority to 55-45)—making this the first time the GOP has managed congressional majorities for consecutive terms since 1928. But while this was happening, President Clinton won reelection, by a margin similar to the one he gained over George Bush four years earlier. What's more, Clinton again won despite persisting doubts about his character—because his political skills surpassed his opponent's, and because the

economy (seen as bad in 1992, good in 1996) was on his side again. (See Chapter 3, pp. 38-39 and Chapter 4, pp. 72-75).

It was a status-quo election, though, in a more fundamental sense. The partisan realignment that ushered in our contemporary system is now fully mature, its essential features set. One large part of it involves a shift in the agenda of politics—what I will call the "philosophical realignment." This part is clear and decisive, but the other principal element, involving the parties' competitive standings, is far more ambiguous. The Democrats have long since lost the majority status they held from the New Deal to the Great Society, but the Republicans have not been able to claim the mantle. Voters again chose in 1996 to divide control of national government between the two major parties. Finally, 1996 repeated the patterns of social group voting that began emerging in the latter 1960s.

The parties and elections system we know today has evolved in response to postindustrialism. The present system is distinguished by (1) (as noted above) a *philosophical realignment* which finds the electorate significantly more conservative than in the preceding era, especially in the sense of being far less inclined to accept claims that more government represents progress; (2) markedly weakened ties of voters to the political parties; (3) television's dominance as the campaign medium; (4) the absence of a true majority party and (5) divided partisan control of government; and (6) a sharply different composition and alignment of social groups than were seen in the New Deal years—reflecting central structural features of the postindustrial economy, and the group conflicts and cultural tensions of this era.[1]

Vote For President, '92 and '96

	Clinton	Dole	Perot	Dem. over Rep. Margin
1996	49.2	40.8	8.5	8.4
1992	43.0	37.4	18.9	5.6

Understanding "Realignment": Definitions and Controversies

Three different definitions of realignment have been in circulation: (1) the dictionary meaning, which is the most general; (2) the understanding common in most media discussions; and (3) the predominant political science usages, which are the most elaborate and the narrowest. As to the first of these, *The Random House Dictionary of the English Language* (2nd edition, unabridged) defines "alignment" as "a state of agreement or cooperation among persons, groups...with a common cause or viewpoint." Realignment occurs, then, when such an alliance is significantly changed or, inferentially, when conflict among competing alliances is transformed. This simple construction would have provided a far better starting point for research than those that have in fact held sway.

Media uses of the term have tended to make it merely a way to connote the emergence of a new majority. Realignment occurs when the party that had been ascendent loses its electoral pre-eminence, and a new majority consolidates its rule.

The political science literature owes much to V. O. Key, Jr., the "Father of Realignment." He wrote three key pieces on the subject in the 1950s. His first was an essay appearing in *The Virginia Quarterly Review* entitled "The Future of the Party," published during the 1952 campaign. In it he introduced the term "party realignment" (p. 166) and described some of what realignment entails. His starting point was the pivotal historical role that he saw played by catastrophe. "For almost a hundred years," Key wrote, "ca-

tastrophe has fixed the grand outlines of the partisan division among American voters." First, it was the Civil War that "burned into the American electorate a pattern of partisan faith that persisted in its main outlines until 1932." The Depression was the second great realigning catastrophe. In general, the U.S. party system was seen to have been permanently reshaped by a few massive sociopolitical events which left deep imprints on Americans' collective memories. Realignment was seen stemming from the emergence of new social needs and breakthroughs in partisan responses to them, as well as demographic shifts that gradually transform the electorate. In this first formulation of realignment, Key did not envision any fixed pattern or singular model.

American political science proceeded to build on this modest foundation an elaborate conceptualization of realignment as the centerpiece of a more general theory of partisan change. Many things besides Key's suggestions caused this to happen. The New Deal's dramatic partisan change was alive in analysts' minds. It was the one such occurrence political scientists of the time had experienced personally. The vividness of the specific instance helped it masquerade convincingly as the general rule. With more perspective, we can now see that the shifts in the party system and voting alignments in the 1930s were in fact *sui generis*. Nothing like the New Deal transformation had ever occurred before, nor has it since.

Understanding Realignment: Historical Background

As I see it, each of the major partisan transformations the US has experienced historically has grown out of broad shifts in the country's socioeconomic setting. Once established, the underlying properties of the new system shape subsequent election results in many ways. They do not, obviously, determine who the winners will be in each election. The personal appeal (or lack thereof) of the candidates is always a key independent element, and parties have opportunities to fashion appeals and build majorities, whatever the sociopolitical setting.

There was plenty of mystery and uncertainty at the start of the 1996 campaign. It was by no means certain in late 1995 that Bill Clinton would win reelection. He responded boldly to his then-sagging electoral fortunes, adopting or emphasizing positions far

> **"**
> *The vividness of the specific instance helped it masquerade convincingly as the general rule. With more perspective, we can now see that the shifts in the party system and voting alignments in the 1930s were in fact sui generis. Nothing like the New Deal transformation ahd ever occurred before, nor has it since.*
> **"**

closer to what majorities in the electorate had called for than he did in his first two White House years. From proclaiming that "the era of Big Government is over," in his January 1996 State of the Union Address, to calling for programs that rally the "vital center" in his December speech to the Democratic Leadership Council (DLC), Mr. Clinton responded to a changed political environment. We can't know precisely how much the subsequent rise in his approval ratings and electoral standing accrued from these changes in direction, but it is apparent that Mr. Clinton helped himself with the voters. (See Chapter 4, pp. 76-77.)

On the Republican side, a variety of important short-term factors hurt the GOP's chances to regain the presidency. Urged by many Republican officials to seek the party's presidential nomination and enjoying a remarkably high level of public encouragement (through the polls), Colin Powell nonetheless said, "no". The GOP found itself with a weak field of candidates and nominated a man who never, in a long and distinguished political career, had shown the ability to rally the nation. Ross Perot, who had mounted so formidable a challenge to George Bush's reelection in 1992, had by 1996 lost much of his appeal. Many Americans, who had seen the economy in trouble in '92, had by the '96 campaign come to feel better about their own economic positions and the country's. All of these factors contributed to Clinton's reelection.

Still, for all the unpredictability which resulted from short-term factors, one can see the imprint of an underlying sociopolitical setting in the elections of a period. Movement from one setting to another precipitates shifts in social needs and problems and in the public's thinking about what should be done, and reshapes the contending coalitions of groups and interests. Early in a realigning era these elements are in flux and we are often startled by departures from predecessor systems, but the mystery vanishes when the transition is largely complete, and we have observed the properties of the new sociopolitical era over a series of elections. That was the situation in 1996.

The US has experienced four great sociopolitical eras. The emergence of each has precipitated broad partisan transformations. The first era involved the post-Revolution maturation of a rural republic, at once unprecedentedly egalitarian in resource distribution and social relations, but which nonetheless permitted slavery. The Jeffersonian/Jacksonian party system was the creature of this era. In contrast, the post-Civil War years saw the growing ascendancy of an urban and industrializ-

ing order in the population centers of the North, and a South isolated by memories of the War and by its non-participation in industrial development. The Republicans assumed leadership of industrial nation building and from this base gradually established a national majority—a decisive one outside the South. The third broad setting emerged with the maturation of the industrial system, which resulted in an America distinguished by institutional scale, interdependence and complexity. These developments placed new demands on government, national government in particular.[2] Over the last

> ## ""
>
> *The 'New Deal party system' was a creature of the industrial era. it was designed to confront problems which were distinctly part of the industrial era, and it chose approaches that struck responsive cords in the population of that day.* ""

several decades, the US has entered a fourth major sociopolitical period that I've chosen to call, following Daniel Bell's seminal work on the subject, the Postindustrial Era.[3] In his brilliant study, Bell contrasted the postindustrial period with its predecessor, writing that whereas "industrial society is the coordination of machines and men for the production of goods," postindustrial society is "organized around knowledge." The key developments defining postindustrialism, Bell argued, are "the exponential growth and branching of science, the rise of a new intellectual technology, the creation of systematic research through R & D budgets, and...the codification of theoretical knowledge." I have found Bell's analysis very useful, as I have said, and I've applied elements of it in my assessments of the American political system, notably the party system, in a

number of works over the years (see Footnote 3).

The "New Deal party system" was a creature of the industrial era. It was designed to confront problems which were distinctly part of the industrial era, and it chose approaches that struck responsive cords in the population of that day. The interest groups that came together included some whose entry into the Democratic fold long pre-dated the Depression. For example, the South, which was a key part of the New Deal majority, became solidly Democratic as a result of the Civil War. But the majority assembled under FDR's leadership was in many ways a distinctively industrial-era majority—marked by the prominent place accorded big-city interests and party organizations and by the cementing of the allegiance to the Democratic party of a growing labor movement.

What's even more important, the industrial era shaped the substance of the policy debate. Central among those influences on public policy was the fact that industrialization brought with it vast concentrations of power and activity in large enterprises. This was dramatically evident in the business sphere, where the factory system had transformed work life and, in turn, generated demand for a like development in labor unions. The field of communications evinced clear parallels, including in the American experience a single dominant telephone company and, later, the "Big Three" networks' ascendancy in broadcasting.

In such an environment, enlargement of the authority and reach of the national government was widely thought—not just by New Deal Democrats—to be appropriately "countervailing." There was argument, to be sure, between the major parties over how much government there should be, doing which things. Throughout the long New Deal era the Democrats were the more committed of the two major parties to new national government programs. Still,

Repblicans were often a "me too" party as governmental expansion took place, something nowhere more fully seen than in "Great Society" programs. The Great Society originated in Lyndon Johnson's administration, but Richard Nixon's first term saw many extensions of this approach. The Environmental Protection Agency had its birth during Nixon's presidency, for example, with Nixon's strong support; and a major increase in federal environmental regulation ensued. It was Nixon who remarked early in 1971 that "Now I am Keynesian"—referring to the great British economist's thinking about government's role in macroeconomic management, and endorsing far more activist government than any Republican president had contemplated previously. In an age of centralization and concentration brought on by the mature industrial order, then, the idea of expanded government had broad appeal and legitimacy.

But if the dominant impulses of industrialization were centralizing and government-enhancing, those of the postindustrial years are the polar opposite. In the economic and technological spheres, dispersion and decentralization have proceeded apace. In this new setting, centering political power in national government bureaucracies has become increasingly anomalous. The late twentieth century is seeing a quite extraordinary movement against monopolies and their sisters, oligopolies. Telephone companies are an obvious case. Until a decade or so ago, experts assumed that one monopoly would survive in the telephone business, even as AT&T's historic dominance of the local telephone market ended. However much competition there might be in other sectors of the phone business, people would have to have their homes and offices wired, wouldn't they, and it wouldn't make sense to have two companies wiring one town. Now, developments in cellular technology, as well as in the regulatory environment, have brought competition to local service.

Looking to business corporations today, we read much about "corporate downsizing" and the strians it entails for employees. We read less of the fact that downsizing reflects not only a global marketplace and its greater competitive pressures, but as well the end of the kind of exclusivity and dominance which certain big corporations had experienced. In general, "Fortune 500" firms have for many years now been losing ground in their share of US employment. Job growth, which has been impressive overall in the past 20 years, continuing now into the second Clinton Administration, has occurred primarily through a vast expansion of small enterprises. Individual entrepreneurial activity has been flourishing—in part because many features of the postindustrial socioeconomic structure, including developments in computer technology, have encouraged it.

In the face of these changes across the social and eocnomic realms, major political shifts were inevitable. The latter have proceeded in stages—centering in a vast transfor-

mation of public thinking on the role and place of government. Caught up as we are in this debate, and inevitably choosing sides in ongoing partisan arguments, we easily lose sight of the fact that pressures for decentralization and dispersion are occurring across society and are in no sense limited to the governmental sphere.

Each of these four eras, described on the above pages, displays features that reach beyond the socioeconomic setting narrowly construed. Each has witnessed, for example, an important redefinition of the thrusts of American individualism, at once extending opportunities and recognition to groups previously excluded and posing new tensions and problems. Each has had its special mix of ethnic groups and its distinctive frontier of ethnic conflict. That the US of the first era was essentially a nation of British ancestry, with a large and enslaved minority of African ancestry, was enormously important to the politics of the time; these elements were not, however, products of the "rural republic" setting. Similarly, politics in the 1990s is being influenced by current shifts of ethnic make-up—which aren't a feature of postindustrialism, though they accompany it. Each of the four eras demarking US politics historically has had, then, along with its distinguishing socioeconomic core, many other important ancillary elements.

The "Philosophical" Realignment of the Postindustrial Era

Calling this change in direction in the public's thinking about government and politics a shift toward "conservatism" is, of course, simplistic—as was describing the New Deal change in terms of "liberalism." In every era, the populace displays considerable variety in political outlook, and many people don't sign on unambiguously and *en masse* to any of the contending positions. These qualifications entered, it makes sense to describe the New Deal setting as liberal and the present one as conservative—as long as the meanings attached to these terms are carefully delineated. In the political era bounded by FDR's election in 1932 and LBJ's "Great Society" of the mid-1960s, public support for expanding governmental programs and initiatives was unusually high, set against American historical experience. When asked, for example, in the Spring of 1941, after eight years of expanding New Deal programs, whether they thought "there is too much power in the hands of the government in Washington," just 32 percent of Gallup's respondents said there was, while 56 percent said not (Chart 1). Politicians seeking to broaden national government programs and services often had the winds of public opinion at their backs.

Our Postindustrial Era is distinguished by far greater skepticism about government, though for most not hostility toward it. This shift has two different sources. For one thing, it took the creation in the Great Society years of "big

Chart 1
Greater Confidence in Government, and Support for More National Government, in the New Deal Era

1941

Question: Do you think there is too much power in the hands of the government in Washington?

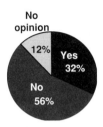

No opinion 12%
Yes 32%
No 56%

Source: Survey by the Gallup Organization, April 10-15.

1954

Question: One problem is keeping any group in the United States from getting too big and too powerful. Where do you feel this problem is greatest today...?

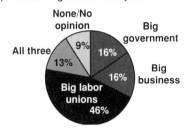

None/No opinion 9%
Big government 16%
Big business 16%
All three 13%
Big labor unions 46%

Source: Survey by the Opinion Research Corporation, August 23-September 3, 1954.

1960

Question: On the whole, do the activities of the national government tend to improve conditions in this country or would we be better off without them?

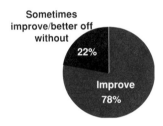

Sometimes improve/better off without 22%
Improve 78%

Source: Survey by the National Opinion Research Center of International Studies, Princeton University, March, 1960.

1964

Question: Which one of the statements listed on this card comes closest to your own views about governmental power today?

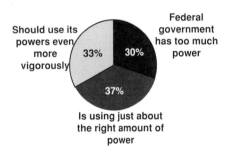

Should use its powers even more vigorously 33%
Federal government has too much power 30%
Is using just about the right amount of power 37%

Source: Survey by the Gallup Organization for Potomac Associates, October 1964.

Question: How much of the time do you think you can trust the government to do what is right—just about always, most of the time, or only some of the time?

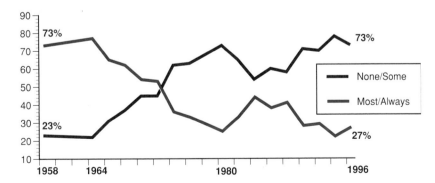

73%
73%
23%
27%

None/Some
Most/Always

1958   1964   1980   1996

Source: University of Michigan National Election Study (NES) for years 1958-1994; 1996 asking from the Gallup/CNN/*USA Today*, May 1996 (1996 NES data were not available at the time this publication went to press.)

government," and its inevitably more visible failings, to swing individualist America away from its relatively brief and historically anomalous enthusiasm for expanding national government. The other source comprises the dispersion and decentralization induced by postindustrialism, that has made central national government bureaucracy seem ever-more cumbersome and out of phase. Americans have not come to see less government as progress—as some Republicans found to their acute disappointment in the public's response to the work of the 104th Congress in its first year. But we have come rather decidedly to reject the idea that more government is progress.

Now in the mid-1990s, the US is no longer seeing significant year-to-year change in public sentiment about government and its proper role. The 1994 congressional elections were widely taken as a call for a Republican-led "revolution" against the New Deal/Great Society state, while much of the commentary in 1996 had Americans calling off this revolution (if indeed they had ever sought it). But survey data show great continuity over this span in public thinking about government (Chart 2). The conservative swing indicated by these data has not, of course, occurred evenly across the population. African-Americans give much more support than most other groups to a broader governmental role. Differences by gender are less striking, but women in 1996 continued to provide more support than men for governmental activism—which probably goes far toward explaining the electoral gender gap evident again in the November 5 balloting (Chart 3). The 1996 election day voters' poll taken by Voter News Service (VNS) found big regional differences on how much government is desirable, with Texans at one end of the continuum and New Yorkers at the other (Chart 4). Overall, though, questions posed by the opinion polls in 1996 confirmed the electorate's desire to stay with a relatively conservative stance on role-of-government questions.

Two sets of surveys—one taken by the Hart and Teeter research companies for NBC News and the *Wall Street Journal*, the other by Gallup for CNN and *USA Today* — point up the extent to which today's relatively conservative mood reaches beyond role-of-government issues. Hart and Teeter asked respondents which political party they thought would do a better job handling 14 issues. The list is a carefully balanced one, reaching across the policy spectrum, including foreign policy, crime, taxes, reforming welfare, Medicare, and education. At this supposed low point in GOP fortunes, pluralities gave the party the edge on 9 of the 14. These 1996 assessments can be compared to those made in 1994, just before voters elected Republican majorities to the House and Senate. In mid-October 1994, when Hart and Teeter asked about 10 of the 14 issues they included again in the May 1996 poll, they found no change on these 10 over this 19-month span. Not only did Republicans lead on the same 7 (of the 10) in both October 1994 and May 1996, but

they led by virtually identical margins. They gained 15 points on the Democrats on "controlling government spending," while losing 8 points on "health care," but on most, the shift was minuscule (Chart 5).

In late April 1996, Gallup conducted an "opinion referendum" for CNN and *USA Today*, in which respondents were asked how, supposing "that on election day this year you could vote on key issues as well as candidates," they would vote on 26 propositions, from a balanced budget amendment to prayer in schools, and from the death penalty for murder, to a ban on assault rifles. As in the Hart-Teeter survey, the overall list was balanced. A few of the propositions, such as "doctor-assisted suicide" and "selling off public lands," don't fit on a liberal-conservative continuum, but by my count 20 of the 26 do. And on only 5 of the 20 did pluralities come down on the liberal side: banning assault rifles, reducing Defense spending, raising the minimum wage, (not) reducing social spending, and (not) banning all abortions except to save the life of the mother. On most of the 15 where the conservative side carried, including the BBA, term limits, reducing all government agencies, and school choice, it did so overwhelmingly (Chart 6).

The Realignment Hasn't Produced a New Majority Party

As noted, while the "philosophical" side of the postindustrial realignment has come swiftly and fairly decisively, the partisan side has yielded no such definitive results. The 1996 balloting reflected the general partisan parity that has prevailed since the postindustrial system took clear form a decade and a half or so ago. Clinton won reelection, while the Republicans retained their Congressional majorities. Republicans now lead the Democrats in governorships by 32 to 17 (with one independent in Maine), one of their largest margins ever; but the Democrats still lead in state legislative seats, 3,883 to 3,470 (though this margin is down sharply from what it was after the 1992 vote).

National surveys asking partisan identification typically find a small Democratic edge, on the order of 2 to 4 percentage points. Thirty-nine percent of those interviewed by the VNS on November 5 called themselves Democrats, 35 percent Republicans. There's been no significant movement in party identification distributions since 1984.

Two different types of explanations may be offered for this state of partisan affairs. One focuses on failures of leadership in both parties, the other on underlying characteristics of the contemporary electorate and the way elections are now conducted. Elements of both may, of course, be valid.

Explanation 1. At any point in time decisions and actions of their leaders will be, in varying degrees, helpful or

Chart 2
Views on Role of Government:
No Change, 1994 to 1996

Question: ...How do you feel about the way the federal government works...enthusiastic, satisfied but not enthusiastic, dissatisfied but not angry, or angry?

1994

Enthusiastic 2%
Angry 20%
Satisfied but not enthusiastic 26%
Dissatisfied but not angry 52%

1996

Enthusiastic 2%
Angry 16%
Satisfied but not enthusiastic 28%
Dissatisfied but not angry 54%

Source: Surveys by ABC News/*Washington Post*, October 1994 and March 1996

Question: Would you say you favor smaller government with fewer services, or larger government with many services?

1995

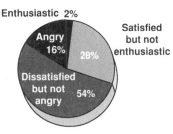

Smaller government 63%
Larger government 27%

Source: Survey by the *Los Angeles Times*, January 1995.

1996

Smaller government 63%
Larger government 32%

Source: Survey by ABC News/*Washington Post*, August 1996.

Question: Which comes closer to your view: Government should do more to solve national problems, or government is doing too many things better left to businesses and individuals?

1994

Should do more 42%
Doing too many things 58%

1994

Don't know/No answer 7%
Government do more 30%
Government doing too many things 63%

1996

Don't know/No answer 10%
Government do more 28%
Government doing too much 62%

Source: Survey by Voter News Service, November 1994.

Source: Surveys by CBS News/*New York Times*, October 1994 and September 1996.

Chart 3
More Women Than Men Support Government Activism

Question: If you had to choose, **would you rather have a smaller government providing fewer services, or a bigger government providing more services**?

Question: Do you agree or disagree that the federal **government should see to it that every person who wants to work has a job**?

Question: Do you think the **government in Washington should guarantee medical care for all people who don't have health insurance**, or isn't that the responsibility of the government in Washington?

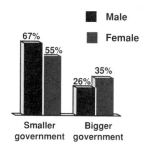

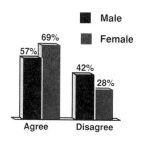

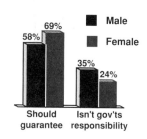

Source: Survey by CBS News/*New York Times*, February 22-24, 1996.

Source: Survey by CBS News/*New York Times*, February 22-24, 1996.

Source: Survey by CBS News/*New York Times*, February 22-24, 1996.

Though Both Sexes Call Government Too Big and Untrustworthy

Question: Which comes closer to your view: **Government should do more to solve national problems, or government is doing too many things** better left to businesses and individuals?

Question: ... Please tell me whether you would vote for or against each of the following propositions... **A reduction in the size and budget of all government agencies**.

Question: How much of the time do you think you can **trust government in Washington to do what is right**: just about always, most of the time, or only some of the time?

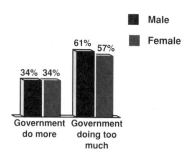

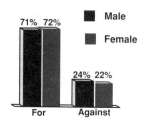

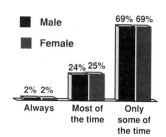

Source: Survey by CBS News/*New York Times*, March 31-April 2, 1996.

Source: Survey by the Gallup Organization, April 23-25, 1996.

Source: Survey by the Gallup Organization for CNN/*USA Today*, May 9-12, 1996.

Chart 4
The Parties Hold Their Ground on Issues

Question: When it comes to [each item], which party do you think would do a better job—the Democratic Party, the Republican Party, both about the same, or neither?

	May 1996			October 1994	
Republican	**Democrat**			**Republican**	**Democrat**
43%	15%	Controlling government spending		34%	21%
43	20	Foreign policy		34	15
36	21	Promoting strong moral values		38	20
31	21	Crime		28	23
34	25	Taxes		38	23
30	26	The Economy		30	22
35	31	Reforming the welfare system		31	28
25	34	Abortion		24	31
24	40	Education		21	34
22	42	Healthcare		25	37
35	18	Immigration		--	--
21	19	Drug problem		18 *	15
26	45	Medicare		22 **	33
17	45	The Environment		15 *	44

*October 22-26, 1993
**June 2-6, 1995

Source: Surveys by NBC News/*Wall Street Journal,* May 10-14, 1996 and October 14-18, 1994.

Chart 5
The 1996 Gallup "Opinion Referendum" Found a Distinctly Conservative Tilt

Question: Suppose that on election day this year you could vote on key issues as well as candidates. Please tell me whether you would vote for or against each one of the following propositions?

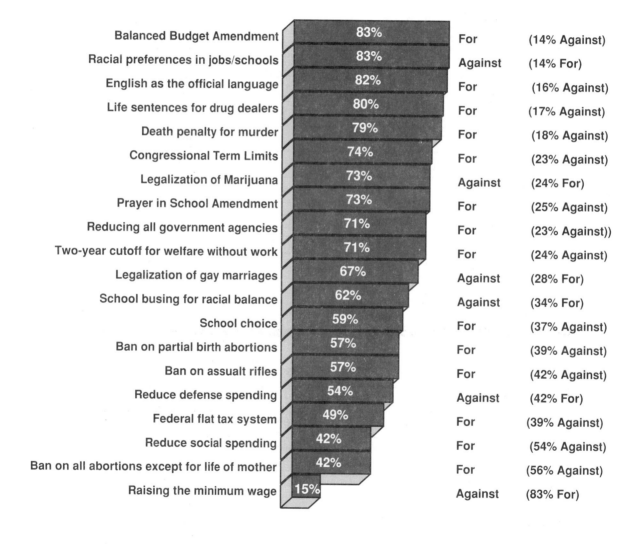

Balanced Budget Amendment	83%	For	(14% Against)
Racial preferences in jobs/schools	83%	Against	(14% For)
English as the official language	82%	For	(16% Against)
Life sentences for drug dealers	80%	For	(17% Against)
Death penalty for murder	79%	For	(18% Against)
Congressional Term Limits	74%	For	(23% Against)
Legalization of Marijuana	73%	Against	(24% For)
Prayer in School Amendment	73%	For	(25% Against)
Reducing all government agencies	71%	For	(23% Against))
Two-year cutoff for welfare without work	71%	For	(24% Against)
Legalization of gay marriages	67%	Against	(28% For)
School busing for racial balance	62%	Against	(34% For)
School choice	59%	For	(37% Against)
Ban on partial birth abortions	57%	For	(39% Against)
Ban on assualt rifles	57%	For	(42% Against)
Reduce defense spending	54%	Against	(42% For)
Federal flat tax system	49%	For	(39% Against)
Reduce social spending	42%	For	(54% Against)
Ban on all abortions except for life of mother	42%	For	(56% Against)
Raising the minimum wage	15%	Against	(83% For)

Note: The bars show the percentage of all respondents taking what is conventionally called the more conservative response on the issue. The numbers shown in parentheses after the bars are the percentages taking the opposing response. Included in the "referendum" but not shown here are the following items: "Withdrawal of U.S. from U.N.," "5-year freeze on legal immigration," "Reestablishing relations with Cuba," "Doctor-assisted suicide," "Mandatory job retraining," and "Selling off public lands."

Source: Survey by the Gallup Organization, April 25-28, 1996.

harmful to the parties' standing. Today, it may be argued that neither party has produced leaders able to reconcile contending themes and impulses in voters' thinking in anything like the persuasive fashion achieved by Franklin Roosevelt, Theodore Roosevelt, Abraham Lincoln, Andrew Jackson, and Thomas Jefferson. Ronald Reagan did strengthen the Republican party, by understanding the extent of the philosophical realignment that was occurring, and by being the kind of political personality—sunny and optimistic—Americans persistently seek in presidents. But he has found no successor. Whereas Reagan grew up politically a Roosevelt Democrat, both George Bush and Bob Dole entered Republican politics in an era of Republican failure. Theirs is, interestingly enough—in a way the older Reagan's never was—a pre-realignment Republicanism. Many post-realignment Republican conservatives have long complained of this. Bush and Dole are clearly in the American conservative tradition, but their roots are in the conservatism-in-retreat era of GOP minority status. The delay in bringing a new generation of Republican leadership to the fore in the presidential party has blunted Republican efforts to expand their base.

Along with these weaknesses in recent Republican presidential leadership, the party's congressional leadership overreached in 1995—mistaking the public's clear rejection of the idea that "more government is progress," for a conclusion it has not reached, that "less government is progress." There may in fact have been an "underreach" in the Republicans' response—one that 1996 presidential hopeful Lamar Alexander discussed in a *Wall Street Journal* op-ed piece following the election. To become the majority, Alexander argued, Republicans need to do more than demonstrate failures of the New Deal/Great Society state. They must offer plausible alternatives to it, ones that meet public expectations for a better society. New solutions need to be offered, clearly and positively. Alexander gave the following example of what, he believes, Republican politicians need to say and do:

> "Nothing is more important to me than making it possible for you to send your child to such a school, one of the best schools in the world—a safe, neighborhood school where every child is expected to behave and learn to high standards. I am ready to make the changes necessary to create those schools and give you those opportunities, and the Democrats are not. There will be time to explain the policies—charter schools, high standards, a GI Bill for Kids—*after* we paint the picture."[4]

As the GOP was encountering its problems, national Democratic leaders were trying to respond to criticisms that had contributed to their party's electoral decline. From the Vietnam War on through the 1980s, the national Democratic party seemed unaware of the extent of the conservative realignment that was occurring. The party appeared "tone deaf." This was the situation in which Bill Clinton and his party found themselves in December 1994, after their "blow-out defeat." Subsequently, though, the President has changed direction. He has been criticized for waffling and lacking firm principles. But it's sometimes hard to tell precisely where "waffling" and "lacking principles" leave off and "pragmatism" and "flexibility" begin. Since the 1994 debacle, the determinedly centrist thrust of his speeches and such decisions as signing the Welfare Reform bill in 1996 helped Clinton give a new look to the national Democratic party.

The President's December 1996 DLC speech is especially instructive on the reach of his effort to redirect the Democratic party so as to bring it into phase with the philosophical realignment. He called upon the party to mobilize the "vital center" by making six main commitments:

*Balance the budget.

*Give young people the best education in the world.

*Reform welfare by demanding "responsibility of welfare recipients," while avoiding the more"punitive" aspects of Republican approach.

*Press the fight against "gangs and guns and drugs and violence."

*Strengthen families.

*Pass "meaningful campaign finance reform legislation and modernize government operations."

While there are liberal elements in such program—e.g., seeking expanded family leave (though "in a very limited way")—his call to the DLC meeting, like much of his 1996 campaign, was largely devoid of a liberal agenda.

Explanation 2. An alternate explanation begins with an entirely different perspective—that the chief reason no party has majority status is that large segments of the electorate are abandoning firm partisan ties altogether. For decades many political scientists and journalists alike were mesmerized by the New Deal realignment, which had seen a new majority emerge so quickly and decisively. *Realignment* became virtually synonymous with *new majority*, but the historical record in fact shows that each of the country's historic realignments had followed its own course. [5] Broad changes in social structure, yielding new demographics, new social problems, and new views of government's role and policy needs, need not result in one party's ascendancy for an extended period.

There's strong evidence that the continuing weakening of voter ties to parties is one key dimension of postindustrialism. Growing segments of the electorate are thereby "up for grabs" in each contest. The postindustrial electorate is far more highly educated, more confident of its ability to make its political judgments independent of party cues. It draws its information not from party-influenced sources but from independent, adversarial mass media. Surveys such as one the Roper Center conducted for the Media Studies Center in November/December 1995 show national journalists heavily Democratic in both party identification and presidential voting.[6] (See Chapter 8, pp. 177-178.) The idea that journalists, however, disciplined professionally, can escape in their reporting the claims of their underlying political preferences, seems to me as silly as claims that those of us teaching American government and politics can approach our students unencumbered by our own political preferences. But journalists are surely right when they insist that their overriding guide *isn't* loyalty to a political party. They see themselves in an adversarial relationship to parties generally. Today, most Americans derive their political information from a source that tends to discourage rather than encourage stable party loyalties.

More than two decades ago, journalist David Broder observed that news persons had becun to serve as the principal source of information about what candidates were saying and doing. They acted as talent scouts, conveying the judgment that some contenders were provising, while dismissing others as having no real talent. They operated as race callers, or handicappers, telling the public how the election contest was going and what was important in it. The press had begun to see itself as public defender, bent on exposing what it considered frailties, duplicities, and sundry other inadequacies of candidates and officeholders.

The growth of a large, independent, often adversarial role by the national press in the country's electoral politics has proceeded apace since Broader wrote the above depiction. The 1992 presidential contest saw an extraordinary institutional innovation, startling even in the context of the established features of the contemporary system. For the first time in American history, a serious presidential nominee was "nominated" on television talk shows, most notably on *Larry King Live*.

The political parties are, quite simply, enormously disadvantaged with regard to communications resources in an age when communications media have such extraordinary capabilities for reaching large audiences. The early newspapers in the US were often avowedly party papers. Today, the press is fiercely independent of party control or influence—whatever the philosophic bent of the editors may be. Most of the money spent in political communications in the US is expended in a fashion entirely independent of party control. Parisan "spin doctors" try valiantly, of course, to get communications media to present political developments as the party would like, but they enjoy only intermittent and always highly limited success in this endeavor. There is extensive argument about the press's role, compared to that of the parties—much handwringing in some circles. I do not wish to enter that argument here. My observation is simply that the diminished presence of the parties generally accrues in large measure from their diminished place in the political communications process, at a time when communications resources are so enormously enhanced by technological and other changes that accompany postindustrialism.

Political parties for the reasons cited just aren't important institutions for most Americans today. Despite their decline and contrary to arguments advanced by Robert Putnam and others, I find evidence that "civic America" remains nonetheless active and vital.[7] Political parties, never huge actors in civic America, are perhaps less relevant now than ever before. There seems to be a general inclination across the public to reject older confines of "us and them" distinctions. We see this in religious group identification, where the proportion describing themselves in terms of Protestant or Catholic is yielding to a growing proportion choosing the label "other Christian." Seventeen percent of voters interviewed by VNS on November 5, 1996, chose this "I don't want to be part of that old divide" response, as did 19 percent in the election-day poll done by the *Los Angeles Times* nationally.[8] Similarly, being tied to the Republican or Democratic side seems to draw less favor than in times past.

Survey work done by the Roper Center for the Media Studies Center in 1996 reveals an electorate remarkably unanchored in partisan terms. Thus 65 percent indicated in the February 1996 poll that they "typically split [their] ticket—that is, vote for candidates from different parties." In 1942, Gallup had found 58 percent of respondents saying they usually voted a straight ticket—only 42 percent describing themselves as ticket splitters. Sixty-three percent said in 1996 they had "voted for different parties for president" in past elections; back in 1952, when the University of Michigan's Center for Political Studies first asked this question, just 29 percent reported having voted for different parties in past contests.

An experiment that the Roper Center conducted in its February 1996 survey gives further indication of how weak party ties are for many voters, even when the voters claim ties in some form. The Center asked the party identification question regularly used by the National Election Studies (NES): "Generally speaking, do you usually think of yourself as a Republican, a Democrat, an independent, or what?" Thirty-six percent identified with the Democratic party, 33 percent with the Republican party, while 24 percent claimed to be independents. The Center also asked another, different party identification question: "In your own mind, do you identify with one of the political parties or not?" If the respondent said yes, a follow-up asked, "Which party...?"

The bivariate relationship between the NES question and the Roper question is highly instructive. Only three-quarters of Republican identifiers on the NES item were recorded as Republican identifiers by the Roper Center question, and only two-thirds of Democrats on the NES measure remained there in the Roper version. Overall, 32 percent of voters did *not* give a consistent response—that is, were not Republican/Republican, Democrat/Democrat, or Independent/No Party, on the two questions. Only 24 percent of registered voters identified with the Republicans on both askings and 24 percent with the Democrats on both. Thus, a slight majority (52 percent) didn't consistently identify with one or the other major party in both measures. And, even those who were "consistent" Democrats or Republicans said they often do not vote the party line: About 60 percent of both groups typically vote split tickets. (See Chapter 9, pp. 190-191.)

In September 1996, the Center recontacted more than 500 randomly selected voters from the February survey in this panel study. We again posed the party identification questions—and found significant movement in the NES measure over this seven-month span. Eighteen percent of those calling themselves Republicans in the February survey said in September that they were Democrats or independents, while 24 percent of February's Democrats were Republicans or independents in the fall.[9]

Such erosion in party loyalties makes it appear unlikely that the US will, in its postindustrial era, experience a majority party of the type that the Democrats had in 1836, the Republicans in 1900, or the Democrats in 1940. The electorate is too weakly tied to parties to, in effect, sit still as the "sun and moon" model that Lubell used in describing the New Deal party system requires.

Divided Government. We present in Chapter 9 (pp. 186-187), a chart showing that the US historically

has had two prolonged periods where divided government has been the rule, not the exception: the half-century or so from the early 1840s through the mid-1890s, and then from the mid-1950s to the present. In both spans major realignment was occurring. And in both, neither of the major parties had attained majority status. The first was a time of slow, incomplete realignment that left both parties at rough parity for an extended span. By the time of the Civil War, although the new Republican party had come far, the Democrats had "won" a truly solid South, and outside Dixie still retained substantial Jacksonian-era-type backing. It wasn't until the industrialization had progressed far enough to erode the socioeconomic fabric of Jacksonian America, that national Republican ascendancy became possible.

Divided government of our era also reflects the fact that changes in party strength have been occurring slowly. The Republicans have again gained ground (this time, of course, not as a new party but from their weak number 2 position during most of the New Deal/Great Society years), but they have climbed only to parity. This relatively even two-party balance doesn't mandate that control of government will be divided, but it makes split results more likely.

Today—in contrast to the late 19th century experience—a growing segment of the electorate really doesn't "belong" to any party, and is disinclined to place much long-term faith in either party's leadership or direction. Historic American political individualism has long helped sustain our Madisonian constitution—through which governmental authority is divided among different institutions (presidency, Congress, federal courts; national government, state and local governments) each with powerful resources to resist the other. Now, Madisonianism has become overlaid with a new feature—the unwillingness of many voters to commit themselves to any party.

Why hasn't the postindustrial realignment yielded a new majority party? Will it in the future? My strong understanding is that large parts of both interpretations just reviewed are valid. Both major parties are groping for a satisfactory response to the electorate's changed outlook, following the decisive but subtle realignment of political outlook. Finding the right leadership and voice could advance either party further toward majority status than it is now. But this said, today's postindustrial sociopolitical environment makes it exceedingly difficult for any party to establish stable, long-term loyalties across much of the population.

Social Group Alignments

Republicans won the three presidential elections of the 1980s, and have lost the two of the 1990s. But while the parties' presidential fortunes have waxed and waned with the popularity of their candidates and voter reactions to current conditions, the underlying structure of social group support has remained essentially unchanged. The groups that in 1996 were the Republicans' best had been their best in the immediately preceding elections; the same is true for the Democrats.

Chart 6, using data from the exit polls done by Voter News Service, shows how closely Clinton's 1996 coalition resembled that of 1992. His share of the popular vote was up among most groups, of course, because it climbed 6.2 percentage points for the entire electorate; Dole's popular vote percentage, compared to George Bush's, rose 3.4 points, while Ross Perot's declined 10.4 points. Perot's support base shrank massively—but in even proportions across the various groups (Chart 8). His 1996 support was 11 points down among whites, where he had gotten a whopping 20 percent in 1992, down 3 points among African-Americans, where he had been extremely weak four years earlier—

Chart 6
Presidential Vote by Social Group, 1996 and 1992 compared

	Clinton '96	Dole '96	Perot '96	Clinton percentage point change, '92 to '96	Perot percentage point change, '92 to '96
Everyone	49%	41%	8%	6	-10
By Gender					
Everyone Male=48%	43%	44%	10%	2	-11
Female=52%	54%	38%	7%	9	-10
Whites only Men=48%	38%	49%	11%	1	-14
Women=52%	48%	43%	8%	7	-11
By Race					
White=83%	43%	46%	9%	4	-11
Black=10%	84%	12%	4%	1	-3
Hispanic=5%	72%	21%	6%	11	-8
By Race and Region					
East					
White=86%	51%	37%	10%	7	-9
Black=9%	85%	12%	3%	7	-6
Hispanic=3%	73%	20%	5%	31	-8
Midwest					
White=90%	45%	43%	10%	5	-12
Black=7%	79%	16%	5%	-9	1
Hispanic=1%					
South					
White=77%	36%	56%	8%	2	-10
Black=17%	87%	10%	3%	4	-3
Hispanic=5%	66%	27%	6%	5	-8
West					
White80%	43%	44%	9%	4	-15
Black=6%	77%	14%	7%	-7	-3
Hispanc=10%	74%	19%	5%	0	-7
By Age					
18-29=17%	53%	34%	10%	10	-12
30-44=33%	48%	41%	9%	7	-12
45-59=26%	48%	41%	9%	7	-10
60+=24%	48%	44%	7%	-1	-5
By Income					
Less than $15,000=11%	59%	28%	11%	1	-8
$15,000-$30,000=23%	53%	36%	9%	8	-11
$30,000-$50,000=27%	48%	40%	10%	7	-11
$50,000-$75,000=21%	47%	45%	7%	7	-11
$75,000-$100,000=9%	44%	48%	7%		
Over $100,000=9%	38%	54%	6%		
Union Member in Household					
Yes=24%	62%	36%	9%	4	-12
No=76%	45%	45%	8%	5	-11
By Education					
No High School=6%	59%	28%	11%	5	-7
High School Graduate=24%	51%	35%	13%	8	-8
Some College=27%	48%	40%	10%	7	-11
College Graduate=26%	44%	46%	8%	5	-12
Post Graduate=17%	52%	40%	5%	2	-9
By Religion					
Protestant=38%	41%	50%	8%	5	-10
Catholic29%	53%	37%	9%	9	-11
Other Christian=16%	45%	41%	12%	6	-11
Jewish=3%	78%	16%	3%	-1	-6
Other=6%	60%	23%	11%	7	-10
None=7%	59%	23%	13%	-2	-7
By Religion-Whites					
Protestant/Christian=56%	36%	53%	10%	3	-11
Catholic=29%	48%	41%	10%	6	-12
Jewish=4%	78%	16%	3%	-2	-7
Other=5%	51%	29%	13%	5	-11
None=7%	56%	26%	14%	-3	-8
By Financial Situation					
Better=33%	66%	26%	6%	42	-8
Worse=20%	27%	57%	13%	-33	-12
Same=45%	46%	45%	8%	5	-9
By Party ID					
Democrat=39%	84%	10%	5%	7	-8
Republican=35%	13%	80%	6%	3	-11
Independent/Other=26%	43%	35%	17%	5	-14
By Ideology					
Liberal=20%	78%	11%	7%	10	-11
Moderate=47%	57%	33%	9%	10	-12
Conservative=33%	20%	71%	8%	2	-19

Note: If candidate did better in '96 among a group than he did in '92, the number shown here is positive. If he did less well, it's a minus number.

Source: Voter New Service exit polls, November 1992 and 1996.

which means it was cut roughly in half in both groups. VNS also found Perot's 1996 drop-off roughly comparable in each income stratum. In both elections, he did better among men than women, and much better among independents than among Democrats or Republicans—and lost support between '92 and '96 in similar proportions in these groups.

Clinton made a big gain among voters of Hispanic background—presumably in reaction to highly publicized Republican-led efforts on immigration reform, such as that by Governor Pete Wilson in California. The President strengthened his position among women voters more than among men. But on the whole, the Clinton, Perot, and Dole votes in 1996 reflected a "universality of trends" from the 1992 balloting—modest increases for both major party candidates among most groups, as Perot plummeted everywhere. (See Chapter 4, pp.80-83.)

Asking voters whether their financial situation was getting better, worse, or staying the same produced an instructive caution on the matter of what causes what. Those who in 1996 said their financial position was getting better gave Clinton a 42-percentage point higher share of their votes than did those who in 1992 had said their finances were improving. A Republican occupied the White House in '92, of course, a Democrat in 1996. Many people who in 1992 had decided to vote for Bush wanted to give him economic credit by declaring that their economic position was improving; and similarly, the very different group of voters who in 1996 had wanted to reelect the incumbent Democrat sought to give *him* economic credit. Whether one's financial situation was improving or getting worse wasn't the operative dimension here—causality ran the other way. Respondents wanted to square their description of their personal economic position, with an otherwise-determined decision on how to vote.

Race, Region, and Religiosity

The racial background of voters, the region in which they live, and the extent of their religious participation have become in the postindustrial-party system especially powerful factors in differentiating such political choices and stances as vote for President and Congress, party identification, and liberalism/conservatism. Neither race nor religiosity had been key variables in the New Deal years; and though region was central then as now, today's regional alignment is virtually a mirror image of the preceding eras.

Even in 1996, when their presidential nominee ran weakly, the Republicans received a plurality of the presidential ballots of non-Hispanic whites and a decisive majority of white voters' congressional ballots (Charts 6 and 7). African-Americans moved into Democratic ranks following the Great Depression, but they were not a major part of the New Deal electorate—because their voting rights were denied in much of the South, and because Republicans retained significant support in the African-American community. Since 1964, however, African-American voters have backed Democratic candidates overwhelmingly almost every time and everywhere. In 1996 congressional votings, Southern whites backed GOP candidates by nearly two to one, leaving the black vote the major support for Democrats in the region. This was the case in Louisiana, for example, when Democrat Mary Landrieu narrowly defeated Republican Woody Jenkins by winning 91 percent of the black vote (VNS exit poll), while gaining only 32 percent of the white vote. Persons of Hispanic background were four to five percent of the electorate in 1996, according to the VNS exit poll. They backed Clinton and Democratic congressional candidates by roughly three to one—substantially greater margins than in past elections (Charts 6 and 7).

Religion—From Denomination to Religiosity. Historically, the "religious factor" has been central in American politics—but with religion, in the form of denominational affiliation, operating largely as a surrogate for ethnicity. Older ethnic groups (in time of arrival in the United States) tended (outside the South) to back the Republicans, newer groups the Democrats; and the former are heavily Protestant, the latter Catholic. This historic ethnic/denominational dimension can still be seen, but it has greatly eroded. In the 1996 vote for the US House of Representatives, for example, non-Hispanic Roman Catholics gave Republicans a small plurality—for only the second time in US history. They first did so in 1994.

Religiosity, not denomination, sharply divides the electorate. Chart 10 shows the extraordinary power of just one measure of religious participation—frequency of religious service attendance. According to the *Los Angeles Times* exit poll, those who don't practice a religion (9 percent of the electorate) backed Clinton by 62 to 22 percent, while those who attend services regularly (once a week or more) gave Dole a large margin (Chart 8). House voting, party identification and liberalism-conservatism all show this same strong pattern.

Region. A solidly Democratic South was a key component of the New Deal Democratic majority, as it had been a major part of the Democrats' coalition in the preceding Republican era. The South has long since swung Republican, however, and in 1996, it solidified its position as the Republicans' best region. When the election was over, there were 15 Republican senators from the 11 states of the old confederacy, just 7 Democrats; 71 Republican members of the US House, 54 Democrats; and 8 Republican governors compared to 3 Democratic. In the state legislatures of the region, Democrats still outnumber Republicans (1,061 to 712), but the GOP has made huge gains since 1992.

Chart 7
House Vote by Social Group, 1996 and 1994 compared

	Democrat	Republican	Democratic percentage point change, '94 to '96
Everyone	49%	49%	3
By Gender			
Everyone Male=48%	45%	53%	4
Female=52%	54%	44%	2
Whites only Men=48%	39%	58%	3
Women=52%	48%	50%	2
By Race			
White=83%	44%	54%	3
Black=10%	81%	18%	-9
Hispanic=4%	72%	26%	13
By Race and Region			
Northeast			
White=86%	51%	46%	6
Black=9%	81%	18%	-9
Hispanic=2%	81%	19%	
South			
White=77%	35%	64%	-1
Black=17%	87%	10%	-6
Hispanic=5%	61%	38%	
Midwest			
White=90%	47%	52%	5
Black=7%	80%	18%	-5
Hispanic=1%			
West			
White=80%	44%	53%	3
Black=6%	71%	28%	-10
Hispanic=10%	77%	21%	8
By Age			
18-29=17%	54%	44%	6
30-44=33%	48%	49%	3
45-59=27%	49%	49%	3
60+=23%	48%	50%	

	Democrat	Republican	Democratic percentage point change, '94 to '96
By Income			
Less than $15,000=11%	61%	36%	1
$15,000-$30,000=22%	54%	43%	4
$30,000-$50,000=27%	48%	40%	4
$50,000-$75,000=21%	47%	45%	2
$75,000-$100,000=9%	44%	48%	4
Over $100,000=9%	38%	54%	2
Union Member in Household			
Yes=24%	62%	36%	4
No=76%	45%	53%	0
By Education			
No High School=6%	64%	34%	8
High School Graduate=23%	53%	44%	7
Some College=27%	49%	49%	9
College Graduate=26%	43%	56%	0
Post Graduate=18%	50%	49%	-5
By Religion			
Protestant=38%	40%	59%	1
Catholic29%	53%	45%	7
Other Christian=16%	48%	49%	1
Jewish=3%	73%	26%	-2
Other=6%	70%	27%	8
None=7%	60%	38%	0
By Religion-Whites			
Protestant/Christian=56%	37%	61%	3
Catholic=29%	48%	50%	4
Jewish=4%	73%	25%	-4
Other=4%	65%	33%	17
None=7%	56%	41%	-3
By Financial Situation			
Better=33%	64%	35%	5
Worse=20%	32%	65%	-2
Same=45%	46%	52%	1
By Party ID			
Democrat=40%	88%	14%	-2
Republican=36%	10%	88%	2
Independent/Other=25%	47%	49%	6
By Ideology			
Liberal=20%	80%	18%	0
Moderate=47%	56%	42%	1
Conservative=34%	21%	78%	2

Note:

Note: If candidate did better in '96 among a group than he did in '92, the number shown here is positive. If he did less well the number is negative.
Source: Voter New Service exit polls, November 1994 and 1996.

Chart 8
Frequency of Religious Attendance Sharply Differentiates Americans Politically

Question: How frequently do you attend religious services, or do you never attend religious services?

	Presidential Vote			Congressional Vote	
	Clinton	Dole	Perot	Democrat	Republican
Never/Don't practice a Religion = 9%	62%	22%	12%	63%	29%
Less than once a year = 9%	54%	31%	15%	55%	38%
Once a year = 7%	57%	30%	11%	56%	39%
Several times a year/Once a month = 27%	53%	36%	9%	54%	41%
Several times a month = 13%	46%	49%	4%	47%	50%
Once a week = 23%	43%	49%	7%	45%	51%
Several times a week or more = 12%	33%	60%	6%	35%	61%

	Party Identification of Voters			Self-Described Ideology of Voters		
	Democrat	Republican	Independent	Liberal	Conservative	Middle-of-the-Road
Never/Don't practice a Religion = 9%	49%	19%	28%	30%	17%	53%
Less than once a year = 9%	42%	29%	28%	16%	24%	60%
Once a year = 7%	46%	32%	22%	20%	26%	53%
Several times a year/Once a month = 27%	44%	32%	23%	19%	29%	52%
Several times a month = 13%	41%	37%	20%	14%	40%	46%
Once a week = 23%	41%	42%	16%	14%	40%	46%
Several times a week or more = 12%	30%	51%	17%	9%	61%	31%

Source: *Los Angeles Times* exit poll, November 5, 1996.

At the same time, the Northeast in general, and New England in particular, have moved steadily Democratic. On November 5, 1996, Massachusetts and Rhode Island gave Bill Clinton his biggest margins among the 50 states, and Clinton's "worst" New England State, New Hampshire, backed him by a margin roughly three points bigger than what he gained nationally. Charts 9 and 10 show the long march of New England and the South away from their historic partisan homes.

Chart 11 shows the powerful interaction of region and religiosity in shaping the contemporary electorate. The narrower frequency of church attendance categories used in Chart 10 have been combined here into three broader groupings: persons that say they never attend religious services or do so rarely; those who attend occasionally (once a month to several times monthly); and those who attend at least weekly. Southerners who rarely or never participate in church services gave Bill Clinton a large plurality in 1996, while those who attend regularly backed Bob Dole by a margin of roughly 20 points. Northeasterners who attend church regularly were the only group of regular attendees to give Clinton a plurality—but they gave him a much smaller margin (7 points) than those in the region who don't attend services (a 35-point Clinton margin).

The Gender Gap—Again

The gender gap has become an important dimension of American politics in the postindustrial era—probably in large part because of the big growth that has occurred in single-parent families, disproportionately female-headed, and the consequent feminization of poverty. But if gender is now an important discriminating variable— which it wasn't in the New Deal system—the divide it locates is by no means among the most prominent. Differences separating whites and blacks are, obviously, far larger; and so are many others, including those

stemming from religiosity and regional subcultures.[10]

The VNS exit poll taken November 5 found women giving both Bill Clinton and Democratic House candidates solid margins; men split evenly in presidential voting, and give Republican House candidates an 8-point edge (Charts 8 and 9). White men backed Dole by an 11-point margin, while white women favored Clinton by 5 points. In US Senate races, Democratic candidates, male and female alike, typically received higher proportions of women's than of men's votes in most states (Chart 12). (See Chapter 4, pp. 102-107.)

Postindustrialism's Political Status-Quo

Americans voted on November 5, 1996, to stay on the political course and continue the alignment that distinguishes our era. They again elected a president of one party, and gave congressional majorities to the other. They again signaled a desire to curb the growth of national government, though not to cut it greatly. They remained remarkably unanchored in partisan terms. Substantial numbers of those who still call themselves party adherents identify with one or the other party very weakly. The social group alignments of the New Deal years have been so altered that "obliterated" is not too strong a verb. Indeed, today's alignment differs from the New Deal's more than the latter differed from the preceding Republican era's. Race, region, and religiosity continued in 1996 to split the US electorate in ways without precedent. The postindustrial party system remains firmly in place.

Endnotes

[1] I've discussed many of the distinguishing features of the social group alignment of the postindustrial system in my previous elections articles in the *PSQ*. See "The Brittle Mandate: Electoral Dealignment and the 1980 Presidential Election," Spring 1981, pp. 1-25; "On Mandates, Realignments, and the 1984 Presidential Election," Spring 1985, pp. 1-25; "The 1988 Elec-

tions: Continuation of the Post-New Deal System," Spring 1989, pp. 1-18; "The 1992 Vote for President Clinton: Another Brittle Mandate?," Spring 1993, pp. 1-28; "The 1994 Congressional Elections: The Realignment Continues," Spring 1995, pp. 1-23.

[2] I have discussed these developments in a number of earlier publications, especially in *American Political Parties: Social Change and Political Response* (New York: W. W. Norton, 1970).

[3] Daniel Bell, *The Coming of Postindustrial Society* (New York: Basic Books, 1973). I have elaborated on implications of Bell's underlying argument for the American parties and election system and contemporary US politics generally in "The 1994 Congressional Elections: The Realignment Continues," *PSQ*, Spring 1995, pp. 3-10.

[4] Lamar Alexander, *The Wall Street Journal*, December 24, 1996, p. A12.

[5] I have criticized this dimension of the realignment literature in "Like Waiting For Godot: The Uselessness of Realignment for Understanding Change in Contemporary American Politics." I meant by the title not realignment as major transformation of the parties and election system, but realignment in the "critical elections," New Deal model understanding. This paper, first presented to the 1989 meeting of the American Political Science Association in Atlanta, was subsequently published in *Polity*, Volume 22 (Spring 1990): 511-25; and in Byron E. Shafer, ed., *The End of Realignment? Atrophy of a Concept and Death of a Phenomenon* (Madison: University of Wisconsin Press, 1991), Chapter 2.

[6] See Kenneth Dautrich and Jennifer Necci Dineen, "Media Bias: What Journalists and the Public Say About It," *The Public Perspective*, October/November 1996, pp. 7-10.

[7] The argument that "civic America," or the country's "social capital," is in decline has been variously advanced by a number of observers but most prominently by Robert D. Putnam, "Bowling Alone: America's Declining Social Capital," *The Journal of Democracy*, January 1995, pp. 76-78; and in a series of articles: "The Strange Disappearance of Civic America," *The American Prospect*, Winter 1996, pp. 34-48; "Tuning In, Tuning Out: The Strange Disappearance of Social Capital in America," *PS: Political Science and Politics*, December 1995, pp. 664-683. My colleagues and I have examined these articles and relevant data and reached con-

Chart 9
Both New England and the South Leave Home

The percentage point margin by which the state's popular vote for the GOP candidate exceeded or trailed the Republican percentages nationally

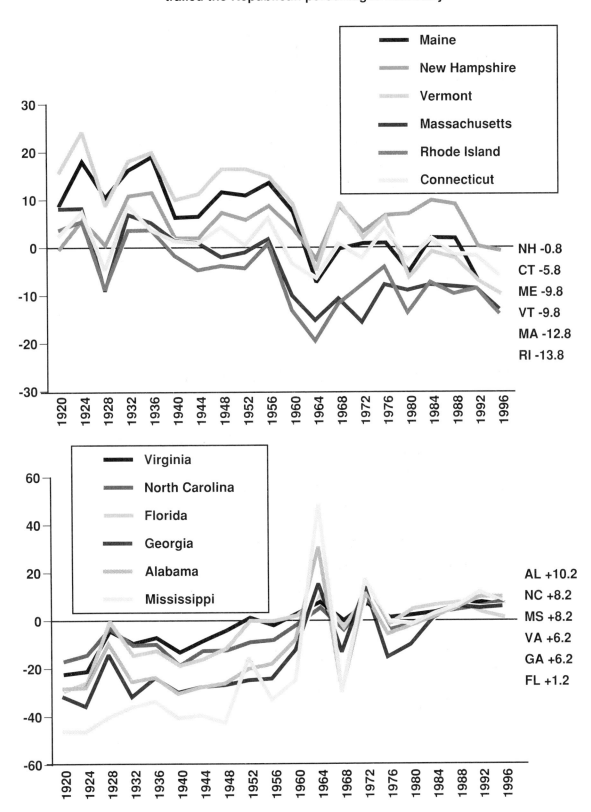

Chart 10
1996 Vote of Non-Hispanic Whites, by Region

				House Vote	
Region	Clinton	Dole	Perot	Democratic	Republican
New England	54%	32%	11%	58%	37%
Mid-Atlantic	49%	42%	7%	44%	51%
Industrial Midwest	48%	39%	12%	51%	43%
Pacific	40%	48%	9%	43%	50%
Midwest Farm	39%	49%	11%	43%	53%
Rim South	37%	53%	9%	41%	55%
Mountain	35%	51%	13%	35%	59%
Deep South	31%	60%	7%	31%	64%

Source: *Los Angeles Times* exit poll, November 5, 1996.

Chart 11
1996 Vote and Political Stance, By Region and Religiosity

					Self-Described Ideology		
Region	Frequency of Church Attendance	Clinton	Dole	Perot	Liberal	Conservative	Moderate
Northeast	Rarely	62%	27%	9%	23%	22%	56%
Midwest	Rarely	60%	27%	12%	22%	23%	55%
Northeast	Occasionally	56%	39%	4%	19%	26%	55%
West	Rarely	51%	32%	13%	20%	26%	54%
Northeast	Regularly	50%	43%	5%	14%	41%	45%
South	Rarely	50%	38%	11%	19%	32%	50%
Midwest	Occasionally	48%	43%	7%	12%	33%	55%
South	Occasionally	44%	52%	4%	14%	40%	46%
West	Occasionally	40%	53%	5%	19%	37%	44%
Midwest	Regularly	39%	50%	10%	11%	47%	42%
South	Regularly	37%	56%	6%	13%	49%	39%
West	Regularly	32%	61%	6%	11%	52%	37%

Source: *Los Angeles Times* exit poll, November 5, 1967.

Chart 12
Democratic Senate Candidates Received Higher Proportions of Women's Votes Than Men's in Most States

		Everyone		Women		Men		Gender Gap
State	Candidates	% Voting for Dem. Cand.	% Voting for Rep. Cand.	% Voting for Dem. Cand.	% Voting for Rep. Cand.	% Voting for Dem. Cand.	% Voting for Rep. Cand.	% Women voting Dem. minus % Men voting Dem.
Delaware	Biden (D) Clatworthy (R)	60%	39%	67%	32%	51%	48%	16
Georgia	Cleland (D) Millner (R)	49%	48%	56%	40%	41%	55%	15
Idaho	Minnick (D) Craig (R)	43%	54%	46%	51%	34%	63%	12
South Dakota	Johnson (D) Pressler (R)	52%	48%	57%	42%	45%	54%	12
Michigan	Levin (D) Romney (R)	56%	43%	63%	34%	52%	46%	11
New Hampshire	Swett (D) Smith (R)	47%	49%	52%	44%	41%	53%	11
Kansas A	Thompson (D) Roberts (R)	38%	61%	39%	59%	30%	66%	9
Louisiana	Landrieu (D) Jenkins (R)	50%	50%	54%	45%	45%	55%	9
Maine	Brennan (D) Collins (R)	47%	48%	48%	43%	39%	56%	9
Massachusetts	Kerry (D) Weld (R)	52%	45%	56%	40%	47%	48%	9
Minnesota	Wellstone (D) Boschwitz (R)	52%	43%	55%	37%	46%	45%	9
North Carolina	Gantt (D) Helms (R)	46%	53%	50%	49%	41%	58%	9
Oklahoma	Boren (D) Inhofe (R)	40%	57%	44%	53%	35%	63%	9
Alabama	Bedford (D) Sessions (R)	45%	53%	49%	49%	41%	57%	8
Colorado	Strickland (D) Allard (R)	48%	49%	50%	48%	42%	54%	8
Mississippi	Hunt (D) Cochran (R)	25%	74%	31%	69%	23%	75%	8
Kansas B	Docking (D) Brownbeck (R)	47%	52%	47%	50%	40%	58%	7
Oregon	Bruggere (D) Smith (R)	48%	49%	51%	45%	44%	53%	7
Illinois	Durbin (D) Salvi (R)	54%	44%	59%	39%	53%	43%	6
Iowa	Harkin (D) Lightfoot (R)	52%	47%	55%	45%	49%	49%	6
Montana	Baucus (D) Rehberg (R)	49%	45%	52%	40%	46%	50%	6
Nebraska	Nelson (D) Hagel (R)	42%	56%	45%	53%	39%	59%	6
Tennessee	Gordon (D) Thompson (R)	37%	62%	40%	59%	34%	65%	6
West Virginia	Rockefeller (D) Burks (R)	76%	24%	79%	20%	73%	26%	6
Texas	Morales (D) Gramm (R)	44%*	55%*	46%	53%	40%	58%	6
Kentucky	Beshear (D) McConnell (R)	45%	55%	45%	53%	40%	58%	5
Virginia	M. Warner (D) J. Warner (R)	47%	53%	49%	49%	44%	55%	5
Arkansas	Bryant (D) Hutchinson (R)	48%	50%	49%	51%	45%	54%	4
South Carolina	Close (D) Thurmond (R)	44%	53%	45%	51%	41%	56%	4
Rhode Island	Reed (D) Mayer (R)	64%	35%	65%	35%	63%	36%	2
New Jersey	Torricelli (D) Zimmer (R)	53%	42%	53%	42%	53%	42%	0
Wyoming	Karpan (D) Enzi (R)	42%	54%	42%	53%	42%	55%	0
New Mexico	Trujillo (D) Domenici (R)	30%	64%	29%	65%	30%	64%	-1
Alaska	Obermeyer (D) Stevens (R)	23%	68%	14%	70%	17%	72%	-3

*Actual vote percentages. All others in the table are exit poll percentages.
Source: Voter News Service, November 5, 1996.

clusions that differ sharply from Putnam's. See Ladd, "The Data Just Don't Show Erosion of America's 'Social Capital'," *The Public Perspective*, Vol. 7 No. 4, June/ July 1996, pp. 1, 5-22; and related articles by other authors in this same issue.
[8]A small proportion of respondents—for example, Mormons, really aren't Protes-

tant or Catholic Christians, but most "other Christians" belong to new, nondenominational churches.
[9]For a further discussion of the party identification data from the Roper Center/Media Studies Center surveys, see Kenneth Dautrich, "Partisan Instability in the 1996 Campaign," *The Public Perspective*, Octo-

ber/November 1996, pp. 52-54.
[10]I've discussed gender differences in contemporary politics in a number of other publications. See, in particular, Everett C. Ladd, "Media Framing of the Gender Gap," Chapter 6 in *Women, Media, and Politics*, Pippa Norris, ed. (New York: Oxford University Press, 1997), pp. 113-128.

Chapter 2

The Story in the Numbers

Popular Vote For President, 1996, by State

(as percentages, and showing Clinton's state percentage point lead or loss (-)

	Clinton	Dole	Perot	Clinton margin
New England				
MA	62%	28%	9%	34
RI	60	27	11	33
VT	54	31	12	23
ME	52	31	14	21
CT	52	35	10	17
NH	50	40	10	10
Mid-Atlantic				
NY	59%	31%	8%	28
NJ	53	36	9	17
PA	49	40	10	9
East North Central				
IL	54%	37%	8%	17
MI	52	38	9	14
WI	49	39	10	10
OH	47	41	11	6
IN	42	47	10	-5
West North Central				
MN	51%	35%	12%	16
IA	50	40	9	10
MO	48	41	10	7
SD	43	46	10	-3
ND	40	47	12	-7
KS	36	54	9	-18
NE	35	53	11	-18
South Atlantic				
D.C.	85%	9%	2%	75
MD	54	38	7	16
DE	52	37	11	15
WV	51	37	11	14
FL	48	42	9	6
GA	46	47	6	-1
VA	45	47	7	-2
NC	44	49	7	-5
SC	44	50	6	-6
East South Central				
TN	48%	46%	6%	2
KY	46	45	9	1
MS	44	49	6	-5
AL	43	51	6	-8
West South Central				
AR	54%	37%	8%	17
LA	52	40	7	12
TX	44	49	7	-5
OK	40	48	11	-8
Mountain				
NM	49%	41%	6%	8
AZ	47	44	8	3
NV	44	43	9	1
CO	44	46	7	-2
MT	41	44	14	-3
WY	37	50	12	-13
ID	34	52	13	-18
UT	33	54	10	-21
Pacific				
HI	57%	32%	8%	25
WA	51	36	9	15
CA	51	38	7	13
OR	47	37	11	10
AK	33	51	11	-18
United States	49.2%	40.8%	8.5%	8.4

Source: *Congressional Quarterly Weekly Report* (Washington, DC: Congressional Quarterly, Inc.), November 9, 1996, p. 3192.

Popular Vote For President, 1992, by State

(as percentages, and showing Clinton's state percentage point lead or loss (-)

	Clinton	Bush	Perot	Clinton margin
New England				
MA	48%	29%	23%	19
RI	47	29	23	18
VT	46	30	23	16
ME	39	30	30	9
CT	42	36	22	6
NH	39	38	23	1
Mid-Atlantic				
NY	50%	34%	16%	16
NJ	43	41	16	2
PA	45	36	18	9
East North Central				
IL	49%	34%	17%	15
MI	44	36	19	8
WI	41	37	22	4
OH	42	38	21	4
IN	37	43	20	-6
West North Central				
MN	44%	32%	24%	12
IA	43	37	19	6
MO	44	34	22	10
SD	37	41	22	-4
ND	32	44	23	-12
KS	34	39	27	-5
NE	29	47	24	-18
South Atlantic				
D.C.	85%	9%	4%	76
MD	50	36	14	14
DE	44	35	20	9
WV	48	35	16	13
FL	39	41	20	-2
GA	44	43	13	1
VA	41	45	14	-4
NC	43	43	14	0
SC	40	48	12	-8
East South Central				
TN	47%	42%	10%	5
KY	45	41	14	4
MS	41	50	9	-9
AL	41	48	11	-7
West South Central				
AR	53%	36%	10%	17
LA	46	41	12	5
TX	37	41	22	-4
OK	34	43	23	-9
Mountain				
NM	46%	37%	16%	9
AZ	37	39	24	-2
NV	37	35	26	-2
CO	40	36	23	4
MT	38	35	26	3
WY	34	40	26	-6
ID	28	42	27	-14
UT	25	43	27	-18
Pacific				
HI	48%	37%	14%	11
WA	43	32	24	11
CA	46	33	21	13
OR	43	33	24	10
AK	30	40	28	-10
United States	43.0%	37.4%	18.9%	5.6

Source: *Statistical Abstract of the United States, 1996-97* (Washington, DC, U.S. Bureau of the Census, 1996), p. 271.

Election Box Scores

1996

1992

Popular Vote
For President

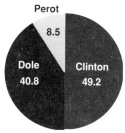

Perot
8.5

Dole
40.8

Clinton
49.2

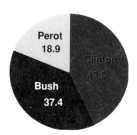

Perot
18.9

Clinton
43.0

Bush
37.4

1996

1994

1992

House Seats

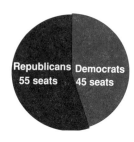

Independents 1

Republicans
227

Democrats
207

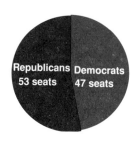

Republicans
230 seats

Democrats
204 seats

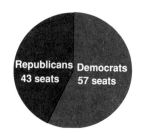

Independents 1

Republicans
176

Democrats
258

Senate Seats

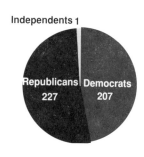

Republicans
55 seats

Democrats
45 seats

Republicans
53 seats

Democrats
47 seats

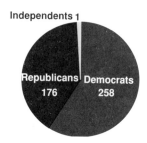

Republicans
43 seats

Democrats
57 seats

Governorships

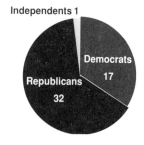

Independents 1

Democrats
17

Republicans
32

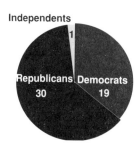

Independents
1

Republicans
30

Democrats
19

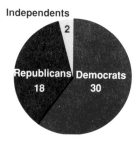

Independents
2

Republicans
18

Democrats
30

Source: *Congressional Quarterly*, November 9, 1996, November 1994, and November 7, 1992.

Summary Results, 1992-1996

1996		1994		1992	
Republicans	Democrats	Republicans	Democrats	Republicans	Democrats
Members of State Legislatures					
3470	3883	3491	3846	3005	4342
Control of State Legislative Chambers by Party					
46	50	47	48	29	66
States with both Legislative House and Governor of Same Party					
12	6	15	7	3	16

	1996	1992
Senators		
Republicans		
Re-elected	12	10
Retired*	8	3
Defeated	1	2
Democrats		
Re-elected	7	13
Retired*	6	5
Defeated	0	1
House Members		
Republicans		
Re-elected	194	129
Retired*	15	28
Defeated	18	8
Democrats		
Re-elected	164	195
Retired*	40	58
Defeated	3	16
Governors		
Republicans		
Re-elected	3	0
Retired*	1	5
Defeated	0	0
Democrats		
Re-elected	4	4
Retired*	3	2
Defeated	0	0

*Retired, resigned, died, sought other office, not re-nominated, etc.

Source: National Conference of State Legislatures, December 17, 1996; *Congressional Quarterly*, November 9, 1996, November 1994, and November 7, 1992.

Popular Vote for US House of Representatives
1932-1996

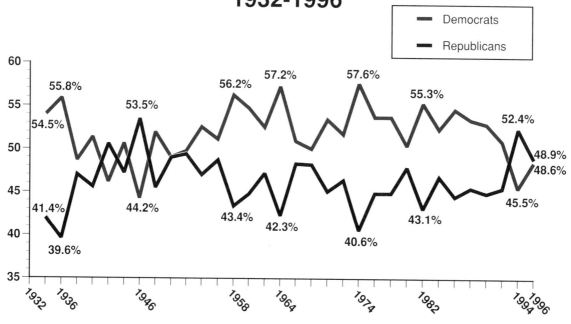

	Democrats	Republicans		Democrats	Republicans
1932	54.5%	41.4%	1964	57.2%	42.3%
1934	53.9	42.0	1966	50.9	48.3
1936	55.8	39.6	1968	50.0	48.2
1938	48.6	47.0	1970	53.4	45.1
1940	51.3	45.6	1972	51.7	46.4
1942	46.1	50.6	1974	57.6	40.6
1944	50.6	47.2	1976	53.7	44.9
1946	44.2	53.5	1978	53.7	44.9
1948	51.9	45.5	1980	50.4	47.9
1950	49.0	49.0	1982	55.3	43.1
1952	49.7	49.4	1984	52.3	46.8
1954	52.5	47.0	1986	54.6	44.5
1956	51.1	48.7	1988	53.4	45.5
1958	56.2	43.4	1990	52.9	44.9
1960	54.7	44.8	1992	50.9	45.5
1962	52.5	47.2	1994	45.5	52.4
			1996	48.5	48.9

Source: 1996 data are from the *Congressional Quarterly*, February 15, 1997. All other data are from the *Statistical Abstract of the United States, 1996-97* and *Historical Statistics of the United States, Colonial Times to present.*

Editor's Note: It's a quite extraordinary string, isn't it? It was an unprecedentedly long span (for a competitive democracy) that one party, the Democrats, dominated US House of Representatives voting—both the popular vote as shown above, and the House seats side shown on the next page.

Party Shares of Seats in the
US House of Representatives, 1932-1996

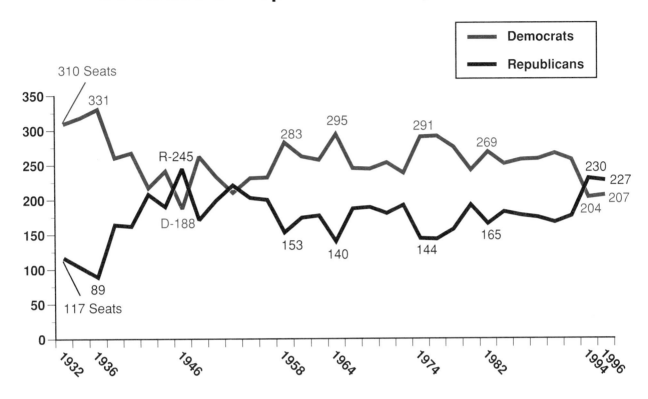

	Democrat	Republican	Independent			Democrat	Republican	Independent
1932	310	117	5		1964	295	140	0
1934	319	103	10		1966	246	187	0
1936	331	89	13		1968	245	189	0
1938	261	164	4		1970	254	180	0
1940	268	162	5		1972	239	192	1
1942	218	208	4		1974	291	144	0
1944	242	190	2		1976	292	143	0
1946	245	188	1		1978	276	157	0
1948	263	171	1		1980	243	192	0
1950	234	199	1		1982	269	165	0
1952	221	211	1		1984	252	182	0
1954	232	203	0		1986	258	177	0
1956	233	200	0		1988	259	174	0
1958	283	153	0		1990	267	167	1
1960	263	174	0		1992	258	176	1
1962	258	177	0		1994	204	230	1
					1996	207	227	1

Seats in the House:
The Parties Swap Regions

For the First Time in 1994, Republicans Won A Majority of House Seats from the South

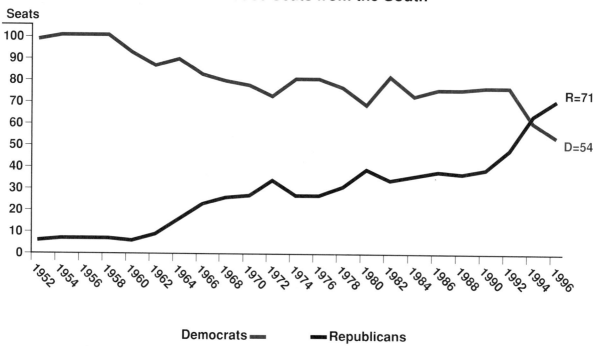

Seats

R=71

D=54

Democrats ▬ ▬ Republicans

The Northeast Has Long Since Swung Democratic —And Remained Democratic in House Seats in 1994

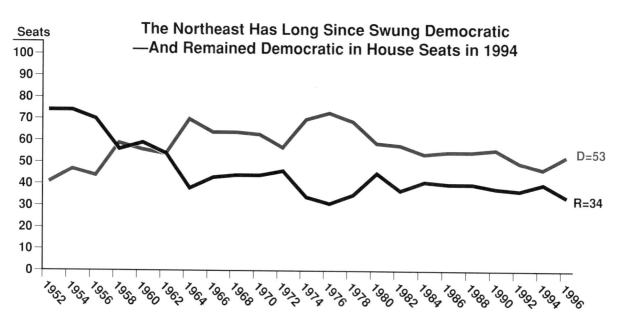

Seats

D=53

R=34

Note: The South is comprised of the 11 states of the Old Confederacy. The Northeast is comprised of the 6 New England states, as well as New Jersey, New York, and Pennsylvania.

Changing Regional Make-Up of the Congressional Parties

Percentage of all House Republicans from Each Region

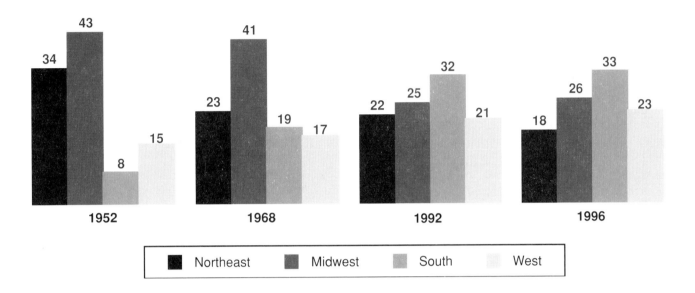

Percentage of All House Democrats from Each Region

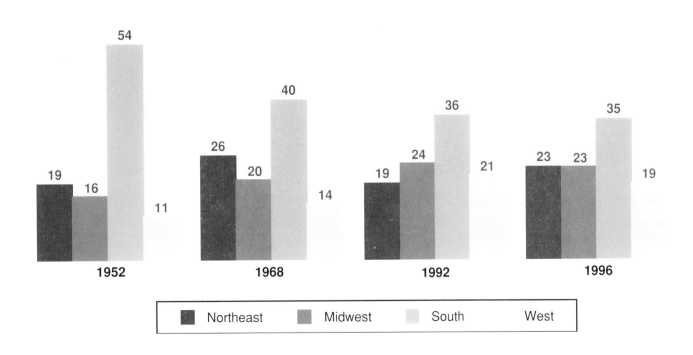

Party Control of the Governorships, 1952-1996

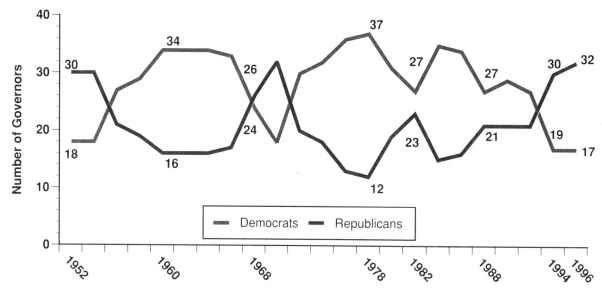

Source:

Party Control of the Governorships of the Ten Largest States, selected years, 1952-1994

	Democrats	Republicans
1996	2	8
1994	2	8
1992	5	5
1980	6	4
1972	5	5
1970	2	8
1960	8	2
1952	6	4

Women in State Legislatures

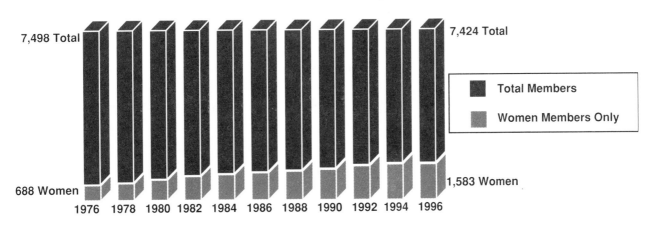

7,498 Total

7,424 Total

| | Total Members |
| | Women Members Only |

688 Women

1,583 Women

1976 1978 1980 1982 1984 1986 1988 1990 1992 1994 1996

Women in the U.S. Congress

	1976		1978		1980		1982		1984		1986		1988		1990		1992		1994		1996	
	D	R	D	R	D	R	D	R	D	R	D	R	D	R	D	R	D	R	D	R	D	R
House																						
Total	292	143	276	159	243	192	269	166	252	182	258	177	260	175	267	167	258	176	204	230	207	227
Women	13	5	11	5	10	9	12	9	11	11	13	11	14	11	20	9	35	12	31	17	35	16
Senate																						
Total	61	38	58	41	46	53	46	54	47	53	55	45	55	45	56	44	57	43	47	53	45	55
Women	0	0	1	1	0	2	0	2	0	2	1	1	1	1	1	1	5	1	5	3	6	3

Note: The numbers reflect the post-election results.

Source: 1976-1994: *Statistical Abstract of the United States*. 1996 data supplied by the Center for the American Woman in Politics (CAWP), National Information Bank on Women in Public Office, Eagleton Institute of Politics, Rutgers University.

African-Americans in the U.S. Congress

	1976		1978		1980		1982		1984		1986		1988		1990		1992		1994		1996	
	D	R	D	R	D	R	D	R	D	R	D	R	D	R	D	R	D	R	D	R	D	R
House																						
Total	292	143	276	159	243	192	269	166	252	182	258	177	260	175	267	167	258	176	204	230	207	227
Blacks	25	0	15	0	17	0	20	0	20	0	22	0	23	0	25	1	38	1	37	2	38	1
Senate																						
Total	61	38	58	41	46	53	46	54	47	53	55	45	55	45	56	44	57	43	47	53	45	55
Blacks	0	1	0	0	0	0	0	0	0	0	0	0	0	0	0	0	0	1	0	1	0	1	0

Note: The numbers reflect the post-election results.

Source: *Vital Statistics on Congress, 1995-1996*, Thomas Mann, Norman Ornstein, and Michael Malbin, eds. (Washington, DC: AEI Press, 1996), p. 38; 1996 data supplied by the Joint Center for Political and Economic Studies, Washington, DC.

Turnout in 1996,
Compared to Past Off-Year Elections

Voter Turnout
1932-1996

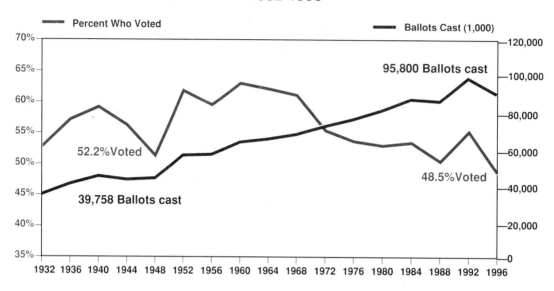

── Percent Who Voted   ── Ballots Cast (1,000)

95,800 Ballots cast

52.2%Voted

39,758 Ballots cast

48.5%Voted

The Turnout Muddle

For a nation which has been holding free elections for more than two centuries, we Americans have a terrible time getting the voter turnout story straight. Everyone recognizes, to be sure, that voter turnout—whether in presidential years, or in off-year elections—reached its 20th-century high in the early 1960s, and stands at a significantly lower level today.

This said, our basic turnout data are seriously flawed. I believe that the estimates developed by Curtis Gans and his colleagues at the Center for the Study of the American Electorate are the best available—better than those developed by the U.S. Bureau of the Census and published in the *Statistical Abstract*—but Gans himself notes problems with the percentages which his organization releases, shown in the figure above. Gans notes in his *1994 Report*, for example, that the base for determining turnout which he uses, following the Census lead, is voting-age population. The problem here is that many resident adults by law cannot vote—and these people should not be considered "non-voters." Gans writes: "They are, however, flawed figures, insofar as they include approximately 11 million documented aliens, 2 million undocumented aliens, convicted felons and people in mental institutions who cannot vote...." I would add that the figure on "undocumented aliens" in the resident population is almost certainly far too low. Overall, as many as 18 or 19 million people who by law cannot vote are categorized as "non-voters" in the most widely used turnout statistics.

Each year analysts are presented with this same puzzle: Should they use a more accurate turnout measure for the current year, but then present a number which is not comparable to the previous year's estimates, or should they continue calculating turnout as usual, maintaining the time-line but again yielding estimates known to be flawed? In my judgment, there is no excuse for the Census to continue to base its turnout statistics on a substantially erroneous base. The base has to be: American ctitizens of voting age who are not otherwise deprived, by law, of the franchise.

In any event, turnout was down in 1996, to the second lowest reported figure of this century. Turnout in 1924 was lower, but this was the first year in which women everywhere had the suffrage and their voting rates were temporarily much lower than men's.

—ECL—

Chapter 3

Charting the Electorate's Mind and Mood

Each presidential election occurs in a setting that's defined by a variety of factors. Among them: the relative underlying strength of the political parties and voters' judgments on their current performance; the public's feelings about the presidential candidates themselves; where the country stands "philosophically," compared to the parties' stands; and whether Americans are in a "things are good—let's continue" mood, or whether "it's time for a change." As to the latter factor, an incumbent running for reelection is obviously advantaged when voters are generally feeling good.

What was the nation's mood in campaign '96? To provide a little context for answering this question, we show the public's response to a series of basic mood indicators in a number of earlier years: 1979-80, when rather deep pessimism reigned; 1985-86, when optimism was notably high; 1992, when public dissatisfaction, prompted in particular by the recession, had risen sharply; and then during the last election two years ago, when the public saw economic gains but expressed strong dissatisfaction with current political performance. Overall, the 1996 numbers on a diverse set of mood indicators show far greater optimism than what prevailed in the late 1970s, though less than what the country experienced in the mid-1980s (pp. 42-46).

Some things change little over time. Asked to assess the fundaments of their society, Americans have declared themselves highly supportive and optimistic at every point when poll soundings have been taken—and this is certainly true now in 1996.

Many surveys showed the public fairly satisfied with the country's current economic performance— vastly more so than it was four years ago (pp. 38-39, 41). Interestingly, when asked how they would rate the economic conditions now prevailing nationally, Republicans and Democrats, and Clinton and Dole supporters, differed little. But when asked in the same Gallup survey whether things *are now improving*—on the Democratic president's watch—partisans differed sharply. Republicans were much more likely than Democrats to say that, at the time, economic conditions in the country were getting worse.

Despite relative overall satisfaction with the economy, the national mood wasn't buoyant this past election year. We thought we were succeeding economically—but we were far less confident about performance in broad social areas sometimes captured by "the moral dimension." A certain element of "values nostalgia" has probably always been present: Maybe we're not performing today up to the standards of yesteryear. Such responses occur in large part, it seems, because the only problems we have to confront are today's; yesterday's are for the history books. Still, it is striking that a comprehensive survey on the national mood taken in early May by Chilton Research for ABC's World News Tonight, found 67% of respondents saying that the country "is in a long-term moral decline," while only 31% declared its moral standing "basically pretty solid." In areas from drug abuse and crime to school performance and the status of the family, Americans saw too much going wrong to really feel good (p. 63).

Throughout Bill Clinton's first term, the two major parties remained at rough parity in underlying support, and their respective bases shifted little (pp. 47-50). And bases now are sharply different, however, from what they were two decades ago (pp. 58-59). Each party is seen having important areas where it performs better than its opponent (pp. 52-55).

In philosophical terms, the US moved little during Clinton's first four years as president. It hued to the generally conservative position to which it had moved over the 1970s and 1980s—something especially evident on role of government questions (p. 61).

—Everett C. Ladd

The Public's Satisfaction With the National Economy Rose Sharply Between 1993 and 1996

Questions: How would you describe economic conditions in the country today—as being very good, fairly good, poor or very poor? Would you describe the state of your own personal finances these days as very secure, fairly secure, fairly shaky or very shaky?

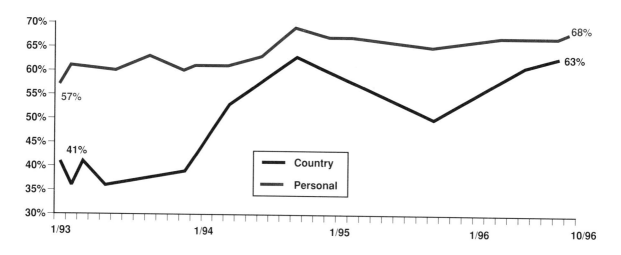

Note: The first asking in each month is shown here, when the question was asked more than once a month.
Source: [Country question] Survey by Yankelovich Partners, Inc. for *Time*/CNN. [Personal finances question] Survey by the *Los Angeles Times*.

Questions: [1/93-4/96] Right now, do you think that economic conditions in the country as a whole are getting better, getting worse, or staying about the same? [5/96-10/96] Right now, do you think that economic conditions in the country as a whole are getting better or getting worse? ["Same" was a voluntary response.]

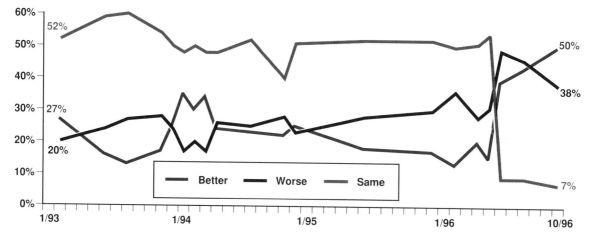

Note: The first asking in each month is shown here, when the question was asked more than once a month.
Source: Surveys by the Gallup Organization for CNN/*USA Today*.

Republicans and Democrats Agreed on Economy's Strength

By Party ID

Question: How would you rate the economic conditions in this country today...?

Legend: Republican, Democrat, Independent

Excellent: 2% 3% 3%
Good: 33% 30% 27%
Only Fair: 49% 49% 46%
Poor: 15% 18% 24%

Everyone

- Excellent/Good: 43%
- Only Fair: 43%
- Poor: 14%

By Presidential Vote

Legend: Dole, Clinton, Perot

Excellent: 2% 4% 2%
Good: 34% 33% 21%
Only Fair: 48% 49% 47%
Poor: 15% 14% 30%

But Differed Sharply When It Comes to Partisan Credit

By Party ID

Question: Right now, do you think that economic conditions in the country as a whole are getting better or getting worse?

Legend: Republican, Democrat, Independent

Better: 32% 52% 36%
Worse: 55% 37% 53%
Same: 10% 8% 9%

Everyone

- Getting Better: 43%
- Same (vol.): 9%
- Getting Worse: 46%

By Presidential Vote

Legend: Dole, Clinton, Perot

Better: 32% 53% 29%
Worse: 57% 36% 60%
Same (vol.): 8% 8% 9%

Still, Democrats Said Economic Problems Worse, Republicans Said Moral Problems Worse

Question: Which concerns you more—the nation's economic problems or the nation's moral problems?

By Party ID

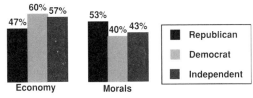

Legend: Republican, Democrat, Independent

Economy: 47% 60% 57%
Morals: 53% 40% 43%

Everyone

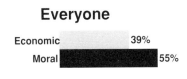

- Economic: 39%
- Moral: 55%

By Presidential Vote Intent

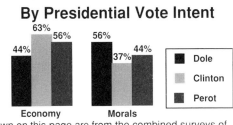

Legend: Dole, Clinton, Perot

Economy: 44% 63% 56%
Morals: 56% 37% 44%

Source: The group responses (by party identification and presidential preference) shown on this page are from the combined surveys of the Gallup Organization, January-August, 1996. The "everyone" responses are for the latest Gallup asking of the questions, July 18-21, 1996.

How Voters Saw the Issues, the Economy, and the State of the Nation

Exit Poll Findings

VNS Questions and Responses   **LAT Questions and Responses**

Political Self-Description

Question: On most political matters, do you consider yourself:

Liberal	20%
Moderate	47%
Conservative	33%

Question: In most political matters, do you consider yourself:

Liberal	17%
Middle-of-the-Road	48%
Conservative	35%

Role of Government

Question: Which comes closer to your view:

Gov't should do more to solve problems	41%
Gov't is doing too many things better left to businesses and individuals	52%

Question: Do you think the gov't can reduce the federal budget deficit and cut taxes at the same time?

Yes	58%
No	39%

Question: Do you think the new federal welfare law...?

Cuts welfare too much	18%
Does not cut welfare enough	39%
Is about right	37%

Question: What do you think is the most important priority for improving the economy...?

To make substantial cuts in the federal budget deficit by cutting gov't spending	51%
To boost gov't spending on things like education, public works and research	25%
To cut taxes	24%

Question: Which concerns you more...?

Bill Clinton will go too far in increasing gov't spending and taxes	51%
Bob Dole will go too far in reducing needed gov't programs	49%

Abortion

Question: Which comes closest to your position? Abortion should be:

Legal in all cases	25%
Legal in most cases	35%
Illegal in most cases	25%
Illegal in all cases	12%

Question: Do you think abortion should be made illegal in all cases, except for rape, incest and to save the life of the mother?

Yes, made illegal with exceptions	39%
Yes, made illegal without any exceptions	11%
No, not made illegal	50%

VNS Questions and Responses	*LAT* **Questions and Responses**

Divided Government

Question: Regardless of how you voted today, are you concerned that a Democratic-controlled Congress will be too liberal?

Yes	49%
No	48%

Question: Regardless of how you voted today, are you concerned that a Republican-controlled Congress will be too conservative?

Yes	41%
No	55%

Question: If Bill Clinton is re-elected, would you rather have the US Congress controlled by...

the Democrats	44%
the Republicans	49%

Question: Do you think it is better when:

One political party controls both the White House and Congress, or	44%
The White House and Congress are divided between the two political parties	56%

Economy

Question: Compared to four years ago, is your family's financial situation:

Better today	33%
Worse today	20%
About the same	45%

Question: Do you think the condition of the nation's economy is...

Excellent	4%
Good	51%
Not so good	36%
Poor	7%

Question: Over the past four years, has your financial situation:

Gotten better	34%
Gotten worse	23%
Stayed the same	43%

National Mood

Question: Do you think things in this country today are:

Generally going in the right direction	53%
Seriously off on the wrong track	43%

Question: Do you expect life for the next generation of Americans to be:

Better than life today	29%
Worse than life today	33%
About the same	35%

Question: Do you think things in this country are generally:

Going in the right direction	52%
Seriously off on the wrong track	48%

Nation's Mood, From the 1970s to the 1990s
1979-80: Striking Pessimism

National Optimism/Pessimism

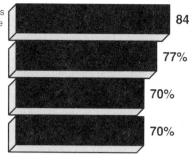

Dissatisfied with the way things are going in the US at this time (Gallup, July 1979) — 84%

Things in this country have pretty seriously gotten off on the wrong track (MOR, Oct.-Nov. 1979) — 77%

Things in the country these days are going badly (YSW, Aug. 1979) — 70%

The country is really in deep and serious trouble today (YSW, Aug. 1979) — 70%

National Economy

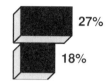

Economy is getting worse, same (24%), better (5%) (CBS/*NYT*, Oct.-Nov. 1979) — 70%

Personal Economic Position

Not satisfied at all with your present financial situation (more or less 44%, pretty well 28%) (NORC, 1980) — 27%

Dissatisfied with the work you do* (NORC, 1980) — 18%

Presidential Disapproval

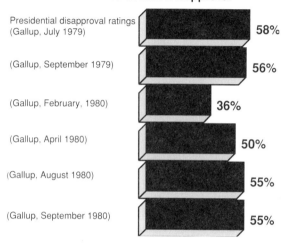

Presidential disapproval ratings (Gallup, July 1979) — 58%

(Gallup, September 1979) — 56%

(Gallup, February, 1980) — 36%

(Gallup, April 1980) — 50%

(Gallup, August 1980) — 55%

(Gallup, September 1980) — 55%

Personal Optimism/Pessimism

Dissatisfied with the way things are going in your own personal life (Gallup, Nov. 1979) — 24%

Nation's Future

Have no real confidence that our country will be strong and prosperous a few years from now (some 42%, a lot 36%) (YSW, Aug. 1979) — 22%

Generally pessimistic about our country's future (uncertain 37%, generally optimistic 44%) (Roper Starch, Aug. 1979) — 18%

Consumer Confidence

Conference Board Consumer Confidence Index, May 1980 (1985 = 100) — 50.1

Political Cynicism

Most public officials are not really interested in the problems of the average man (NORC, Feb.-Apr. 1980) — 71%

Note: MOR=Market Opinion Research for the Republican National Committee; YSW = Yankelovich Skelly White.

*Asked of those currently working, temporarily not at work, or keeping house (85%).

Question: Some people say there is a crisis of confidence in the country, that is, the people lack confidence in themselves and their future. Others say there is a crisis, but that it is a crisis of confidence in the elected officials. And others say there is no crisis at all. How about you...?

Question: [Do you]... agree or disagree with each of these statements...The American way of life is being seriously threatened by the energy and economic situation.

Question: Do you have more confidence or less confidence than you had a year ago in the government's ability to solve the inflation problem?

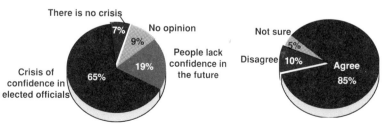

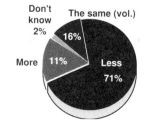

Source: Survey by CBS News/*New York Times*, October 29-November 3, 1979.

Source: Survey by ABC News/Louis Harris and Associates, September 18-28, 1979.

Source: Survey by Cambridge Reports for the American Retail Federation, April 17-May 5, 1980.

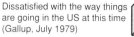

1985-86: Morning in America

National Optimism/Pessimism

Dissatisfied with the way things are going in the US at this time (Gallup, June 1986)

Things in this country have pretty seriously gotten off on the wrong track (ABC/*WP*, July 1985)

Things in the country these days are going badly (YSW, July 1985)

The country is really in deep and serious trouble today (YSW, July 1985)

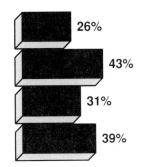
26%
43%
31%
39%

Presidential Disapproval

Presidential disapproval ratings (Gallup, Jan. 1985))

(Gallup, March 1985)

(Gallup, August 1985)

(Gallup, November 1985)

(Gallup, March 1986)

(Gallup, May 1986)

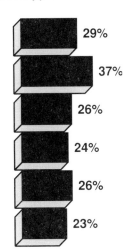
29%
37%
26%
24%
26%
23%

Consumer Confidence

Conference Board Consumer Confidence Index, July 1985 (1985 = 100)

103.2

National Economy

Economy is getting worse, same (33%), better (42%) (ABC/*WP*, March 1986)

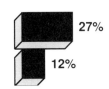
24%

Personal Economic Position

Not satisfied at all with your present financial situation (more or less 43%, pretty well 30%) (NORC, 1986)

Dissatisfied with the work you do* (NORC, 1986)

27%
12%

Personal Optimism/Pessimism

Dissatisfied with the way things are going in your own personal life (Gallup, March 1986)

15%

Nation's Future

Have no real confidence that our country will be strong and prosperous a few years from now (some 51%, a lot 35%) (YSW, April 1986)

Generally pessimistic about our country's future (uncertain 36%, generally optimistic 47%) (Roper Starch, Feb. 1986)

14%
13%

Political Cynicism

Most public officials are not really interested in the problems of the average man

NA

*Asked of those currently working, temporarily not at work, or keeping house (83%).

Question: Overall, would you say this country is in better shape, worse shape, or about the same shape as when President Reagan took office in January 1981?

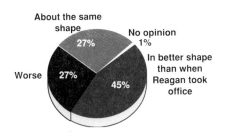

About the same shape 27%
No opinion 1%
Worse 27%
In better shape than when Reagan took office 45%

Source: Survey by ABC News, January 24-26, 1986.

Question: Do you approve or disapprove of the way Ronald Reagan is handling the nation's economy?

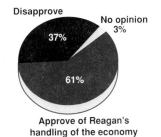

Disapprove 37%
No opinion 3%
Approve of Reagan's handling of the economy 61%

Source: Survey by ABC News/*Washington Post*, May 15-16, 1986.

Question: Do you approve or disapprove of the way Ronald Reagan is handling foreign policy?

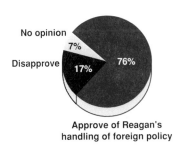

No opinion 7%
Disapprove 17%
Approve of Reagan's handling of foreign policy 76%

Source: Survey by CBS News/*New York Times*, April 15, 1986.

1992: Again, Widespread Dissatisfaction

National Optimism/Pessimism

Dissatisfied with the way things are going in the US at this time (Gallup, June 1992) — **84%**

Things in this country have pretty seriously gotten off on the wrong track (ABC, April 1992) — **81%**

Things in the country these days are going badly (YCS, Jan. 1992) — **72%**

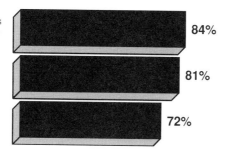

The country is really in deep and serious trouble today — **NA**

National Economy

Economy is getting worse, same (34%), better (9%) (ABC/Money, Jan.-Feb. 1992 — **57%**

Personal Economic Position

Dissatisfied with your family or household income (Gallup, Dec. 1991) — **33%**

Dissatisfied with the work you do (Gallup, Dec. 1991) — **16%**

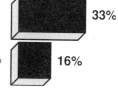

Presidential Disapproval

Presidential disapproval ratings (Gallup, July 1992) (Gallup, Aug.1992) — **59%**

— **58%**

(Gallup, Aug.-Sept. 1992) — **54%**

(Gallup, Oct. 1992) — **58%**

(Gallup, Oct. 1992) — **56%**

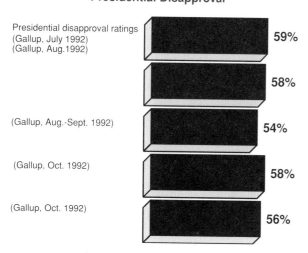

Personal Optimism/Pessimism

Dissatisfied with the way things are going in your own personal life (Gallup, Jan. 1992) — **22%**

Nation's Future

Have no real confidence that our country will be strong and prosperous a few years from now (some, a lot) — **NA**

Generally pessimistic about our country's future (uncertain, generally optimistic)

Consumer Confidence

Conference Board Consumer Confidence Index, Feb.(1985=100) — **47.3**

Political Cynicism

Most public officials are not really interested in the problems of the average man (ABC, April 1992) — **65%**

Question: Some people say the Bush administration is drifting without clear policies, while other people say it is moving carefully to develop its plans. Which do you think is more accurate?

Source: Survey by CBS News/*New York Times*, April 20-23, 1992.

Question: In general, do you approve or disapprove of the job Congress is doing?

Source: Survey by NBC News/*Wall Street Journal*, April 11-14, 1992.

Question: How satisfied are you with the candidates in this year's presidential election—very satisfied, somewhat satisfied, somewhat dissatisfied, or very dissatisfied?

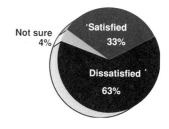

Source: Survey by Louis Harris and Associates, April 22-27, 1992.

1994: Economic Brightening and Political Dissatisfaction

National Optimism/Pessimism

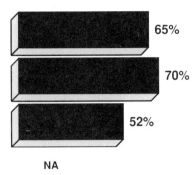

Dissatisfied with the way things are going in the U.S. at this time (Gallup, July 1994) — **65%**

Things in this country have pretty seriously gotten off on the wrong track (ABC News, July 1994) — **70%**

Things in the country these days are going badly (YP, Aug. 1994) — **52%**

The country is really in deep and serious trouble today — **NA**

Presidential Disapproval

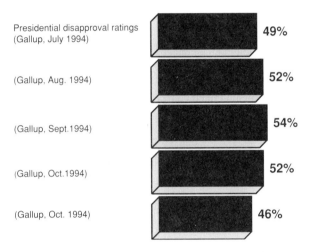

Presidential disapproval ratings (Gallup, July 1994) — **49%**

(Gallup, Aug. 1994) — **52%**

(Gallup, Sept.1994) — **54%**

(Gallup, Oct.1994) — **52%**

(Gallup, Oct. 1994) — **46%**

Consumer Confidence

Conference Board Consumer Confidence Index — **89.5**

National Economy

Economy is getting worse [same (56%), better (22%)] (CBS News/ *NYT*, July 1994) — **21%**

Personal Economic Position

Not satisfied at all with your present financial situation (more or less 46%, pretty well 28%) (NORC 1994) — **26%**

Dissatisfied with the work you do* (NORC 1994) — **15%**

Personal Optimism/Pessimism

Dissatisfied with the way things are going in your own personal life (Roper Center, Aug. 1994) — **15%**

Nation's Future

Have no real confidence that our country will be strong and prosperous a few years from now (some, a lot) — **NA**

Generally pessimistic about our country's future (uncertain , generally optimistic) — **NA**

Political Cynicism

Most public officials are not really interested in the problems of the average man (NORC 1994) — **74%**

*Asked of those who are currently working, temporarily not at work or keeping house (82%).

Question: Do you agree or disagree with the following statements?...

Government is the problem, not the solution to our problems.

Don't know 7%
Disagree 27%
Agree 66%

Question: How do you feel about the problem of low moral and ethical standards in this country today? Do you think this problem is about the same as it has been, that the country is making progress in this area, or that the country is losing ground in this area?

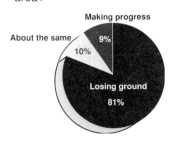

Making progress 9%
About the same 10%
Losing ground 81%

Question: How much of a problem is crime in the US?

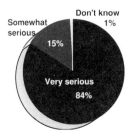

Don't know 1%
Somewhat serious 15%
Very serious 84%

Source: Survey by the Tarrance Group & Melman, Lazarus & Lake for *U.S. News and World Report,* October 21-23, 1994.

Source: Survey by Princeton Survey Research Associates for Times Mirror, September 9-11, 1994.

Source: Survey by the Wirthlin Group, September 6-9, 1994.

1996: Economic Gains Lift Clinton's Ratings

National Optimism/Pessimism

Dissatisfied with the way things are going in the U.S. at this time (Gallup, Aug. 1996) — **57%**

Things in this country have pretty seriously gotten off on the wrong track (NBC/*WSJ*, Aug. 1996) — **43%**

Things in the country these days are going badly (YP, July 1996) — **37%**

The country is really in deep and serious trouble today (YP, July 1996) — **51%**

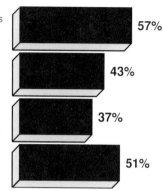

National Economy

Economy is getting worse [same (57%), better (17%)] (CBS/*NYT*, Aug. 1996) — **23%**

Personal Economic Position

Not satisfied at all with your present financial situation (NORC, 1996) — **28%**

Dissatisfied with the work you do* (NORC, 1996) — **15%**

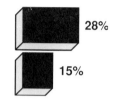

Presidential Disapproval

Presidential disapproval ratings (Gallup, June 1996) — **37%**

(Gallup, June 1996) — **42%**

(Gallup, Aug. 1996) — **36%**

(Gallup, Aug. 1996) — **39%**

(Gallup, Sept. 1996) — **31%**

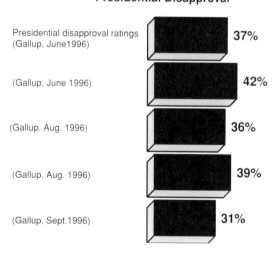

Personal Optimism/Pessimism

Dissatisfied with the way things are going in your own personal life (Gallup, March 1996) — **12%**

Nation's Future

Generally pessimistic about our country's future (ABC News, Apr.-May 1996) — **27%**

Political Cynicism

Most public officials are not really interested in the problems of the average man — **NA**

Consumer Confidence

Conference Board Consumer Confidence Index, Aug. 1996 (1985 = 100) — **109.4**

*Asked of those currently working, temporarily not at work, or keeping house (83%).

Question: Do you personally agree or disagree with those who feel that there is something wrong with the country at this time?

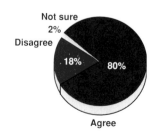

Not sure 2%
Disagree 18%
Agree 80%

Source: Survey by Yankelovich Partners, Inc. for *Time*/CNN, July 10-11, 1996.

Question: Thinking about everything going on in this country, how would you rate the state of the nation today...?

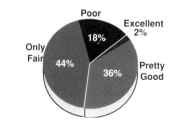

Poor 18%
Excellent 2%
Only Fair 44%
Pretty Good 36%

Source: Survey by Louis Harris and Associates, July 9-13, 1996.

Question: Would you say that you and your family are better off or worse off than you were four years ago?

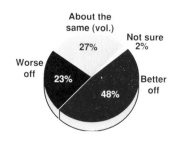

About the same (vol.) 27%
Not sure 2%
Worse off 23%
Better off 48%

Source: Survey by NBC News/*Wall Street Journal*, August 2-6, 1996.

Party Identification Constant Over Clinton's First Term

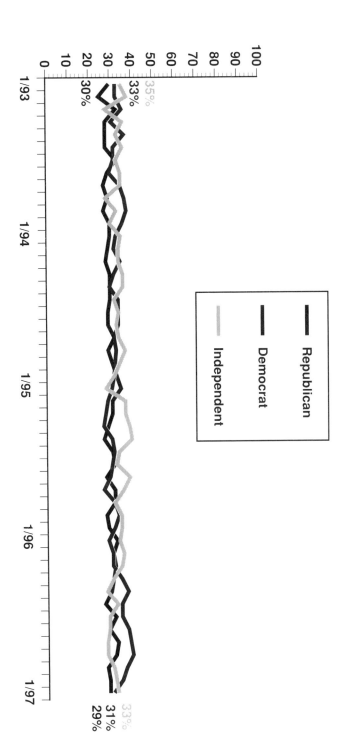

Source: Surveys by the Gallup Organization for CNN/USA Today.

Party Identification By Age

The Democrats Remain Strongest in the New Deal Generation

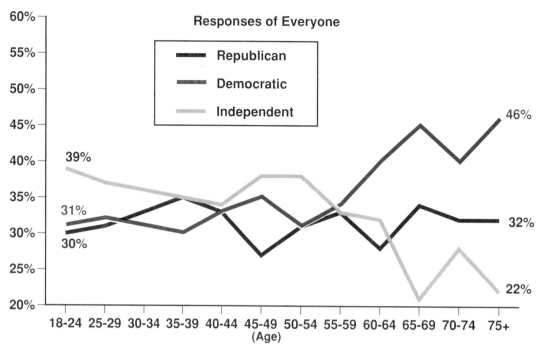

Among the Young, Women Are Democrats, Men Identify as Republicans

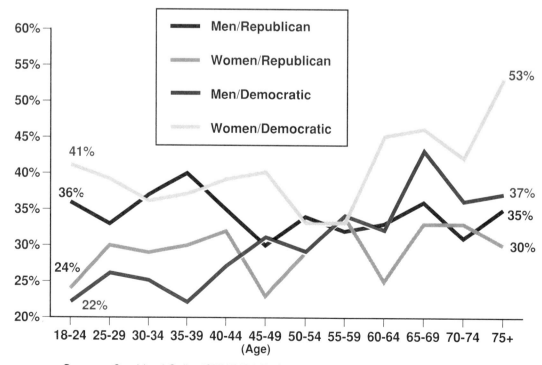

Source: Combined Gallup/CNN/*USA Today* surveys of January-June 1996

In 1996 Gallup Surveys, Republicans Were Most Numerous Among College Grads, Those With Higher Incomes,...

Party Identification

	Everyone		Men		Women	
	Republican	Democrat	Republican	Democrat	Republican	Democrat
By Whites/Income						
Less than $10,000	22%	45%	24%	35%	22%	50%
$10-15,000	27%	39%	30%	34%	25%	42%
$15-20,000	28%	35%	29%	26%	28%	42%
$20-30,000	33%	30%	31%	27%	34%	34%
$30-50,000	38%	29%	42%	23%	34%	36%
$50-75,000	41%	24%	44%	18%	39%	31%
$75,000+	43%	22%	47%	18%	39%	27%
By Blacks/Income						
Less than $15,000	8%	67%	13%	57%	5%	73%
$15-30,000	6%	71%	8%	71%	4%	71%
$30,000+	4%	71%	7%	70%	1%	73%
By Ethnicity						
Non-Hispanic White	36%	30%	39%	23%	33%	36%
Hispanic	18%	41%	20%	40%	17%	42%
African-American	6%	70%	8%	68%	4%	71%
By Denomination						
Protestant	36%	33%	40%	28%	32%	37%
Catholic	28%	35%	33%	28%	24%	42%
By Region						
East	29%	36%	32%	30%	27%	42%
Midwest	31%	32%	35%	26%	28%	38%
South	32%	36%	36%	30%	29%	41%
West	34%	33%	35%	28%	33%	38%
Whites (Non-Hispanic)/By Region						
East	33%	32%	36%	25%	30%	38%
Midwest	34%	28%	37%	21%	31%	33%
South	38%	29%	43%	23%	34%	35%
West	38%	31%	39%	25%	38%	37%
By Marital Status						
Married	38%	30%	41%	24%	34%	36%
Divorced	26%	38%	26%	34%	25%	41%
Widowed	28%	43%	21%	40%	29%	43%
Never Married	26%	34%	32%	28%	20%	42%

Source: Combined Gallup/CNN/*USA Today* surveys of January-June 1996

...Non-Hispanic Whites, Southern Whites, And Married Persons

Party Identification

	Everyone		Men		Women	
	Republican	Democrat	Republican	Democrat	Republican	Democrat
By Education						
Less than H.S.	22%	45%	24%	40%	21%	50%
High School Grad	30%	36%	32%	31%	29%	40%
Some College	34%	31%	39%	24%	30%	37%
College Grad	39%	28%	41%	20%	37%	35%
Post Grad	33%	32%	37%	27%	27%	40%
By Age/Education						
18-34/Less than H.S.	27%	24%	28%	22%	24%	28%
18-34/H.S. Grad	28%	33%	31%	27%	26%	37%
18-34/Some College	32%	33%	38%	24%	27%	41%
18-34/College Grad	39%	28%	42%	20%	35%	37%
18-34/Post Grad	35%	32%	40%	25%	28%	40%
35-49/Less than H.S.	19%	43%	24%	34%	13%	52%
35-49/H.S. Grad	29%	34%	32%	28%	27%	39%
35-49/Some College	36%	30%	40%	24%	32%	35%
35-49/College Grad	39%	30%	40%	21%	38%	36%
35-49/Post Grad	28%	36%	33%	30%	22%	44%
50-64/Less than H.S.	22%	46%	21%	45%	23%	46%
50-64/H.S. Grad	31%	39%	30%	40%	33%	39%
50-64/Some College	32%	27%	38%	22%	28%	32%
50-64/College Grad+	37%	26%	40%	22%	33%	32%
65+/Less than H.S.	21%	58%	21%	58%	21%	59%
65+/H.S. Grad	34%	42%	38%	34%	32%	46%
65+/Some College	40%	36%	42%	30%	40%	39%
65+/College Grad+	43%	27%	42%	23%	43%	32%
By Income						
Less than $20,000	22%	44%	24%	36%	21%	49%
$20-29,999	29%	36%	28%	33%	30%	39%
$30-49,999	34%	33%	37%	27%	30%	40%
$50-74,999	38%	27%	41%	22%	35%	33%
$75,000+	41%	25%	45%	21%	37%	30%

Source: Combined Gallup/CNN/*USA Today* surveys of January-June 1996

Among exit poll voters, Democrats had their biggest share of party ID in the Border states; Republicans in the Mountain states

	Democrat	Republican	Independent		Liberal	Moderate	Conservative
National	**39%**	**35%**	**26%**		**20%**	**47%**	**33%**
W. Virginia	55%	31%	15%		16%	48%	36%
Louisiana	53%	29%	18%		18%	36%	46%
Kentucky	51%	33%	16%		14%	45%	41%
Maryland	49%	32%	19%		26%	51%	24%
New Mexico	46%	34%	20%		22%	45%	32%
Arkansas	45%	28%	27%		8%	51%	41%
Oklahoma	45%	38%	17%		11%	45%	44%
California	44%	38%	18%		24%	44%	33%
Hawaii	44%	20%	36%		24%	47%	29%
Mississippi	44%	39%	16%		17%	33%	50%
Michigan	43%	32%	24%		16%	52%	32%
Rhode Island	43%	14%	43%		23%	48%	29%
Delaware	42%	37%	21%		14%	50%	36%
Missouri	42%	34%	25%		15%	49%	36%
New York	42%	29%	28%		25%	48%	27%
No. Carolina	42%	39%	18%		16%	47%	38%
Pennsylvania	42%	39%	19%		18%	47%	35%
Alabama	41%	36%	23%		16%	40%	44%
Maine	41%	28%	32%		20%	51%	30%
Florida	39%	39%	23%		18%	48%	34%
Minnesota	39%	35%	26%		19%	52%	30%
Oregon	39%	33%	27%		21%	47%	32%
Tennessee	39%	37%	24%		18%	47%	34%
Georgia	38%	34%	28%		14%	47%	39%
Illinois	38%	34%	27%		19%	53%	28%
Nevada	38%	43%	20%		16%	42%	42%
New Jersey	38%	30%	31%		21%	54%	26%
Ohio	37%	37%	26%		16%	51%	33%
So. Dakota	37%	45%	19%		12%	45%	43%
Texas	37%	41%	22%		15%	41%	44%
Massachusetts	36%	18%	46%		26%	50%	24%
Washington	36%	32%	32%		22%	49%	30%
Connecticut	35%	31%	34%		24%	42%	34%
So. Carolina	35%	39%	25%		13%	44%	43%
Vermont	35%	29%	36%		29%	42%	28%
Virginia	35%	36%	29%		19%	43%	38%
Wisconsin	35%	34%	30%		19%	48%	33%
Iowa	34%	34%	31%		17%	46%	38%
Kansas	33%	47%	20%		13%	55%	32%
Arizona	32%	45%	23%		14%	45%	40%
Montana	32%	33%	34%		14%	48%	38%
Indiana	31%	45%	24%		13%	43%	44%
No. Dakota	31%	36%	33%		13%	49%	38%
Colorado	30%	41%	29%		22%	46%	32%
Nebraska	30%	45%	25%		13%	46%	41%
Wyoming	30%	46%	23%		14%	44%	42%
Utah	28%	48%	24%		10%	40%	50%
Idaho	27%	48%	25%		10%	40%	50%
Alaska	25%	35%	40%		18%	42%	40%
New Hampshire	25%	35%	40%		19%	50%	31%

Source: Voter News Service exit poll, November 5, 1996.

Which Party Does a Better Job On...?

Advantage Republicans in 1996

In percent

Survey Organization/Date	Issue	R	D
CBS News 8/26-28	Insure a strong economy	43	41
CBS 8/26-27	Insure a strong economy	43	40
CBS/NYT 8/16-18	**Reform the welfare system**	50	31
	Insure a strong economy	48	38
	Reducing deficit	50	29
	Caring more about needs and problems of men	41	35
CBS 8/12-14	Insure a strong economy	43	36
	Caring more about needs and problems of men	42	33
PSRA/Newsweek 8/8-9	Budget deficit	43	34
	Reducing crime/violence	37	31
CBS/NYT 8/3-5	Reforming welfare	47	35
	Insure a strong economy	46	38
	Caring more about needs and	39	35
PSRA/Pew 7/25-28*	Governing honestly	38	37
	Well organized	40	35
	Managing gov't well	45	32

In percent

Survey Organization/Date	Issue	R	D
NBC/WSJ 5/10-14	Dealing with economy	30	26
	Dealing with crime	31	21
	Dealing with immigration	35	18
	Reforming welfare	35	31
	Dealing with foreign policy	43	20
	Reducing drug problem	21	19
	Controlling gov't spending	43	15
	Promoting strong moral values	36	21
	Dealing with taxes	34	25
US News and World Report 1/27-29	**Reducing deficit**	47	30
	Fighting crime/drugs	35	34
	Holding the line on taxes	46	32
	Reforming welfare	42	41
	Dealing with foreign affairs	47	33
	Getting things done	39	31
	Bringing about change	45	34
	Keeping America prosperous	42	35
	Improving the economy	42	40

The Parties at Parity—Part I

Questions: [Variants of these two questions have been asked by different polling organizations over time] Which party, the Democrats or the Republicans, do you think can do a better job handling the major problems facing the country; Which political party do you think can do a better job of handling the problem you think is most important...?

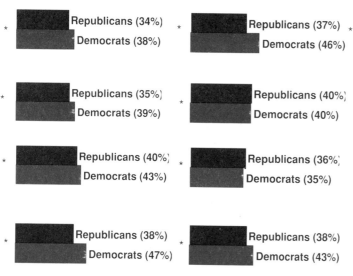

* Republicans (34%)
Democrats (38%)

* Republicans (37%)
Democrats (46%)

* Republicans (35%)
Democrats (36%)

Republicans (38%)
Democrats (45%)

* Republicans (35%)
Democrats (39%)

* Republicans (40%)
Democrats (40%)

Republicans (41%)
Democrats (45%)

* Republicans (40%)
Democrats (43%)

* Republicans (36%)
Democrats (35%)

* Republicans (38%)
Democrats (47%)

* Republicans (38%)
Democrats (43%)

Note: All are registered voters, except where noted by * = National Adult Sample.

Sources: [Reading from left, top to bottom] Surveys by the *Los Angeles Times*, April 13-16, 1996; Yankelovich Partners for *Time*/CNN, May 8-9, 1996; Gallup Organization/CNN/*USA Today*, May 9-12, 1996; ABC News/*Washington Post*, May 20-22, 1996, June 27-30, 1996; Associated Press, July 12-16, 1996; Princeton Survey Research Associates for the Pew Research Center, July 25-28, 1996; ABC News/*Washington Post*, August 1-5, 1996; *Los Angeles Times*, August 3-6, 1996; ABC News/*Washington Post*, September 3-4, 1996; ABC News, September 11-15, 1996.

The Public is Remarkably Consistent in How It Assigns Credit

Advantage Democrats in 1996

In percent

Survey Organization/Date	Issue	R	D
CBS News/NYT 9/2-4	Insuring a strong economy	39	42
CBS News 8/26-28	Insuring fair tax system	36	46
8/26-27	Insuring fair tax system	35	47
	Helping people achieve American Dream	36	49
8/16-18	Right decisions about Medicare	37	45
	Insuring fair tax system	38	45
	Helping people achieve American Dream	41	46
	Caring more about needs and problems of women	23	58
CBS News 8/12-14	Insuring fair tax system	38	40
	Helping people achieve American Dream	37	46
	Caring more about women	24	53
PSRA/Newsweek 8/8-9	Dealing with economy/jobs	38	45
	Dealing with abortion	30	39
	Dealing with Medicare/Social Security	36	44
	Programs for the poor	35	47
CBS/NYT 8/3-5	**Dealing with Medicare**	34	50
	Insuring fair tax system	33	49

In percent

Survey Organization/Date	Issue	R	D
CBS/NYT 8/3-5	**Helping people achieve**	35	50
	Caring more about needs and problems of women	18	60
PSRA/Pew 7/25-28*	Concerned with needs of business/powerful groups	65	19
	Concerned with needs of disadvantaged	23	63
NBC/WSJ 5/10-14	Dealing with abortion	25	34
	Dealing with education	24	40
	Dealing with Medicare	26	45
	Protecting the environment	17	45
	Dealing with health care	22	42
LAT 4/13-16*	Handling family values/morality	37	39
US News/World Report	**Protecting middle class**	31	51
	Improving health care	29	50
	Improving education	31	51
	Right priority between helping people and cutting spending	37	45
	Dealing with Medicare	31	50
	Protecting the environment	21	61

And, Parity—Part II

Question: Please tell me whether you have a favorable or unfavorable opinion of each of the following parties...?

August 16-18, 1996

■ **Favorable**   ■ **Unfavorable**

	Favorable	Unfavorable
Republican Party	55%	41%
Democratic Party	55%	41%

August 5-7, 1996

	Favorable	Unfavorable
Republican Party	51%	44%
Democratic Party	57%	38%

April 9-10, 1996*

	Favorable	Unfavorable
Republican Party	52%	41%
Democratic Party	55%	38%

April 17-19, 1995*

	Favorable	Unfavorable
Republican Party	52%	42%
Democratic Party	51%	43%

July 6-8, 1992

	Favorable	Unfavorable
Republican Party	53%	39%
Democratic Party	54%	38%

Note: All are registered voters, except where noted by * = National Adult Sample.

Source: Surveys by the Gallup Organization.

Group Differences on "Which Party is Better on..."

Note: The numbers show the difference between the percentage in each group responding that the Republican party would do a better job handling each issue, and the percentage responding that the Democratic party would. The negative numbers are the areas where **Democrats** get higher marks from that group.

Advantage Republicans

	Controlling Spending	Foreign Policy	Promoting Strong Moral Values	Crime	Taxes	Economy	Reforming Welfare
EVERYONE	28	23	15	10	9	4	4
By Gender							
Male	37	31	20	23	23	12	16
Female	20	16	11	-1	-2	-2	-7
By Race							
White	34	28	24	14	17	11	11
Black	3	-4	-28	-28	-33	-37	-35
By Age							
18-29 yrs. of age	30	36	14	8	-3	5	-11
30-39	31	42	26	11	9	8	0
40-49	42	30	15	16	12	4	0
50-59	22	5	8	14	8	7	14
60+	18	4	11	1	16	-1	16
By Region							
East	30	16	9	18	-6	-4	-2
Midwest	27	22	17	8	8	4	-2
South	32	25	14	7	18	10	7
West	26	29	21	9	11	3	11
By Education							
Less than H.S. (n=72)	-14	-33	-26	-6	9	-13	0
H.S. Grad	26	26	12	-3	3	2	0
Some College	26	16	12	14	5	-3	2
College Grad	40	42	33	19	23	22	13
Post Grad	47	34	22	17	12	7	2
By Income							
Less than $10,000 (n=67)	6	3	9	-16	0	-16	-28
$10,000-$19,999	13	6	8	5	-3	-6	-14
$20,000-$29,999	20	19	-6	-2	2	-3	-4
$30,000-$49,999	33	30	15	9	13	8	10
$50,000-$74,999	46	28	32	20	11	8	15
$75,000+ (n=83)	35	26	33	39	12	10	24
By Union Household	36	27	11	-1	-5	-4	-18
Non-Union Household	27	22	16	12	14	6	9
By Ideology							
Liberal	-4	-2	-17	-14	-21	-29	-34
Moderate	22	14	3	5	-2	-9	3
Conservative	59	51	49	37	53	47	40

Source: Survey by NBC News/*Wall Street Journal*, May 10-14, 1996.

The negative numbers are the areas where **Republicans** get higher marks.

Advantage Democrats

	Environment	Healthcare	Medicare	Education	Abortion
EVERYONE	28	20	19	16	9
By Gender					
Male	31	23	14	13	5
Female	25	19	22	20	13
By Race					
White	25	13	11	9	5
Black	36	59	54	44	25
By Age					
18-29 yrs. of age	24	31	11	15	16
30-39	28	16	16	18	6
40-49	41	20	13	19	8
50-59	34	22	23	16	11
60+	18	16	27	15	6
By Region					
East	27	31	30	21	17
Midwest	24	12	9	14	0
South	25	21	16	12	3
West	38	17	21	22	19
By Education					
Less than H.S. (n=72)	15	55	51	40	12
H.S. Grad	26	10	12	7	0
Some College	24	28	23	19	8
College Grad	23	10	7	9	11
Post Grad	53	28	23	30	25
By Income					
Less than $10,000 (n=67)	30	28	27	19	-2
$10,000-$19,999	18	26	31	17	8
$20,000-$29,999	26	30	28	22	8
$30,000-$49,999	34	9	12	11	9
$50,000-$74,999	28	21	12	15	9
$75,000+ (n=83)	29	39	19	20	15
By Union Household	34	30	32	23	12
Non-Union Household	26	18	14	14	8
By Ideology					
Liberal	35	47	42	41	45
Moderate	39	37	29	32	26
Conservative	10	-10	-15	-22	-33

Source: Survey by NBC News/*Wall Street Journal*, May 10-14, 1996.

Partisan Commitment...

At Every Point Since the New Deal, Party Identification...

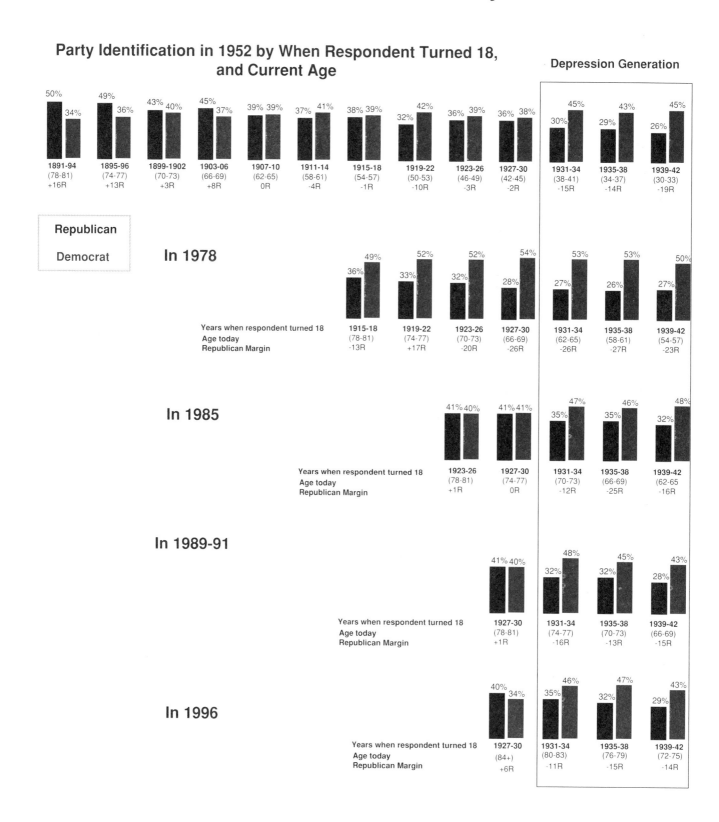

Party Identification in 1952 by When Respondent Turned 18, and Current Age

Depression Generation

Period	% R	% D	Margin
1891-94 (78-81)	50%	34%	+16R
1895-96 (74-77)	49%	36%	+13R
1899-1902 (70-73)	43%	40%	+3R
1903-06 (66-69)	45%	37%	+8R
1907-10 (62-65)	39%	39%	0R
1911-14 (58-61)	37%	41%	-4R
1915-18 (54-57)	38%	39%	-1R
1919-22 (50-53)	32%	42%	-10R
1923-26 (46-49)	36%	39%	-3R
1927-30 (42-45)	36%	38%	-2R
1931-34 (38-41)	30%	45%	-15R
1935-38 (34-37)	29%	43%	-14R
1939-42 (30-33)	26%	45%	-19R

Republican

Democrat

In 1978

Years when respondent turned 18 / Age today / Republican Margin

Period	% R	% D	Margin
1915-18 (78-81)	36%	49%	-13R
1919-22 (74-77)	33%	52%	+17R
1923-26 (70-73)	32%	52%	-20R
1927-30 (66-69)	28%	54%	-26R
1931-34 (62-65)	27%	53%	-26R
1935-38 (58-61)	26%	53%	-27R
1939-42 (54-57)	27%	50%	-23R

In 1985

Years when respondent turned 18 / Age today / Republican Margin

Period	% R	% D	Margin
1923-26 (78-81)	41%	40%	+1R
1927-30 (74-77)	41%	41%	0R
1931-34 (70-73)	35%	47%	-12R
1935-38 (66-69)	35%	46%	-25R
1939-42 (62-65)	32%	48%	-16R

In 1989-91

Years when respondent turned 18 / Age today / Republican Margin

Period	% R	% D	Margin
1927-30 (78-81)	41%	40%	+1R
1931-34 (74-77)	32%	48%	-16R
1935-38 (70-73)	32%	45%	-13R
1939-42 (66-69)	28%	43%	-15R

In 1996

Years when respondent turned 18 / Age today / Republican Margin

Period	% R	% D	Margin
1927-30 (84+)	40%	34%	+6R
1931-34 (80-83)	35%	46%	-11R
1935-38 (76-79)	32%	47%	-15R
1939-42 (72-75)	29%	43%	-14R

...As Electoral Backdrop

...Reflects Time When Voters Entered the Electorate

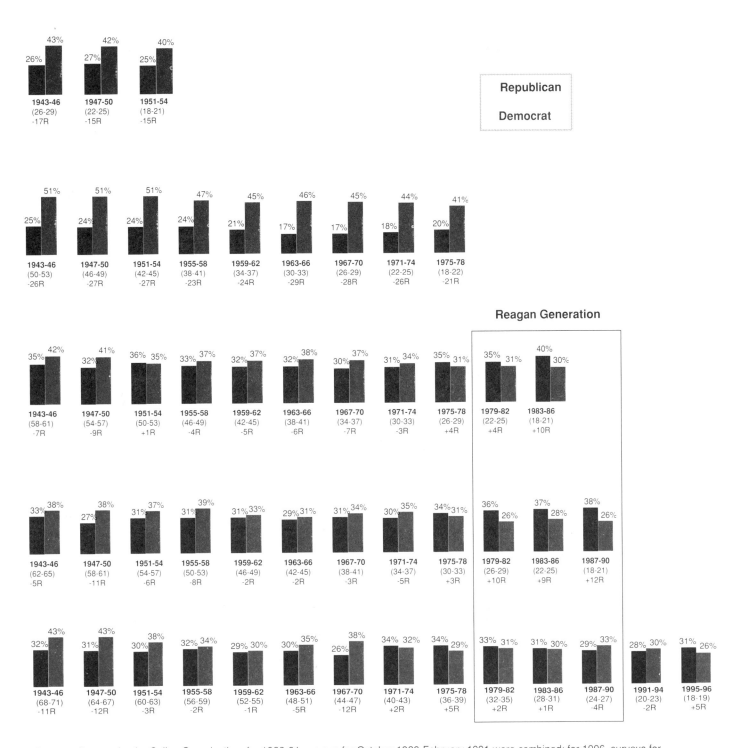

Source: Surveys by the Gallup Organization; for 1989-91 surveys for October 1989-February 1991 were combined; for 1996, surveys for January-August 1996 were combined.

Over the Last Two Decades, Republicans' Strength in Party Identification...

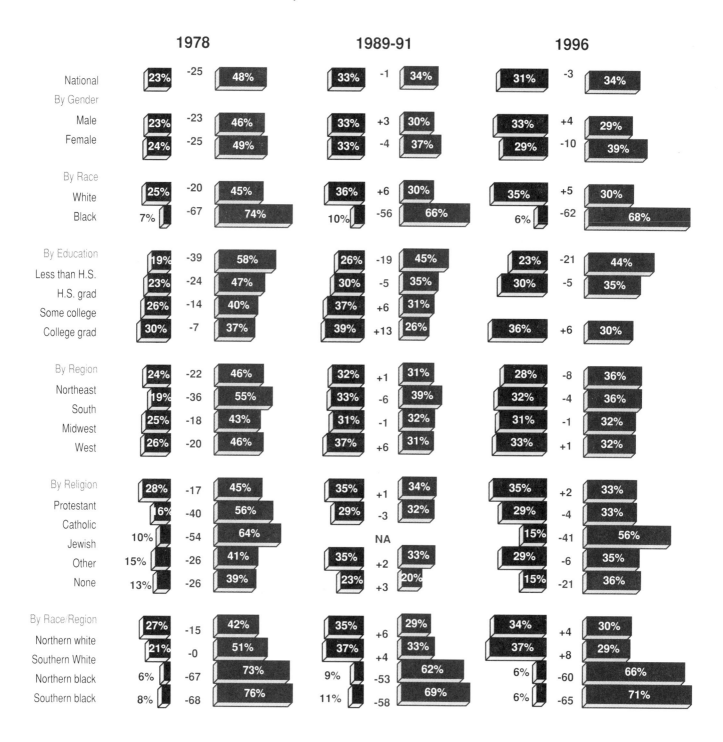

% identifying as Republican   % identifying as Democrat

	1978		1989-91		1996	
National	23%	−25 48%	33%	−1 34%	31%	−3 34%
By Gender						
Male	23%	−23 46%	33%	+3 30%	33%	+4 29%
Female	24%	−25 49%	33%	−4 37%	29%	−10 39%
By Race						
White	25%	−20 45%	36%	+6 30%	35%	+5 30%
Black	7%	−67 74%	10%	−56 66%	6%	−62 68%
By Education						
Less than H.S.	19%	−39 58%	26%	−19 45%	23%	−21 44%
H.S. grad	23%	−24 47%	30%	−5 35%	30%	−5 35%
Some college	26%	−14 40%	37%	+6 31%		
College grad	30%	−7 37%	39%	+13 26%	36%	+6 30%
By Region						
Northeast	24%	−22 46%	32%	+1 31%	28%	−8 36%
South	19%	−36 55%	33%	−6 39%	32%	−4 36%
Midwest	25%	−18 43%	31%	−1 32%	31%	−1 32%
West	26%	−20 46%	37%	+6 31%	33%	+1 32%
By Religion						
Protestant	28%	−17 45%	35%	+1 34%	35%	+2 33%
Catholic	16%	−40 56%	29%	−3 32%	29%	−4 33%
Jewish	10%	−54 64%	NA		15%	−41 56%
Other	15%	−26 41%	35%	+2 33%	29%	−6 35%
None	13%	−26 39%	23%	+3 20%	15%	−21 36%
By Race/Region						
Northern white	27%	−15 42%	35%	+6 29%	34%	+4 30%
Southern White	21%	−0 51%	37%	+4 33%	37%	+8 29%
Northern black	6%	−67 73%	9%	−53 62%	6%	−60 66%
Southern black	8%	−68 76%	11%	−58 69%	6%	−65 71%

...Up Among Men, Catholics, Southern Whites

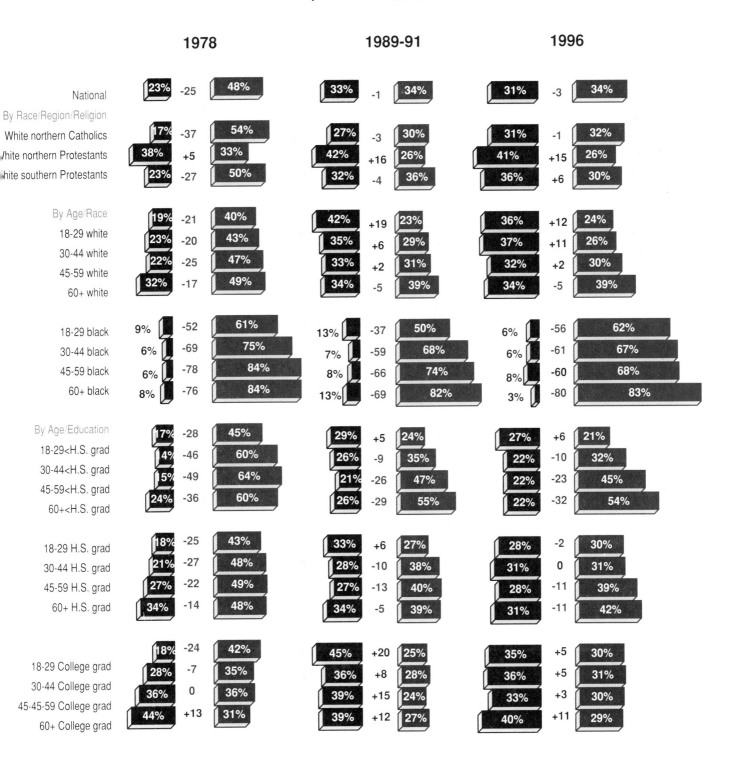

	% identifying as Republican	% identifying as Democrat

	1978			1989-91			1996		
National	23%	-25	48%	33%	-1	34%	31%	-3	34%
By Race/Region/Religion									
White northern Catholics	17%	-37	54%	27%	-3	30%	31%	-1	32%
White northern Protestants	38%	+5	33%	42%	+16	26%	41%	+15	26%
White southern Protestants	23%	-27	50%	32%	-4	36%	36%	+6	30%
By Age/Race									
18-29 white	19%	-21	40%	42%	+19	23%	36%	+12	24%
30-44 white	23%	-20	43%	35%	+6	29%	37%	+11	26%
45-59 white	22%	-25	47%	33%	+2	31%	32%	+2	30%
60+ white	32%	-17	49%	34%	-5	39%	34%	-5	39%
18-29 black	9%	-52	61%	13%	-37	50%	6%	-56	62%
30-44 black	6%	-69	75%	7%	-59	68%	6%	-61	67%
45-59 black	6%	-78	84%	8%	-66	74%	8%	-60	68%
60+ black	8%	-76	84%	13%	-69	82%	3%	-80	83%
By Age/Education									
18-29<H.S. grad	17%	-28	45%	29%	+5	24%	27%	+6	21%
30-44<H.S. grad	14%	-46	60%	26%	-9	35%	22%	-10	32%
45-59<H.S. grad	15%	-49	64%	21%	-26	47%	22%	-23	45%
60+<H.S. grad	24%	-36	60%	26%	-29	55%	22%	-32	54%
18-29 H.S. grad	18%	-25	43%	33%	+6	27%	28%	-2	30%
30-44 H.S. grad	21%	-27	48%	28%	-10	38%	31%	0	31%
45-59 H.S. grad	27%	-22	49%	27%	-13	40%	28%	-11	39%
60+ H.S. grad	34%	-14	48%	34%	-5	39%	31%	-11	42%
18-29 College grad	18%	-24	42%	45%	+20	25%	35%	+5	30%
30-44 College grad	28%	-7	35%	36%	+8	28%	36%	+5	31%
45-45-59 College grad	36%	0	36%	39%	+15	24%	33%	+3	30%
60+ College grad	44%	+13	31%	39%	+12	27%	40%	+11	29%

Source: Surveys by the Gallup Organization; for 1989-91, surveys for October 1989-February 1991 were combined; for 1996, surveys for January-August 1996 were combined.

Self-Described Conservatives Outnumbered Liberals by Nearly 2-1 as Clinton's First Term Ended

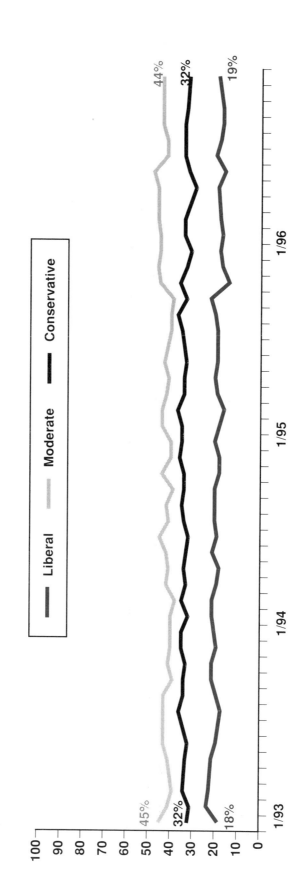

Source: Surveys by *CBS News* and *CBS News/New York Times.*

How Much Government? A Yes to Less

Question: Would you say you favor smaller government with fewer services, or larger government with many services?

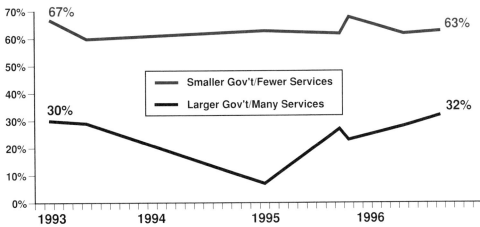

Source: Surveys by ABC News/*Washington Post*, February 25-28, 1993; the *Los Angeles Times*, June 12-14, 1993, January 19-22, 1995, September 16-18, 1995, October 27-30, 1995, April 13-16, 1996, and August 1-5, 1996.

Question: Which comes closer to your view: Government should do more to solve national problems or government is doing too many things better left to businesses and individuals?

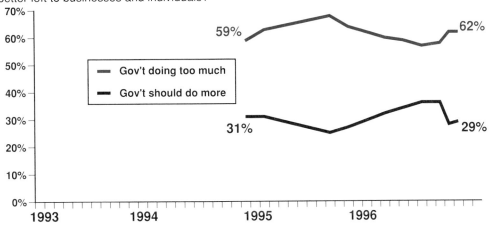

Source: Surveys by CBS News, November 27-28, 1994, January 2-3, 1995; CBS News/*New York Times*, August 5-9, 1995, October 22-25, 1995; NBC News/*Wall Street Journal*, December 1-5, 1995; CBS News/*New York Times*, February 22-24, 1996, March 31-April 2, 1996, May 31 - June 3, 1996, August 16-18, 1996, September 2-4, 1996, and October 10-13, 1996.

Question: Some people think the government is trying to do too many things that should be left to individuals and businesses. Others think that government should do more to solve our country's problems. Which comes closer to your own view?

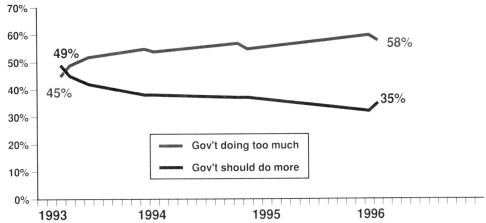

Source: Surveys by Gallup/CNN/*USA Today*, March 22-24, 1993, April 22-24, 1993; Yankelovich Partners/*Time*/CNN, June 17-21, 1993; Gallup/CNN/*USA Today*, December 17-19, 1993, January 15-17, 1994, October 22-25, 1994, November 2-26, 1994, December 15-18, 1995, January 12-15, 1996.

Among Exit Poll Voters, "Less Government" Got Strong Backing in Texas, The Upper Midwest, and Northern New England

Question: Which comes closer to your view: Government should do more to solve problems; government is doing too many things better left to business and individuals?

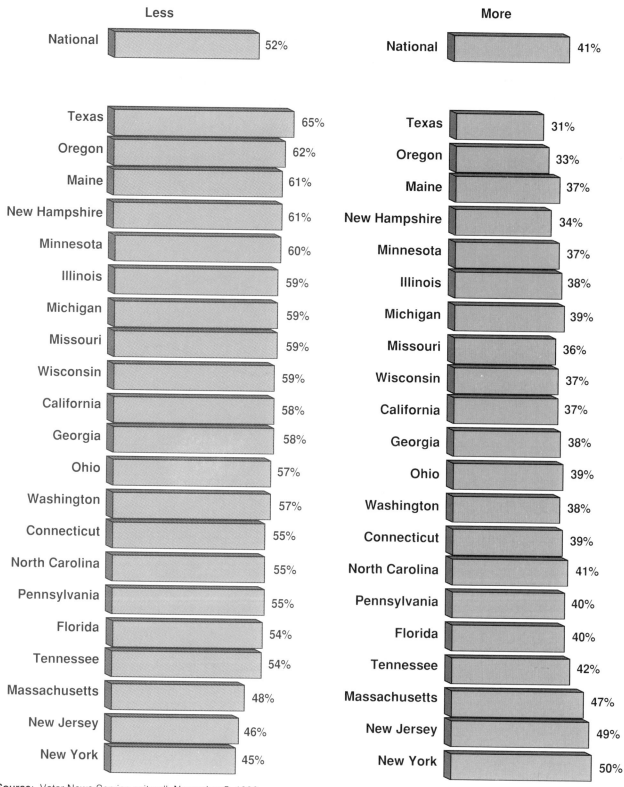

	Less		More
National	52%	National	41%
Texas	65%	Texas	31%
Oregon	62%	Oregon	33%
Maine	61%	Maine	37%
New Hampshire	61%	New Hampshire	34%
Minnesota	60%	Minnesota	37%
Illinois	59%	Illinois	38%
Michigan	59%	Michigan	39%
Missouri	59%	Missouri	36%
Wisconsin	59%	Wisconsin	37%
California	58%	California	37%
Georgia	58%	Georgia	38%
Ohio	57%	Ohio	39%
Washington	57%	Washington	38%
Connecticut	55%	Connecticut	39%
North Carolina	55%	North Carolina	41%
Pennsylvania	55%	Pennsylvania	40%
Florida	54%	Florida	40%
Tennessee	54%	Tennessee	42%
Massachusetts	48%	Massachusetts	47%
New Jersey	46%	New Jersey	49%
New York	45%	New York	50%

Source: Voter News Service exit poll, November 5, 1996.

Real National Unease—Especially on "the Moral Dimension"

Question: Do you personally agree or disagree with those who feel that there is something wrong with the country at this time?

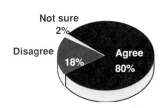

Source: Survey by Yankelovich Partners, Inc. for *Time*/CNN, July 10-11, 1996.

Question: Do you think the US is in a long-term moral decline, or do you think the country's moral standing is basically pretty solid?

Source: Survey by Chilton Research Services for ABC World News Tonight "Listening to America" poll, April 30-May 6, 1996.

Question: Which concerns you more—the nation's economic problems or the nation's moral problems?

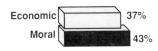

Note: Asked of registered voters.

Source: Survey by NBC News/*Wall Street Journal*, June 20-25, 1996.

Question: Thinking about everything going on in this country, how would you rate the state of the nation today—excellent, pretty good, only fair or poor?

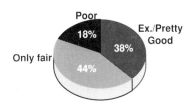

Source: Survey by Louis Harris and Associates, July 9-13, 1996.

Question: Would you say this country's main problems are caused more by a lack of economic opportunity, or more by a lack of morality?

Question: Which concerns you more—the nation's economic problems or the nation's moral problems?

Source: Survey by the Gallup Organization for CNN/*USA Today*, July 18-21, 1996.

Question: If this country's economic problems were solved, do you believe that most of the country's moral problems would also be solved, many of them would be solved, only a few would be solved, or none at all?

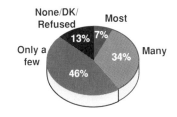

Source: Survey by the Gallup Organization for CNN/*USA Today*, May 9-12, 1996.

In the Deepest Sense, Americans in '96 Remained Confident in Their Nation's Ideals and Promise and Their Place in It

Questions: Would you say that you are optimistic or pessimistic about (the future of this country/your own personal future)?

Country's Future

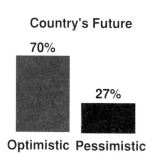

70%
27%
Optimistic Pessimistic

Personal Future

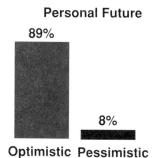

89%
8%
Optimistic Pessimistic

Question: Think of your parents when they were your age. Would you say you are better off financially than they were, or not?

Question: And what about your children? Do you think they will be better off than you are financially when they reach your age, or not? [For people who say they have no children] Suppose you did have children...?

■ Better Off   ■ Not Better Off

Date	Better Off	Not Better Off
5/6/96	69%	29%
1/4/95	67%	31%
5/5/91	70%	26%
3/24/86	81%	18%
1/16/85	74%	23%
12/18/83	73%	25%
3/8/82	69%	30%
3/29/81	64%	35%

■ Better Off   ■ Not Better Off

Date	Better Off	Not Better Off
5/6/96	60%	33%
1/4/95	54%	39%
5/5/91	66%	25%
3/24/86	74%	19%
1/16/85	62%	29%
12/18/83	65%	29%
3/8/82	43%	41%
3/29/81	47%	43%

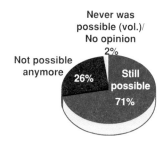

Never was possible (vol.)/ No opinion 2%

Not possible anymore 26%

Still possible 71%

Question: Do you think it's still possible for most people in this country to achieve the American Dream, or do you think that's not possible any more?

Question: ...[Do you agree or disagree]...It is true in this country that if you work hard, eventually you will get ahead?

■ Agree   ■ Disagree

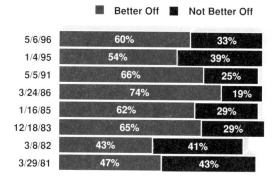

Date	Agree	Disagree
5/6/96	66%	33%
2/19/95	61%	38%
10/6/91	62%	36%
6/23/86	62%	37%
1/16/85	71%	27%
12/18/83	70%	28%
1/30/82	57%	41%
3/29/81	62%	36%

Source for page: Survey by Chilton Research for ABC World News Tonight "Listening to America," April 30-May 6, 1996.

Chapter 4
Charting the Presidential and Congressional Races through the Election Day: Group Alignments

Character Issue Failed to Topple Clinton
By Jim Norman

When GOP leaders gathered in November 1995, their game plan for the coming presidential campaign seemed obvious. "Republican political strategists" *Washington Post* political reporter David Broder wrote, "... are beginning to plan a 1996 campaign in which President Clinton's character is the main issue for voters."

Over the next 12 months, GOP strategists claimed to be winning half the battle—convincing voters that their candidate, Bob Dole, was the better choice on character issues. But winning the other half—convincing Americans that character was the main issue—proved tougher. As a result, Clinton won a decisive 8-point victory even when exit polls were showing less than half of voters thought him honest and trustworthy.

> " *From Clinton's forthrightness about Whitewater to the general impression of his honesty to comparisons with his predecessors, there's ample evidence that a character problem does exist.* "

Throughout the campaign, prominent Republicans cropped up at regular intervals to urge Dole and running mate Jack Kemp to hit the "character issue" harder. Meanwhile, journalists turned the controversy—whether couched as "moral values," "family values," or character—into a staple of 1996 campaign coverage. Magazines, newspapers and television all took their best shots at explaining why Clinton was leading so convincingly when voters favored his opponent on moral values. The following theories were among those proposed by the media to explain what the *Wall Street Journal's* Paul Gigot termed "the mystery of the political year":

—Michael Kinsley, in the April 29 issue of *Time*, maintained that Clinton's character was unfairly hurting him in the polls because his "professional and personal failings" were typical of presidents and presidential candidates.

—In the June 24 *US News & World Report*, Gloria Borger and Linda Kulman contended that "(Voters) do not care about character as much as Dole would like, and they do not define it the way Clinton fears."

—Richard Benedetto, writing in *USA Today* on September 9, suggested that "character apparently matters less than it used to. Or, at least, voters seem to hold lower character expectations for Clinton than they did for other presidents."

These and numerous other articles dealt with the subject from a seemingly endless array of angles. Ultimately, however, three fundamental questions were at the heart of the "mystery": Did Clinton really have a character problem? Did he lose the character issue to Dole? How important was the character issue to the voters?

Was the Character Problem Real?

Clinton backers could offer some poll findings to argue that the President may not have had a "character problem" at all. For example:

—ABC tracking polls began asking voters in August 1996 whether they agreed that "Bill Clinton does not have the kind of personal character and core values a president should have." Throughout the duration of the polls, less than half agreed with the statement.

—Fifty-three percent of registered voters said Clinton was providing "very strong" or "somewhat strong" moral leadership in a September *USA Today*/CNN/Gallup poll.

—In another *USA Today*/CNN/Gallup poll in October, 55% of likely voters said Clinton "is honest and trustworthy enough to be president."

These results, however, must be weighed against a mass of other public opinion measures that demonstrate Americans' lack of confidence in Clinton's integrity. From his forthrightness about Whitewater to the general impression of his honesty to comparisons with his predecessors, there's ample evidence that a character problem does exist.

—The impression that Clinton has not been totally honest about Whitewater goes back to mid-1995 when a *USA Today*/CNN/Gallup poll showed 51% of the public thought he was hiding something. The trend continued through the 1996 election, with the Voter News Service exit poll showing 60% of voters believed Clinton has "not told the truth."

—The *USA Today*/CNN/Gallup poll asked the basic question of whether Clinton is honest and trustworthy 13 times since March 1994, and not once did a

More Than Half of the Electorate Didn't Think Clinton Is Honest— A Fifth of Clinton Voters Agreed

Question: Regardless of how you voted today, do you think Bill Clinton is honest and trustworthy?

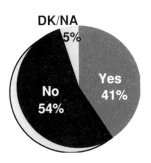

DK/NA 5%

No 54%

Yes 41%

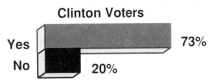

Clinton Voters

Yes 73%

No 20%

Source: Voter News Service exit poll, November 5, 1996.

majority of the public say that he is. Other pollsters during the same time period found the same lack of confidence in the president's honesty.

—A majority of VNS exit poll participants said Clinton was not honest and trustworthy including a fifth of those who voted for him.

—In a March 1996 ABC/*Washington Post* poll, only 44% said Clinton has "high personal moral and ethical standards."

Looking at the question of honesty from another dimension, Clinton scored poorly when compared with previous presidents. Although the wide variation in question wording could explain some of the difference between Clinton and his predecessors, there seems to be considerable evidence that, unlike Clinton, previous presidents enjoyed high levels of confidence in their integrity:

—In an October 1964 Harris survey, 71% described Lyndon Johnson as "personally honest."

—Richard Nixon (often cited as another recent president re-elected in spite of concerns about his character) was picked on a 7-point, sliding-scale question as more honest than insincere by 57% of respondents in a May 1971 ORC poll.

—Sixty-two percent of the respondents in a March 1976 CBS/*New York Times* poll said Gerald Ford struck them as "being more honest and having more integrity than most."

—In a September 1980 CBS/*NYT* poll, 73% found Jimmy Carter "very honest."

—Ronald Reagan was considered "honest and open" by 56% in a December 1986 Gallup poll for *Newsweek*.

Who Won the "Character Issue" Battle?

Pollsters compared Dole and Clinton throughout 1996 on a wide array of character measures. And on the questions of integrity and moral leadership, Dole was the clear victor:

—Dole was consistently identified as the candidate who would "provide the best moral leadership for the country" in the *USA Today*/CNN/Gallup daily tracking poll during the campaign's last month. In the final poll, 45% chose Dole, 34% Clinton and 10% Ross Perot.

—Only 31% of Americans said Clinton had a higher moral character than Dole according to a June 1996 *USA Today*/CNN/Gallup poll.

—Sixty-six percent of voters said Dole was honest and trustworthy in a late-October *USA Today*/CNN/Gallup poll, but only 45% said Clinton was.

In other election-year polls, Dole garnered more support than Clinton for protecting family values (June CBS/*NYT* poll), for setting a moral and religious tone for the country (June CBS/*NYT* poll), and for having better character (May Harris poll).

But Clinton supporters did not automatically cede the character issue. Instead, they defined it in much broader terms thereby putting the President on at least an equal footing with his GOP challenger. A January *US News & World Report* poll, for instance, showed registered voters favoring Dole over Clinton 49% to 31% on the question of which candidate best represented the values of ethics and honesty. But

different, more personal context. Respondents were asked which candidate they favored when viewed from experiences in their own lives. The results

said Clinton.

—Asked who they would trust more to get them to their destination on a car trip, 46% picked Clinton and 43% selected Dole.

> **" Voters do have a threshold for character that a presidential candidate must meet, a threshold more important even than a candidate's stand on the issues. But once the character threshold is reached, other polls suggest, voters care less about comparisons of candidates' character than other comparisons. "**

on the value of "hope" Clinton led 47% to 36%, on the value of "community" the President was ahead 48% to 35%, and on the value of "fairness" he led 50% to 35%. Additionally, Clinton was favored slightly when the same respondents picked the candidate who most shared their values.

An intriguing set of questions asked in a June 1996 *US News & World Report* poll illustrated the point from a

showed the mix of feelings Americans had toward the two candidates:

—If opening a business, respondents were asked whether they would rather have Clinton or Dole keep the books. Fifty-five percent would rather Dole keep their business' books; 24% wanted Clinton.

—When asked who would devote more time and energy to making the business a success, 48% chose Dole and 33%

—Forty-two percent trusted Clinton to know where they needed to go on the trip; 41% said Dole.

—Another question from the poll seemed to show whose character the public admired the most. Forty-two percent said they wanted their child to grow up to be more like Bob Dole; only 33% chose Clinton.

How Much Did Character Matter?

Americans clearly said character mattered in the 1996 campaign; 87% in a May *USA Today*/CNN/Gallup poll claimed a candidate's stand on moral values was important to their vote in the presidential election. And the concern about moral values in general appeared to be growing. Not only did a majority in the May Gallup poll say

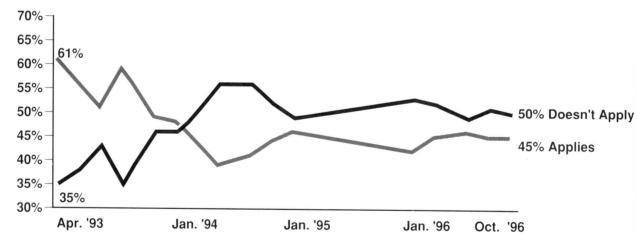

Since Early 1994 a Majority of the Public Has Questioned Clinton's Honesty

Question: ...[P]lease tell me whether you think it applies or doesn't apply to Bill Clinton...honest and trustworthy?

Note: October 1996 asking is of likely voters.
Source: Surveys by the Gallup Organization for *USA Today*/CNN, latest that of October 26-29, 1996.

they were more concerned about the state of moral values in the US than they were about economic issues, but the number who mentioned moral values as the most important problem facing the nation climbed to an all-time high in 1996 Gallup polls.

Further, a Princeton Survey Research poll for Knight-Ridder in January 1996 showed that more voters thought it important for the president to have a strong character than for the respondent to share views with the president. This finding, however, must be examined carefully. It seems to confirm that voters do have a threshold for character that a presidential candidate must meet, a threshold more important even than a candidate's stand on the issues. But once the character threshold is reached, other polls suggest, voters care less about comparisons of candidates' character than other comparisons. Consider the following findings:

—A 1976 CBS/*NYT* poll—at a point in polling history when concern over presidential character may have been at its height following the Watergate scandal—showed 57% considered the positions of candidates on major issues most important while 36% said the candidate's personal qualities and character mattered the most.

—Fifty-nine percent favored a candidate who took better positions on major issues, according to a 1980 *Los Angeles Times* poll, while 34% preferred a candidate with strong personal qualities and character.

—A candidate's views on the issues was more important to 59% of the respondents in a January 1988 Gordon S. Black poll for *USA Today;* only 16% selected character.

—In an October 1996 *USA Today/CNN/*Gallup poll, respondents were asked whether moral values, positions on issues, or ability to manage the government were most important in rating how a president was handling his job. Forty-five percent said ability to manage, 25% listed positions on issues, and only 21% named moral values.

Additionally, a regression analysis of the 1996 Gallup Labor Day poll by David Moore showed that moral character ranked among the least significant predictors of voter behavior.

Finally, in the VNS general election exit poll, only 20% of voters listed honesty and integrity as the most important candidate quality in deciding their vote, with the other 80% picking from such choices as "is in touch with the 1990s" and "cares about people like me."

How the Character Issue Played Out

Even though voters considered presidential character important, and even though Dole was favored by voters on most dimensions, Clinton won the election. A few possible explanations for this development follow:

—Other comparisons were more important. Issues and, even more power-

fully, leadership abilities, were given greater weight by voters once the candidates had passed the character threshold.

—Clinton battled Dole on equal terms when the character question was broadened to include such factors as fairness. Even on the narrower character issues where Dole clearly led Clinton, the challenger didn't score that highly. On the Gallup question of who would provide better moral leadership, fewer than half chose Dole. One in five picked neither Dole nor Clinton, and Dole was a big loser with this group— fewer than 10% planned to vote for him.

—Voters seemed to set the character threshold for a presidential candidate below their general character threshold. In an October *USA Today/CNN/*Gallup poll, half the respondents were asked whether Clinton was honest and trustworthy enough to be president, and the other half were simply asked whether he was honest and trustworthy. Only 47% said he was honest and trustworthy, but 55% said he was honest and trustworthy enough to be president.

—Voters don't see Clinton as any worse than his predecessors (possibly having reassessed their views of how honest and ethical previous presidents were). A late-October *Los Angeles Times* poll asked voters whether Clinton "is less ethical than most other modern-day presidents, or more ethical, or just about as ethical." Fifty-nine percent said he was "just about as ethical," 30% "less ethical," and 7% "more ethical."

Personal Dimensions of Leadership: Clinton Gets High Marks for Caring, Low for Honesty

Question: I'm going to read off some personal characteristics and qualities. As I read each one, please tell me whether you think it applies or doesn't apply to Bill Clinton ...

Survey Date	Applies	Doesn't apply
Can get things done		
Oct. 26-29, 1996	65%	31%
Aug. 5-7, 1996	55%	41%
March 15-17, 1996	48%	50%
Jan. 12-15, 1996	41%	56%
Feb. 3-5, 1995	45%	51%
Dec. 2-5, 1994	45%	53%
Sept. 6-7, 1994	42%	54%
July 15-17, 1994	43%	54%
April 22-24, 1994	52%	44%
March 7-8, 1994	57%	39%
Jan. 28-30, 1994	64%	31%
Jan. 15-17, 1994	62%	33%
Jan. 6-8, 1994	63%	35%
Nov. 19-21, 1993	66%	30%
Nov. 2-4, 1993	49%	46%
Oct. 8-10, 1993	56%	38%
Aug. 8-10, 1993	46%	49%
June 29-30, 1993	46%	49%
June 5-6, 1993	42%	51%
April 22-24, 1993	55%	40%

Survey Date	Applies	Doesn't apply
Shares your values		
Aug. 5-7, 1996	51%	45%
June 18-19, 1996	53%	43%
March 15-17, 1996	47%	51%
Jan. 12-15, 1996	44%	53%
Feb. 3-5, 1995	45%	50%
Dec. 2-5, 1994	41%	56%
July 15-17, 1994	40%	56%
April 22-24, 1994	44%	50%
March 7-8, 1994	49%	47%
Jan. 28-30, 1994	53%	42%
Jan. 15-17, 1994	44%	52%
Nov. 2-4, 1993	49%	48%
Aug. 8-10, 1993	46%	51%
April 22-24, 1993	53%	42%

Survey Date	Applies	Doesn't apply
Cares about the needs of people like you		
Aug. 5-7, 1996	62%	36%
June 18-19, 1996	64%	32%
March 15-17, 1996	57%	41%
Jan. 12-15, 1996	56%	42%
Dec. 2-5, 1994	54%	44%
Jan. 28-30, 1994	65%	32%
July 15-17, 1994	51%	47%
April 22-24, 1994	55%	41%
March 7-8, 1994	60%	38%
Jan. 15-17, 1994	53%	43%
June 5-6, 1993	56%	41%
April 22-24, 1993	64%	33%

Survey Date	Applies	Doesn't apply
Honest and trustworthy		
Oct. 26-29, 1996	45%	50%
Aug. 5-7, 1996	45%	51%
June 18-19, 1996	46%	49%
March 15-17, 1996	45%	52%
Jan. 12-15, 1996	40%	55%
Feb. 3-5, 1995	46%	49%
Dec. 2-5, 1994	44%	53%
July 15-17, 1994	39%	56%
April 22-24, 1994	46%	49%
March 7-8, 1994	48%	47%
Jan. 15-17, 1994	53%	41%
Jan. 6-8, 1994	49%	46%
Nov. 19-21, 1993	54%	41%
Nov. 2-4, 1993	56%	39%
Oct. 8-10, 1993	59%	35%
Aug. 8-10, 1993	51%	43%
June 5-6, 1993	56%	38%
April 22-24, 1993	61%	35%

Survey Date	Applies	Doesn't apply
Tough enough for the job		
Jan. 12-15, 1996	51%	47%
Dec. 2-5, 1994	50%	48%
Oct. 11, 1994	50%	48%
Sept. 6-7, 1994	44%	55%
July 15-17, 1994	46%	52%
April 22-24, 1994	53%	44%
March 7-8, 1994	51%	46%
Jan. 28-30, 1994	62%	36%
Jan. 15-17, 1994	63%	35%
Jan. 6-8, 1994	59%	38%
Nov. 19-21, 1993	56%	41%
Nov. 2-4, 1993	53%	43%
Oct. 8-10, 1993	54%	41%
Aug. 8-10, 1993	50%	46%
June 29-30, 1993	54%	42%
June 5-6, 1993	47%	47%
April 22-24, 1993	61%	35%

Survey Date	Applies	Doesn't apply
Keeps his promises		
Jan. 12-15, 1996	33%	61%
July 15-17, 1994	30%	67%
April 22-24, 1994	37%	57%
March 7-8, 1994	40%	54%
Jan. 28-30, 1994	45%	48%
Jan. 15-17, 1994	35%	60%
Nov. 2-4, 1993	38%	57%
Aug. 8-10, 1993	33%	63%
April 22-24, 1993	44%	51%

Survey Date	Applies	Doesn't apply
Effective Manager		
Jan. 12-15, 1996	42%	55%
March 7-8, 1994	49%	46%
Jan. 15-17, 1994	58%	37%
Nov. 19-21, 1993	55%	40%
Nov. 2-4, 1993	50%	45%
Aug. 8-10, 1993	45%	50%

Source: Surveys by the Gallup Organization for CNN/*USA Today*, latest that of October 26-29, 1996.

Character Rating Remains Low

Question: How confident are you that Bill Clinton has the **right set of personal characteristics to be President of the United States**—extremely confident, quite confident, only somewhat confident, or not at all confident?

	Extremely confident	Quite confident	Only somewhat confident	Not at all confident
Sep. 12-17, 1996	12%	24%	30%	30%
Oct. 27-30, 1995	9	19	4	3
Jan. 14-17, 1995	11	20	37	31
Oct. 14-18, 1994	11	17	36	34
June 10-14, 1994	11	19	37	31
April 30-May 3, 1994	12	22	39	25
Jan. 15-18, 1994	11	24	38	25
Jan. 23-26, 1993	16	31	37	13

December 1996

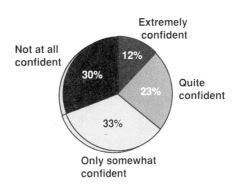

Source: Surveys by NBC News/*Wall Street Journal*, latest that of December 5-9, 1996.

Question: [Do you think each of the following personal characteristics and qualities] applies to Bill Clinton, somewhat applies, or doesn't apply...?

Honest and Trustworthy

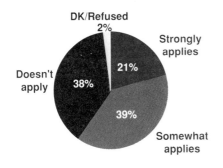

Shares Your Values

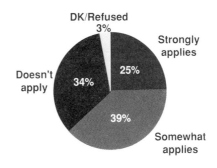

Cares About People Like You

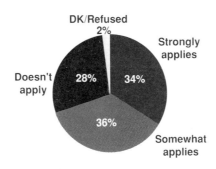

Source: Survey by the Gallup Organization for CNN/*USA Today*, January 10-13, 1997.

Clinton's Image

Positive Marks

Questions: (A) Do you think Bill Clinton cares about the needs and problems of people like yourself? (B) ...[P]lease tell me whether you think [the following personal characteristic or quality] ...applies or doesn't apply to Bill Clinton...?

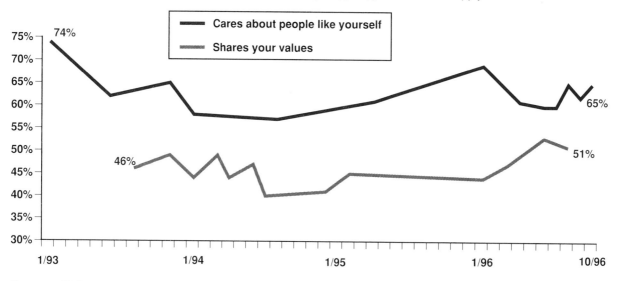

Sources: (A) Surveys by CBS News/*New York Times*. The question was asked 17 times from January 1993 through September 2-4, 1996. Here, the first asking in each month was used if asked more than once during a month. (B) Surveys by Gallup/CNN/*USA Today*. The question was asked 14 times from August 1993 through August 5-7, 1996. Again, the first asking in each month was used if asked more than once during a month.

Negative Marks

Questions: (A) ...[P]lease tell me whether you think [the following personal characteristic or quality]...applies or doesn't apply to Bill Clinton...Honest and trustworthy? (B) How confident are you that Bill Clinton has the right set of personal characteristics to be President of the US—extremely confident, quite confident, only somewhat confident, or not at all confident?

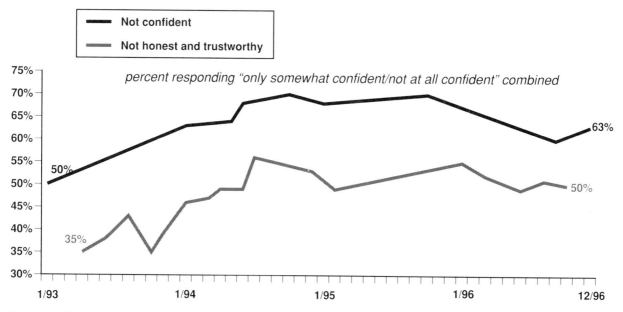

Sources: (A) Surveys by the Gallup Organization/CNN/*USA Today*. The question was asked 22 times from April 1993 through October 26-29, 1996. Here, the first asking in each month was used if asked more than once during a month. (B) Surveys by NBC News/*Wall Street Journal*. The question was asked 9 times from January 1993 through December 5-9, 1996. Again, the first asking in each month was used if asked more than once during a month.

Looking Backward:
How Americans Viewed Clinton in 1992

Question: Do you think Bill Clinton as president will bring about the kind of change the country needs?

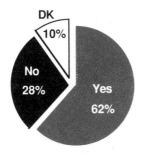

Source: Survey by CBS News/*New York Times,* December 7-9, 1992.

Question: In your view, which of these descriptions apply and which do not apply to Bill Clinton:... someone you would be proud to have as president.

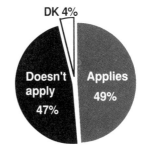

Source: Survey by Yankelovich Clancy Shulman for CNN/*Time,* October 20-22, 1992.

Question: Do you think Bill Clinton says what he really believes most of the time, or does he say what he thinks people want to hear?

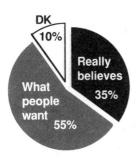

Source: Survey by CBS News/*New York Times,* October 2-4, 1992.

Question: Bill Clinton says he's less likely than past Democratic candidates to raise taxes and increase government spending. Do you believe this, or not?

Source: Survey by CBS News/*New York Times,* September 9-13, 1992.

Question: Do you think Bill Clinton can be trusted to deal with all the problems a president has to deal with, or are you concerned that he might make serious mistakes?

Source: Survey by CBS News/*New York Times,* October 29-November 1, 1992.

Question: Do you think Bill Clinton waffles on the issues, or not?

Source: Survey by the *Los Angeles Times*, October 24-26, 1992.

And From 1994:

Question: (Now, I'm going to read off some personal characteristics and qualities. As I read each one, please tell me whether you think it applies or doesn't apply to (President) Bill Clinton.) Is a nice guy...?

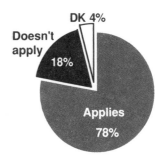

Source: Survey by the Gallup Organization, June 3-6, 1994.

Do You Approve or Disapprove of Clinton's Handling of the Presidency?

	Everyone		Men		Women	
	Approve	Disapprove	Approve	Disapprove	Approve	Disapprove
By Whites/Income						
Less than $10,000	58%	42%	56%	44%	59%	41%
$10-14,999	59%	41%	56%	44%	61%	39%
$15-19,999	59%	41%	55%	45%	63%	37%
$20-29,999	53%	47%	48%	52%	57%	43%
$30-49,999	50%	50%	44%	56%	56%	44%
$50-74,999	49%	51%	46%	54%	51%	49%
$75,000+	49%	51%	44%	56%	56%	44%
By Blacks/Income						
Less than $15,000	81%	19%	83%	27%	79%	21%
$15-29,999	85%	15%	88%	12%	83%	17%
$30,000+	88%	12%	88%	12%	87%	13%
By Ethnicity						
Non-Hispanic White	52%	48%	47%	53%	57%	43%
Hispanic	71%	29%	68%	32%	73%	27%
African-American	86%	14%	88%	12%	83%	17%
By Denomination						
Protestant	47%	53%	43%	57%	52%	48%
Catholic	57%	43%	52%	48%	61%	39%
By Region						
East	62%	38%	57%	43%	67%	33%
Midwest	57%	43%	53%	47%	61%	39%
South	51%	49%	48%	52%	54%	46%
West	56%	44%	51%	49%	60%	40%
Whites (Non-Hispanic)/By Region						
East	57%	43%	51%	49%	63%	37%
Midwest	54%	46%	49%	51%	58%	42%
South	45%	55%	40%	60%	48%	52%
West	53%	47%	48%	52%	58%	42%
By Marital Status						
Married	45%	55%	40%	60%	51%	49%
Divorced	61%	39%	55%	45%	62%	38%
Widowed	55%	45%	52%	48%	57%	43%
Never Married	61%	39%	57%	43%	66%	34%
By Age/Marital Status						
18-39/Married	44%	56%	39%	61%	48%	52%
40-59/Married	45%	55%	40%	60%	50%	50%
18-39/Divorced	45%	55%	41%	59%	48%	52%
40-59/Divorced	60%	40%	60%	40%	61%	39%

Exploring Group Differences

Clinton Approval

	Everyone		Men		Women	
	Approve	**Disapprove**	**Approve**	**Disapprove**	**Approve**	**Disapprove**
By Education						
Less than H.S.	66%	34%	64%	36%	68%	32%
High School Grad	55%	45%	52%	48%	58%	42%
Some College	53%	47%	48%	52%	58%	42%
College Grad	53%	47%	48%	52%	58%	42%
Post Grad	58%	42%	51%	49%	66%	34%
By Age/Education						
18-34/Less than H.S.	61%	39%	60%	41%	63%	37%
18-34/H.S. Grad	55%	45%	50%	51%	60%	40%
18-34/Some College	57%	43%	52%	48%	61%	39%
18-34/College Grad	55%	45%	52%	48%	58%	42%
18-34/Post Grad	61%	39%	56%	44%	68%	32%
35-49/Less than H.S.	54%	46%	51%	49%	56%	44%
35-49/H.S. Grad	52%	48%	51%	49%	53%	47%
35-49/Some College	51%	49%	47%	53%	55%	45%
35-49/College Grad	54%	46%	49%	51%	58%	42%
35-49/Post Grad	61%	39%	53%	47%	70%	30%
50-64/Less than H.S.	69%	31%	70%	31%	69%	31%
50-64/H.S. Grad	58%	42%	57%	43%	59%	41%
50-64/Some College	52%	48%	44%	56%	58%	42%
50-64/College Grad+	52%	48%	47%	53%	60%	40%
65+/Less than H.S.	71%	29%	69%	31%	73%	27%
65+/H.S. Grad	59%	41%	53%	47%	63%	37%
65+/Some College	51%	49%	42%	59%	58%	42%
65+/College Grad+	48%	52%	43%	57%	56%	44%
By Income						
Less than $20,000	64%	36%	61%	39%	65%	35%
$20-29,999	57%	43%	54%	46%	60%	40%
$30-49,999	54%	46%	48%	52%	60%	41%
$50-74,999	51%	49%	49%	51%	54%	46%
$75,000+	51%	49%	46%	54%	58%	42%

Source: Combined Gallup/CNN/*USA Today* surveys of January-June 1996

Gallup Data (percent approving) Show Clinton (first term) Compared to His Predecessors

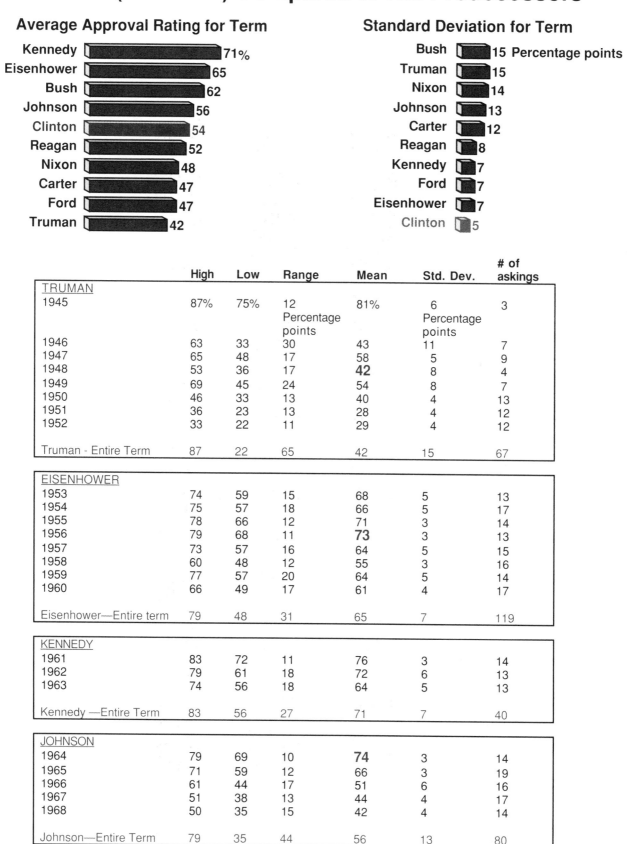

Average Approval Rating for Term

Kennedy	71%
Eisenhower	65
Bush	62
Johnson	56
Clinton	54
Reagan	52
Nixon	48
Carter	47
Ford	47
Truman	42

Standard Deviation for Term

Bush	15 Percentage points
Truman	15
Nixon	14
Johnson	13
Carter	12
Reagan	8
Kennedy	7
Ford	7
Eisenhower	7
Clinton	5

	High	Low	Range	Mean	Std. Dev.	# of askings
TRUMAN						
1945	87%	75%	12 Percentage points	81%	6 Percentage points	3
1946	63	33	30	43	11	7
1947	65	48	17	58	5	9
1948	53	36	17	**42**	8	4
1949	69	45	24	54	8	7
1950	46	33	13	40	4	13
1951	36	23	13	28	4	12
1952	33	22	11	29	4	12
Truman - Entire Term	87	22	65	42	15	67
EISENHOWER						
1953	74	59	15	68	5	13
1954	75	57	18	66	5	17
1955	78	66	12	71	3	14
1956	79	68	11	**73**	3	13
1957	73	57	16	64	5	15
1958	60	48	12	55	3	16
1959	77	57	20	64	5	14
1960	66	49	17	61	4	17
Eisenhower—Entire term	79	48	31	65	7	119
KENNEDY						
1961	83	72	11	76	3	14
1962	79	61	18	72	6	13
1963	74	56	18	64	5	13
Kennedy —Entire Term	83	56	27	71	7	40
JOHNSON						
1964	79	69	10	**74**	3	14
1965	71	59	12	66	3	19
1966	61	44	17	51	6	16
1967	51	38	13	44	4	17
1968	50	35	15	42	4	14
Johnson—Entire Term	79	35	44	56	13	80

	High	Low	Range	Mean	Std. Dev.	# of askings
NIXON						
1969	67	56	11 Percentage points	61	3 Percentage points	18
1970	64	51	13	57	4	18
1971	56	48	8	50	2	13
1972	62	49	13	**56**	4	10
1973	67	27	40	42	12	20
1974 (to August)	28	24	4	26	1	17
Nixon—Entire Term	67	24	43	48	14	96
FORD						
1974 (from August)	71	42	29	54	10	8
1975	52	37	15	43	5	19
1976	53	45	8	**48**	3	9
Ford—Entire Term	71	37	34	47	7	36
CARTER						
1977	75	51	24	63	6	24
1978	55	39	16	46	5	25
1979	54	28	26	37	8	25
1980	58	31	27	**41**	9	17
Carter—Entire Term	75	28	47	47	12	91
REAGAN						
1981	68	49	19	58	6	19
1982	49	41	8	44	2	19
1983	54	35	19	44	5	22
1984	62	52	10	**55**	3	21
1985	65	52	13	60	4	15
1986	68	47	21	61	6	13
1987	53	43	10	48	3	11
1988	63	48	15	52	4	15
Reagan—Entire Term	68	35	33	52	8	135
BUSH						
1989	71	51	20	64	7	12
1990	80	53	27	66	8	29
1991	89	50	39	72	10	42
1992	49	29	20	**40**	5	28
Bush—Entire Term	89	29	60	62	15	111
CLINTON						
1993	59	37	22	49	6	27
1994	58	39	19	46	5	29
1995	53	44	9	48	3	36
1996	60	42	18	**54**	4	35
Clinton—First Term	60	37	23	49	5	108

Note: High = highest approval rating; Low = lowest approval rating; Range = difference between the high and low scores; Mean = average approval rating; Standard Deviation = measure of the dispersion of ratings. Mean and standard deviation are rounded to the nearest whole number. Election year means bolded. Surveys include both in-person (generally, President Carter and earlier) and telephone (generally, President Reagan and after, although a small portion of Gallup surveys during the 1980s and 1990s are in-person).
Source: Surveys conducted by the Gallup Organization.

Both Clinton and Dole Had Areas of Distinct Strength and Weakness; Perot Trailed on All Dimensions

Question: ...Please tell me whether or not each applies to each presidential candidate...

...He is honest and trustworthy...?

Perot	Clinton	Dole
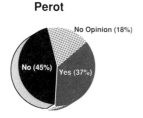	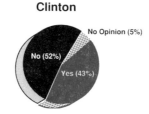	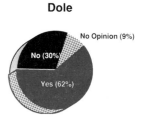

...He has high personal moral and ethical standards...?

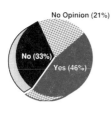	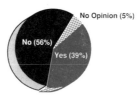	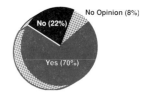

...He stands up for what he believes in...?

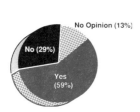	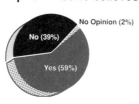	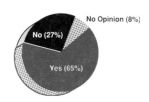

...He has a vision for the future of the country...?

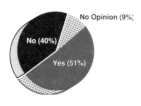	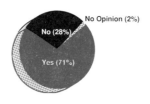	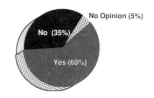

...He has new ideas...?

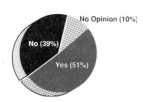	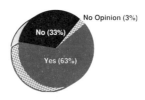	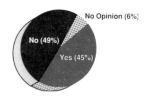

...He understands the problems of people like you...?

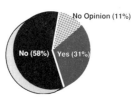	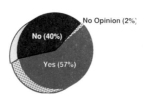	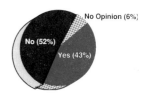

Source: Survey by ABC News/*Washington Post*, September 3-4, 1996.

Perot Was Far Weaker This Time Among All Groups
Vote Intentions Summer 1996 and 1992

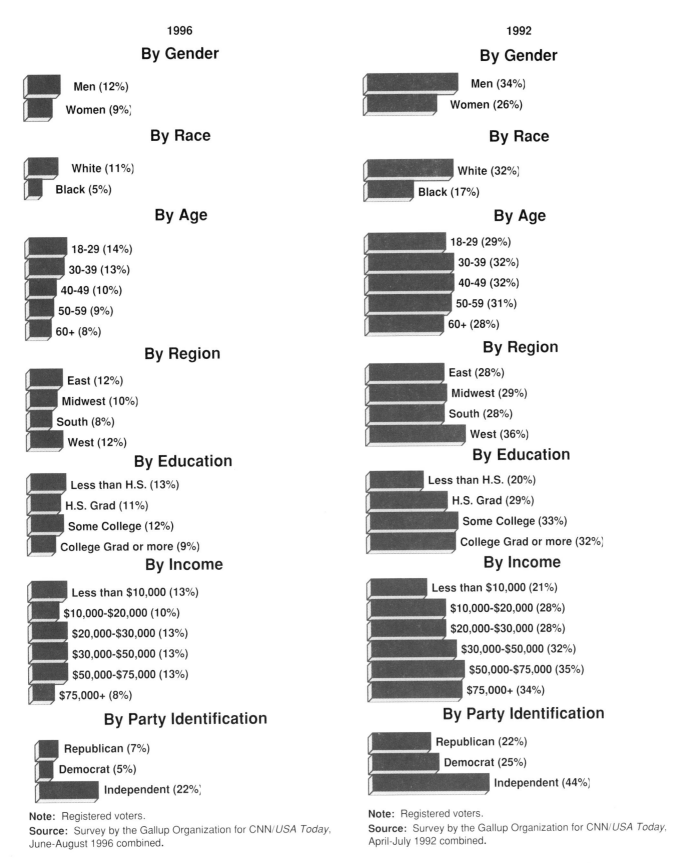

1996

By Gender
Men (12%)
Women (9%)

By Race
White (11%)
Black (5%)

By Age
18-29 (14%)
30-39 (13%)
40-49 (10%)
50-59 (9%)
60+ (8%)

By Region
East (12%)
Midwest (10%)
South (8%)
West (12%)

By Education
Less than H.S. (13%)
H.S. Grad (11%)
Some College (12%)
College Grad or more (9%)

By Income
Less than $10,000 (13%)
$10,000-$20,000 (10%)
$20,000-$30,000 (13%)
$30,000-$50,000 (13%)
$50,000-$75,000 (13%)
$75,000+ (8%)

By Party Identification
Republican (7%)
Democrat (5%)
Independent (22%)

Note: Registered voters.
Source: Survey by the Gallup Organization for CNN/*USA Today*, June-August 1996 combined.

1992

By Gender
Men (34%)
Women (26%)

By Race
White (32%)
Black (17%)

By Age
18-29 (29%)
30-39 (32%)
40-49 (32%)
50-59 (31%)
60+ (28%)

By Region
East (28%)
Midwest (29%)
South (28%)
West (36%)

By Education
Less than H.S. (20%)
H.S. Grad (29%)
Some College (33%)
College Grad or more (32%)

By Income
Less than $10,000 (21%)
$10,000-$20,000 (28%)
$20,000-$30,000 (28%)
$30,000-$50,000 (32%)
$50,000-$75,000 (35%)
$75,000+ (34%)

By Party Identification
Republican (22%)
Democrat (25%)
Independent (44%)

Note: Registered voters.
Source: Survey by the Gallup Organization for CNN/*USA Today*, April-July 1992 combined.

Huge Dropoff in Perot Support Among College-Trained Independents

Vote Intentions Summer 1996 and 1992

1996

By Gender/Education

Men (14%)
Women (10%) — No College

Men (11%)
Women (8%) — College

By Age/Education

18-34 (17%)
35-59 (11%) — No College
60+ (9%)

18-34 (12%)
35-59 (9%) — College
60+ (7%)

By Party Identification/Education

Republican (7%)
Democrat (5%) — No College
Independent (28%)

Republican (7%)
Democrat (5%) — College
Independent (17%)

By Self-Described Ideology/Party ID

Conservative (5%)
Moderate (13%) — Republican
Liberal (15%)

Conservative (7%)
Moderate (7%) — Democrat
Liberal (6%)

Conservative (24%)
Moderate (22%) — Independent
Liberal (26%)

Note: Registered voters.
Source: Surveys by the Gallup Organization for CNN/*USA Today*, June-Aug,1996 combined.

1992

By Gender/Education

Men (32%)
Women (23%) — No College

Men (36%)
Women (29%) — College

By Age/Education

18-34 (29%)
35-59 (29%) — No College
60+ (24%)

18-34 (30%)
35-59 (34%) — College
60+ (34%)

By Party Identification/Education

Republican (17%)
Democrat (25%) — No College
Independent (40%)

Republican (25%)
Democrat (26%) — College
Independent (47%)

By Self-Described Ideology/Party ID

Liberal (21%)
Moderate (25%) — Republican
Conservative (20%)

Liberal (22%)
Moderate (27%) — Democrat
Conservative (28%)

Liberal (41%)
Moderate (47%) — Independent
Conservative (42%)

Note: Registered voters.
Source: Survey by the Gallup Organization for CNN/*USA Today*, April-July 1992 combined.

In '96 Most Americans Didn't See Perot as Presidential

Question: Do you think Ross Perot has the kind of personality and temperament it takes to serve effectively as president, or not?

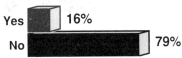

Yes   16%
No   79%

Source: Survey by ABC News/*Washington Post*, September 3-4, 1996.

Question: I'd like you to rate your feelings toward...(Ross Perot)... either very positive, somewhat positive, neutral, somewhat negative, or very negative.

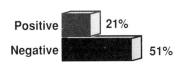

Positive   21%
Negative   51%

Source: Survey by NBC News/*Wall Street Journal*, August 20-21, 1996.

Question: Is your opinion of Ross Perot favorable, not favorable, undecided, or haven't you heard enough about Ross Perot yet to have an opinion?

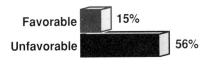

Favorable   15%
Unfavorable   56%

Source: Survey by CBS News, August 26-28, 1996.

Question: Is your opinion of Ross Perot favorable, not favorable, undecided, or haven't you heard enough about Ross Perot yet to have an opinion?

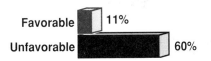

Favorable   11%
Unfavorable   60%

Source: Survey by CBS News/*New York Times*, September 2-4, 1996.

Question: ...please tell me if you have a favorable or unfavorable impression of ...Ross Perot...or perhaps you don't know enough to say?

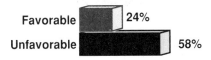

Favorable   24%
Unfavorable   58%

Source: Survey by ABC News/*Washington Post,* September 3-4, 1996.

What a Difference Four Years Make

Question: Regardless of how you plan to vote, do you think Ross Perot can win the presidential election in November, or don't you think so ?

1992

Cannot win 51%
Can win 49%

1996

Can win 7%
Cannot win 93%

Note: For display purposes, "don't know" responses are calculated out.

Source: Survey by Yankelovich Clancy Shulman for *Time*/CNN, July 8-9, 1992.

Source: Survey by Yankelovich Partners, Inc. for *Time*/CNN, July 26-30, 1996.

How the Public Saw Bob Dole

Not Too Old

Question: Do you feel Bob Dole is too old to be president, or not?

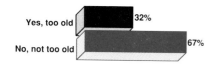

Source: Survey by the Gallup Organization for CNN/*USA Today,* Oct. 19-20, 1996.

Keeps His Word

Question: Do you think Bob Dole can be trusted to keep his word as president, or not?

Source: Survey by CBS News/*New York Times,* Oct. 30-Nov. 2, 1996.

Has Made Goals Clear

Question: Do you think Bob Dole has made it clear what he wants to accomplish in the next four years as President?

Source: Survey by CBS News/*New York Times,* Oct. 30-Nov. 2,1996.

Can Get Things Done

Question: ...please tell me whether you think it applies or doesn't apply to Bob Dole...Can get things done?

Source: Survey by the Gallup Organization for CNN/*USA Today,* Oct. 26-29, 1996.

Honest & Trustworthy

Question: ...please tell me whether you think it applies or doesn't apply to Bob Dole...Honest and trustworthy?

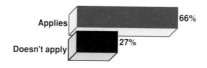

Source: Survey by the Gallup Organization for CNN/*USA Today,* Oct. 26-29, 1996.

Character

Question: Would you say that...Bob Dole's...character is better, worse, or about the same as most other political leaders in this country?

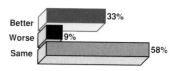

Source: Survey by Louis Harris and Associates, Oct 17-20, 1996.

Shares Americans' Moral Values

Question: Do you think Bob Dole shares the moral values most Americans try to live by, or doesn't he?

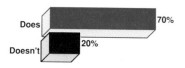

Source: Survey by CBS News/*New York Times,* Oct.10-13,1996.

Able to Deal Wisely in International Crisis

Question: Do you have confidence in Bob Dole's ability to deal wisely with an international crisis, or are you uneasy about his approach?

Source: Survey by CBS News/*New York Times,* Oct.10-13,1996.

Age Won't Matter

Question: If Bob Dole is elected President he will be 73 years old when he takes office. Do you think his age would help him be an effective president,... would be an obstacle,... or wouldn't his age matter that much?

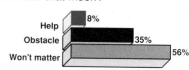

Source: Survey by CBS News/*New York Times,* Oct.17-20,1996.

Not Addressing Issues That Matter

Question: In the presidential campaign, do you think Bob Dole is addressing the issues that matter to you?

Source: Survey by CBS News/*New York Times,* Oct.30-Nov. 2,1996.

Has No Clear Plan

Question: ...please tell me whether you think it applies or doesn't apply to Bob Dole...Has a clear plan for solving this country's problems?

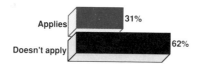

Source: Survey by the Gallup Organization for CNN/*USA Today,* Oct. 26-29, 1996.

Policies Too Conservative

Question: Overall, do you think Bob Dole's policies are too liberal for you, or too conservative for you, or are Bob Dole's policies just about right for you?

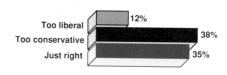

Source: Survey by *Los Angeles Times,* Oct. 24-27, 1996.

How Social Groups Voted for President 1976-1996

1996

	Clinton/Gore (National=49.2%)	Dole/Kemp (National= 40.8%)	Perot/Choate (National= 8.5%)
By party			
Democratic=39%	84%	10%	5%
Republican=35%	13%	80%	6%
Independent=26%	43%	35%	17%
By political philosophy			
Liberal=20%	78%	11%	7%
Moderate=47%	57%	33%	9%
Conservative=33%	20%	71%	8%
By gender			
Male=48%	43%	44%	10%
Female=52%	54%	38%	7%
By race			
White=83%	43%	46%	9%
Black=10%	84%	12%	4%
Hispanic=5%	72%	21%	6%
Asian=1%	43%	48%	8%
By union household			
Union=23%	59%	30%	9%
Nonunion=77%	46%	45%	8%
By region	N/A		
By income			
Under $15,000=11%	59%	28%	11%
$15,000-$30,000=23%	53%	36%	9%
$30,000-$50,000=27%	48%	40%	10%
$50,000-$75,000=21%	47%	45%	7%
$75,000-$100,000=9%	44%	48%	7%
Over $100,000=9%	38%	54%	6%
By age			
18-29 years old=17%	53%	34%	10%
30-44=33%	48%	41%	9%
45-59=26%	48%	41%	9%
Over 60=24%	48%	44%	7%

Note: Sample = 14,651 voters as they left booths. National numbers shown in parentheses at the top of each column, pp. 85-87, are the actual popular vote percentages.
Source: Voter News Service exit poll, November 5, 1996.

1992

	Clinton/Gore (National=43.0%)	Bush/Quayle (National=37.4%)	Perot/Stockdale (National=18.9%)
By party			
Democratic=**38%**	77%	10%	13%
Republican=35%	10%	73%	17%
Independent=23%	38%	32%	30%
By political philosophy			
Liberal=21%	68%	14%	18%
Moderate=49%	47%	31%	21%
Conservative=30%	18%	64%	18%
By gender			
Male=47%	41%	38%	21%
Female=53%	45%	37%	17%
By race			
White=87%	39%	40%	20%
Black=8%	83%	10%	7%
Hispanic=2%	61%	25%	14%
Asian=1%	31%	54%	15%
By union household			
Union=18%	55%	24%	21%
Nonunion=82%	41%	40%	19%
By region			
East=24%	47%	35%	18%
Midwest=27%	42%	37%	21%
South=29%	41%	43%	16%
West=20%	43%	34%	23%
By income			
Under $15,000=14%	58%	23%	19%
$15,000-29,999=24%	45%	35%	20%
$30,000-$49,999=30%	41%	38%	21%
$50,000-$74,999=20%	40%	41%	18%
$75,000+=12%	36%	48%	16%
By age			
18-24 years old=11%	46%	33%	21%
25-29=10%	41%	36%	23%
30-49=46%	41%	38%	21%
50-64=20%	43%	39%	18%
65+=14%	50%	39%	11%

Note: Sample=15,490 voters as they left booths.

Source: Survey by Voter Research & Surveys, a consortium of ABC News, CBS News, CNN, and NBC News November 3, 1992.

1988

Dukakis/Bentsen (National=45.6%) — Bush/Quayle (National=53.4%)

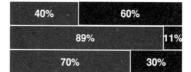

Category	Dukakis/Bentsen	Bush/Quayle
By party		
Democratic=37%	83%	17%
Republican=35%	8%	92%
Independent=26%	43%	57%
By political philosophy		
Liberal=18%	82%	18%
Moderate=45%	51%	49%
Conservative=33%	19%	81%
By gender		
Male=48%	42%	58%
Female=52%	49%	51%
By race		
White=85%	40%	60%
Black=10%	89%	11%
Hispanic=3%	70%	30%
By union household		
Union=25%	57%	43%
Nonunion	NA	
By region		
East=25%	49%	51%
Midwest=28%	47%	53%
South=28%	41%	59%
West=19%	47%	53%
By income		
Under $12,500=12%	63%	37%
$12,500-24,999=20%	51%	49%
$25,000-$34,999=20%	43%	57%
$35,000-$49,999=20%	43%	57%
$50,000-$100,000=19%	39%	61%
Over $100,000=5%	33%	67%
By age		
18-29 years old=20%	47%	53%
30-44 years old=35%	46%	54%
45-59 years old=22%	42%	58%
Over 60=22%	49%	51%

Note: Sample size=11,645 voters as they left voting booths.
Source: Survey by CBS News/*NYT*, November 8, 1988.

1984

Mondale/Ferraro (National=40.6%) — Reagan/Bush (National=58.8%)

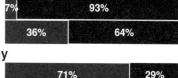
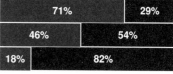

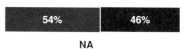
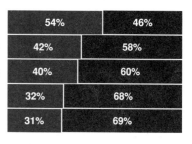
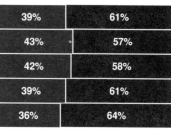

Category	Mondale/Ferraro	Reagan/Bush
By party		
Democratic=38%	74%	26%
Republican=35%	7%	93%
Independent=26%	36%	64%
By political philosophy		
Liberal=16%	71%	29%
Moderate=42%	46%	54%
Conservative=33%	18%	82%
By gender		
Male=47%	38%	62%
Female=53%	42%	58%
By race		
White=86%	34%	66%
Black=10%	91%	9%
Hispanic=3%	66%	34%
By union household		
Union=26%	54%	46%
Nonunion	NA	
By region		
East=26%	47%	53%
Midwest=30%	38%	62%
South=27%	36%	64%
West=17%	38%	62%
By income		
Under $12,500=15%	54%	46%
$12,500-$24,999=27%	42%	58%
$25,000-$34,999=20%	40%	60%
35,000-$50,000=17%	32%	68%
Over $50,000=12%	31%	69%
By age		
18-24 years old=11%	39%	61%
25-29 years old=12%	43%	57%
30-49 years old=34%	42%	58%
50-64 years old=23%	39%	61%
60 and over =19%	36%	64%

Note: Sample size=8,671 as they left voting booths. The survey was not conducted in the states of Washington, Alaska or Hawaii. Someone else/No vote for president (both 1%or less) calculated out for comparison purposes.
Source: Survey by CBS News/*NYT*, November 6. 1984.

1980
Carter/Mondale (National=41.0%) **ReaganBush** (National=50.7%) **Anderson/Lucey** (National=41.0%)

1976
Carter/Mondale (National=50.1%) **Ford/Dole** (National=48.0%)

By party
1980	Carter/Mondale	ReaganBush	Anderson/Lucey
Democratic=43%	67%	27%	6%
Republican=28%	11%	85%	4%
Independent=23%	31%	56%	13%

By party
1976	Carter/Mondale	Ford/Dole
Democratic=37%	80%	20%
Republican=22%	11%	89%
Independent=41%	48%	52%

By political philosophy
1980	Carter/Mondale	ReaganBush	Anderson/Lucey
Liberal=17%	60%	28%	12%
Moderate=46%	43%	49%	8%
Conservative=28%	23%	73%	4%

By political philosophy
1976	Carter/Mondale	Ford/Dole
Liberal=20%	74%	26%
Moderate=49%	53%	47%
Conservative=31%	30%	70%

By gender
1980	Carter/Mondale	ReaganBush	Anderson/Lucey
Male=51%	38%	55%	7%
Female=49%	46%	47%	7%

By gender
1976	Carter/Mondale	Ford/Dole
Male=51%	52%	48%
Female=49%	52%	48%

By race
1980	Carter/Mondale	ReaganBush	Anderson/Lucey
White=88%	36%	56%	8%
Black=10%	83%	14%	3%
Hispanic=2%	56%	37%	7%

By race
1976	Carter/Mondale	Ford/Dole
White=89%	48%	52%
Black=9%	83%	17%
Hispanic=1%	82%	18%

By union household
1980	Carter/Mondale	ReaganBush	Anderson/Lucey
Union=26%	48%	45%	7%
Nonunion=62%	36%	56%	8%

By union household
1976	Carter/Mondale	Ford/Dole
Union=29%	62%	38%
Nonunion=71%	48%	52%

By region
1980	Carter/Mondale	ReaganBush	Anderson/Lucey
East=32%	44%	48%	8%
Midwest=20%	42%	52%	6%
South=27%	45%	52%	3%
West=11%	36%	54%	10%

By region
1976	Carter/Mondale	Ford/Dole
East=28%	54%	46%
Midwest=30%	49%	51%
South=23%	54%	46%
West=18%	50%	50%

By income
1980	Carter/Mondale	ReaganBush	Anderson/Lucey
Under $10,000=13%	52%	42%	6%
$10,000-$14,999=14%	48%	43%	8%
$15,000-$24,999=30%	39%	54%	7%
$25,000-$50,000=24%	33%	59%	8%
Over $50,000=5%	26%	66%	8%

By income
1976	Carter/Mondale	Ford/Dole
Under $8,000=17%	62%	38%
$8000-12,000=24%	57%	43%
$12,001-$20,000=35%	50%	50%
Over $20,000=24%	38%	62%

By age
1980	Carter/Mondale	ReaganBush	Anderson/Lucey
18-21 years old=6%	45%	44%	11%
22-29 years old=17%	44%	44%	11%
30-44 years old=31%	38%	55%	7%
45-59 years old=23%	39%	55%	6%
60 and over=18%	41%	55%	4%

By age
1976	Carter/Mondale	Ford/Dole
18-21years old=9%	49%	51%
22-29 years old=23%	56%	44%
30-44 years old=29%	52%	48%
45-59 years old=26%	48%	52%
60 and over=14%	48%	52%

Note: Sample size=12,782 voters as they left voting booths.
Source: Survey by CBS News/*NYT*, November 4, 1980.

Note: Sample size =15,199 voters as they left voting booths.
Source: Survey by CBS News/*NYT*, November 2, 1976.

How We Voted for President in 1992 and 1996: 41% of the 1996 Electorate Gave Clinton their Votes in Both of His Runs; 30% Went For Dole in '96 and Bush in 1992

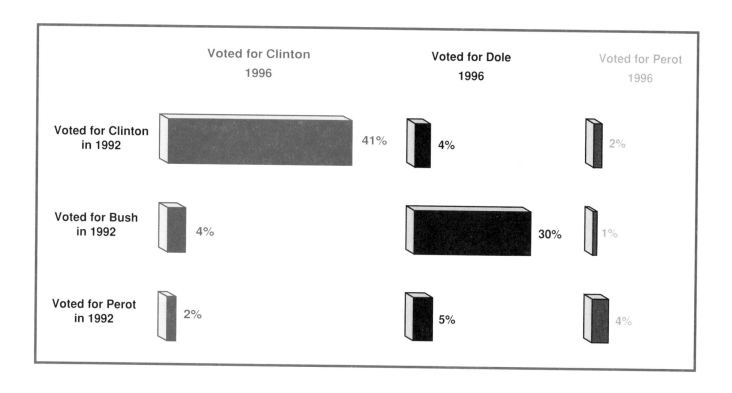

Source: Survey by the *Los Angeles Times* exit poll, November 5, 1996.

1996 Presidential Vote by Party Identification

Party ID in '96	Voted for Clinton '96	Voted for Dole '96	Voted for Perot '96
Democrat	88%	7%	5%
Republican	8%	86%	6%
Independent	42%	35%	20%

1996 Presidential Vote by Ideology

Self-Described Ideology in '96	Voted for Clinton '96	Voted for Dole '96	Voted for Perot '96
Liberal	83%	8%	6%
Middle-of-the-road	58%	31%	11%
Conservative	18%	74%	7%

1996 House Vote by Ideology

Self-Described Ideology	Voted Democratic	Voted Republican	Voted for another
Liberal	85%	10%	5%
Middle-of-the-road	58%	38%	4%
Conservative	22%	76%	2%

Source: Survey by the *Los Angeles Times* exit poll, November 5, 1996.

1996 Presidential Vote by 1992 Presidential Vote

Voted in '92 for	Voted for Clinton '96	Voted for Dole '96	Voted for Perot '96
Clinton	85%	9%	4%
Bush	13%	82%	4%
Perot	22%	44%	33%

1996 Presidential Vote by House Vote

House Vote in '96	Voted for Clinton '96	Voted for Dole '96	Voted for Perot '96
Democrat	84%	8%	7%
Republican	15%	76%	8%

1996 Presidential Vote by Party Identification

Party ID in '96	Voted for Clinton '96	Voted for Dole '96	Voted for Perot '96
Democrat	84%	10%	5%
Republican	13%	80%	6%
Independent/other	43%	35%	17%

Source: Survey by Voter News Service exit poll, November 5, 1996.

1996 Presidential Vote by Ideology

Self-Described Ideology in '96	Voted for Clinton '96	Voted for Dole '96	Voted for Perot '96
Liberal	78%	11%	7%
Moderate	57%	33%	9%
Conservative	20%	71%	8%

1996 House Vote by Ideology

Self-Described Ideology in '96	Democrat	Republican
Liberal	80%	18%
Moderate	56%	42%
Conservative	21%	78%

1996 Presidential Vote by Clinton Honesty Question

Clinton: Honest?	Clinton	Dole	Perot
Yes	88%	6%	4%
No	18%	67%	12%

Source: Survey by Voter News Service exit poll, November 5, 1996.

State Realignments Across 20 Elections:

Note: The data shown in these tables are the percentage point margin by which the state's Republican share of the two-party vote for president exceeded (positive number) or trailed (-) the Republican percentage nationally.

	1920	1924	1928	1932	1936	1940	1944	1948	1952
National	**60.3**	**54.0**	**58.2**	**39.6**	**36.5**	**44.8**	**45.9**	**45.1**	**55.1**
Alabama	-28.4	-28.0	-9.7	-25.5	-23.7	-30.5	-27.7	-26.1	-20.1
Alaska									
Arizona	-4.9	-12.7	0.6	-9.1	-9.6	-8.8	-5.0	-1.3	3.2
Arkansas	-21.0	-24.7	-18.9	-26.9	-18.6	-23.8	-16.1	-24.1	-11.3
California	5.9	3.2	6.5	-2.2	-4.8	-3.5	-2.9	2.0	1.2
Colorado	-1.0	3.0	6.5	1.8	0.6	6.1	7.3	1.4	5.2
Connecticut	2.4	7.5	-4.6	8.9	3.8	1.5	1.0	4.4	0.6
Delaware	-4.6	3.7	7.6	11.0	8.4	0.3	-0.6	4.9	-3.3
Florida	-29.5	-25.9	-0.3	-14.6	-12.6	-18.8	-16.2	-11.5	-0.1
Georgia	-31.6	-35.8	-14.2	-31.8	-23.9	-29.9	-27.6	-26.8	-24.8
Hawaii									
Idaho	5.8	-6.7	6.0	-1.4	-3.3	0.5	2.1	2.2	10.3
Illinois	7.5	4.8	-1.3	2.4	3.2	3.7	2.1	4.1	-0.3
Indiana	-5.2	1.3	1.5	3.3	5.4	5.7	6.5	4.5	3.0
Iowa	10.6	1.0	3.6	0.4	6.2	7.2	6.1	2.5	8.7
Kansas	4.5	7.5	13.8	4.5	9.5	12.1	14.3	8.5	13.7
Kentucky	-11.0	-5.2	1.1	0.6	3.4	-2.5	-0.7	-3.6	-5.3
Louisiana	-29.8	-33.8	-34.5	-32.6	-25.3	-30.7	-26.5	-27.6	-8.0
Maine	8.6	18.0	10.4	16.2	19.0	6.3	6.5	11.6	10.9
Maryland	-5.2	-8.7	-1.1	-3.6	0.5	-4.0	2.2	4.3	0.3
Massachusetts	8.2	8.3	-9.0	7.0	5.3	1.6	1.1	-1.9	-0.9
Michigan	12.5	21.4	12.2	4.8	2.3	5.1	3.3	4.1	0.3
Minnesota	10.3	-2.8	-0.4	-3.3	-5.5	2.9	1.0	-5.2	0.2
Mississippi	-46.2	-46.4	-40.4	-36.1	-33.7	-40.6	-39.5	-42.5	-15.5
Missouri	-5.7	-4.5	-2.6	-4.5	1.7	2.7	2.5	-3.6	-4.4
Montana	0.8	-11.5	0.2	-3.5	-8.9	-4.6	-1.0	-2.0	4.3
Nebraska	4.4	-6.8	5.0	-4.3	4.2	12.4	12.7	9.1	14.1
Nevada	-3.4	-12.2	-1.7	-9.0	-9.3	-4.9	-0.5	2.2	6.3
New Hampshire	-0.5	5.8	0.5	10.8	11.5	2.0	2.0	7.3	5.8

Republicans and Democrats Swap Heartlands

Number of times state voted more Republican than the country

1956	1960	1964	1968	1972	1976	1980	1984	1988	1992	1996	1920-1992 out of 19 elections	1920-1952 out of 9 elections	1968-1996 out of 8 elections
57.4	**49.5**	**38.5**	**43.4**	**60.7**	**48.0**	**50.7**	**58.8**	**53.4**	**37.4**	**40.8**			
-18.0	-7.8	31.0	-29.4	11.7	-5.4	-1.9	1.7	5.8	10.2	10.2	5	0	5
	1.4	-4.4	1.9	-2.6	9.9	3.6	7.9	6.2	2.1	10.2	7	NA	7
3.6	6.0	11.9	11.4	4.0	8.4	9.9	7.6	6.6	1.1	3.2	12	2	8
-11.6	-6.4	4.9	-12.6	8.2	-13.1	-2.6	1.7	3.0	-1.9	-3.8	4	0	3
-2.0	0.6	2.3	4.4	-5.7	1.3	2.0	-1.3	-2.3	-4.8	-2.8	10	5	3
2.6	5.1	-0.3	7.1	1.9	6.0	4.4	4.6	-0.3	-1.5	5.2	15	8	6
6.3	-3.2	-6.4	0.9	-2.1	4.1	-2.5	1.9	-1.4	-1.6	-5.8	12	8	3
-2.3	-0.5	0.3	1.7	-1.1	-1.4	-3.5	1.0	2.5	-2.1	-3.8	10	6	3
-0.2	2.0	10.4	-2.9	11.2	-1.4	4.8	6.5	7.5	3.5	1.2	7	0	6
-24.1	-12.1	15.6	-13.0	14.3	-15.0	-9.7	1.4	6.4	5.5	6.2	5	0	5
	0.5	-17.3	-4.7	1.8	0.1	-7.8	-3.7	-8.6	-0.7	-8.8	3	NA	2
3.8	4.3	10.6	13.4	3.5	11.3	15.8	13.6	8.7	4.6	11.2	16	6	8
2.1	0.3	2.0	3.7	-1.7	2.1	-1.1	-2.6	-2.7	-3.1	-3.8	12	7	2
2.5	5.5	5.1	6.9	5.4	5.3	5.3	2.9	6.4	5.5	6.2	18	8	8
1.7	7.2	-0.6	9.6	-3.1	1.5	0.6	-5.5	-8.9	-0.1	-0.8	14	9	3
8.0	10.9	6.6	11.4	7.0	4.5	7.2	7.5	2.4	1.5	13.2	19	9	8
-3.1	4.1	-2.8	0.4	2.7	-2.4	-1.6	1.2	2.1	3.9	4.2	9	3	5
-4.1	-20.9	18.3	-19.9	4.6	-2.0	0.5	2.0	0.9	3.6	-0.8	6	0	6
13.5	7.5	-7.3	-0.3	0.8	0.9	-5.1	2.0	1.9	-7.0	-8.8	15	9	4
2.6	-3.1	-4.0	-1.5	0.6	-1.3	-6.5	-6.3	-2.3	-1.8	-2.8	6	4	1
1.9	-9.9	-15.1	-10.5	-15.5	-7.6	-8.8	-7.6	-8.0	-8.4	-12.8	7	6	0
-1.8	-0.7	-5.4	-1.9	-4.5	3.8	-1.7	0.4	0.2	-1.0	-2.8	12	9	3
-3.7	-0.3	-2.5	-1.9	-9.1	-6.0	-8.1	-9.3	-7.5	-5.5	-5.8	4	4	0
-32.9	-24.8	48.6	-29.9	17.5	-0.3	-1.3	3.1	6.5	12.3	8.2	5	0	5
-7.5	0.2	-2.5	1.5	1.5	-0.5	0.5	1.2	-1.6	-3.5	0.2	8	3	5
-0.3	1.6	2.1	7.2	-2.8	4.8	6.1	1.7	-1.3	-2.3	3.2	9	3	5
8.1	12.6	8.9	16.4	9.8	11.2	14.8	11.8	6.8	9.2	12.2	17	7	8
0.6	-0.7	2.9	4.1	3.0	2.2	11.8	7.0	5.5	-2.7	2.2	10	2	7
8.7	3.9	-2.4	8.7	3.3	6.7	7.0	9.8	9.0	0.2	-0.8	17	8	7

In 1920, Maine, Massachusetts, Michigan, Minnesota, Vermont and Wisconsin were the Most Republican

	1920	1924	1928	1932	1936	1940	1944	1948	1952
New Jersey	7.3	8.2	1.6	8.0	3.1	3.1	3.1	5.2	1.7
New Mexico	-5.6	-5.5	0.8	-3.8	0.0	-1.5	0.5	-2.2	0.3
New York	4.3	1.8	-8.4	1.7	2.5	3.2	1.4	0.9	0.4
North Carolina	-17.1	-14.4	-3.3	-10.3	-9.9	-18.8	-12.6	-12.4	-9.0
North Dakota	17.5	-6.3	-3.4	-11.6	-9.9	10.3	7.9	7.1	15.9
Ohio	-1.8	4.3	6.7	7.4	0.9	3.0	4.3	4.1	1.7
Oklahoma	-10.1	-11.2	5.5	-12.9	-3.8	-2.6	-1.7	-7.8	-0.5
Oregon	-0.1	-3.0	6.0	-2.7	-6.9	0.8	1.0	4.7	5.4
Pennsylvania	5.5	11.3	7.0	11.2	4.3	1.5	2.5	5.8	-2.4
Rhode Island	3.7	5.6	-8.7	3.7	3.8	-1.6	-4.6	-3.7	-4.2
South Carolina	-56.4	-51.8	-49.7	-37.7	-35.1	-40.4	-41.4	-41.3	-5.8
South Dakota	0.4	-4.3	2.0	-5.2	6.0	12.6	12.4	6.7	14.2
Tennessee	-9.1	-10.5	-2.9	-7.1	-5.7	-12.4	-6.7	-8.2	-5.1
Texas	-36.7	-34.1	-6.3	-28.4	-24.2	-25.9	-29.3	-20.8	-2.0
Utah	-4.4	-4.7	-4.6	1.4	-6.7	-7.2	-6.5	-0.1	3.8
Vermont	15.5	24.2	8.7	18.1	19.9	10.0	11.2	16.4	16.4
Virginia	-22.4	-21.2	-4.3	-9.5	-7.1	-13.2	-8.5	-4.1	1.2
Washington	-4.3	-1.8	8.9	-5.7	-6.6	-4.2	-3.7	-2.4	-0.8
West Virginia	-5.0	-4.5	0.2	4.9	2.7	-1.9	-0.8	-2.9	-7.0
Wisconsin	10.8	-16.9	-4.7	-8.4	-6.2	3.5	4.5	1.2	5.9
Wyoming	2.1	-1.6	5.5	1.2	1.0	2.1	5.3	2.2	7.6
D.C.									

In 1996, Alabama, Mississippi, Nebraska, North Dakota, South Carolina, and Virginia Led the Republican Parade

1956	1960	1964	1968	1972	1976	1980	1984	1988	1992	1996	Number of times state voted more Republican than the country		
											1920-1992	1920-1952	1968-1996
											out of 19 elections	out of 9 elections	out of 8 elections
7.3	-0.3	-4.6	2.7	0.9	2.1	1.3	1.3	2.8	3.2	-4.8	17	9	7
0.4	-0.1	1.9	8.4	0.3	2.5	4.2	0.9	-1.5	-0.1	0.2	10	4	6
3.8	-2.2	-7.2	0.9	-2.2	-0.5	-4.0	-5.0	-5.9	-3.5	-9.8	10	8	1
-8.1	-1.6	5.3	-3.9	8.8	-3.8	-1.4	3.1	4.6	6.0	8.2	5	0	5
4.3	5.9	3.4	12.5	1.4	3.6	13.5	6.0	2.6	6.8	6.2	15	5	8
3.7	3.8	1.4	1.8	-1.1	0.7	0.8	0.1	1.6	0.9	0.2	17	8	7
-2.3	9.5	5.8	4.3	13.0	2.0	9.8	9.8	4.5	5.2	7.2	10	1	8
-2.2	3.1	-2.5	6.4	-8.3	-0.2	-2.4	-2.9	-6.8	-4.9	-3.8	7	5	1
-0.9	-0.8	-3.8	0.6	-1.6	-0.3	-1.1	-5.5	-2.7	-1.3	-0.8	9	8	1
0.9	-13.1	-19.4	-11.6	-7.7	-3.9	-13.5	-7.1	-9.5	-8.4	-13.8	5	4	0
-32.2	-0.7	20.4	-5.3	10.1	-4.9	-1.3	4.8	8.1	10.6	9.2	5	0	5
1.0	8.7	5.9	9.9	-6.5	2.4	9.8	4.2	-0.6	3.3	5.2	14	6	6
-8.2	3.4	6.0	-5.6	7.0	-5.1	-2.0	-1.0	4.5	5.0	5.2	5	0	4
-2.1	-1.0	-2.0	-3.5	5.5	0.0	4.6	4.8	2.6	3.2	8.2	5	0	6
7.2	5.3	6.8	13.1	6.9	14.4	22.1	15.7	12.8	6.0	13.2	12	2	8
14.8	9.1	-4.8	9.4	2.0	6.4	-6.3	-0.9	-2.3	-7.0	-9.8	14	9	3
-2.0	2.9	7.7	0.0	7.1	1.3	2.3	3.5	6.3	7.6	6.2	9	1	7
-3.5	1.2	-1.1	1.7	-3.8	2.0	-1.0	-3.0	-4.9	-5.4	-4.8	4	1	2
-3.3	-2.2	-6.4	-2.6	2.9	-6.1	-5.4	-3.7	-5.9	-2.0	3.8	4	3	2
4.2	2.3	-0.8	4.5	-7.3	-0.2	-2.8	-4.6	-5.6	-0.6	-1.8	8	5	1
2.7	5.5	4.9	12.4	8.3	11.3	11.9	11.7	7.1	2.2	9.2	18	8	8
		-24.0	-25.2	-39.1	-31.5	-37.3	-45.1	-39.1	-28.3	-31.8	0	0	0

Note: The data shown in these tables are the percentage point margin by which the state's Republican share of the two-party vote for president exceeded (positive number) or trailed (-) the Republican percentage nationally.

The Religious Factor: 1996 Vote and Liberalism/ Conservatism By Education and Frequency of Church Attendance

Education	Church Attendance	
Less than High School Grad.	**Less than weekly**	**Weekly and more**
Presidential Vote		
Clinton	68%	65%
Dole	**18%**	**32%**
Perot	13%	3%
Congressional Vote		
Democratic	68%	65%
Republican	**23%**	**32%**
Political Self-Description		
Liberal	22%	23%
Conservative	**30%**	**38%**
Middle-of-the-road	47%	39%
High School Grad.		
Presidential Vote		
Clinton	57%	43%
Dole	**31%**	**48%**
Perot	12%	8%
Congressional Vote		
Democratic	**58%**	**46%**
Republican	35%	49%
Political Self-Description		
Liberal	15%	9%
Conservative	**27%**	**46%**
Middle-of-the-road	58%	45%
Some College		
Presidential Vote		
Clinton	53%	35%
Dole	35%	56%
Perot	10%	8%
Congressional Vote		
Democratic	53%	38%
Republican	**40%**	**57%**
Political Self-Description		
Liberal	18%	11%
Conservative	27%	39%
Middle-of-the-road	55%	49%
Graduate Degree		
Presidential Vote		
Clinton	56%	45%
Dole	**34%**	**51%**
Perot	8%	3%
Congressional Vote		
Democratic	57%	39%
Republican	**40%**	**57%**
Political Self-Description		
Liberal	29%	20%
Conservative	**24%**	**38%**
Middle-of-the-road	47%	42%

Source: *Los Angeles Times* exit poll, November 5, 1996.

The Religious Factor: 1996 Vote and Party Identification, Whites Only, By Married/Not Married and Frequency of Church Attendance

MARRIED	Rarely	Frequently	Regularly
Presidential Vote			
Clinton	49%	34%	29%
Dole	38%	61%	63%
Perot	11%	5%	7%
Congressional Vote			
Democratic	51%	37%	31%
Republican	44%	61%	65%
Party ID			
Democrat	39%	30%	27%
Republican	35%	48%	55%
Independent	25%	21%	17%

NOT MARRIED	Rarely	Frequently	Regularly
Presidential Vote			
Clinton	54%	46%	38%
Dole	29%	46%	52%
Perot	14%	8%	9%
Congressional Vote			
Democratic	53%	46%	38%
Republican	39%	47%	56%
Party ID			
Democrat	42%	41%	31%
Republican	28%	33%	48%
Independent	28%	26%	21%

1996 Vote and Liberalism/Conservativsm, By Race and Frequency of Church Attendance

NON-HISPANIC WHITES	Rarely	Frequently	Regularly
Presidential Vote			
Clinton	51%	38%	31%
Dole	34%	56%	60%
Perot	12%	6%	7%
Congressional Vote			
Democratic	52%	40%	33%
Republican	42%	56%	62%
Political Self-Description			
Liberal	20%	13%	9%
Conservative	27%	38%	50%
Middle-of-the-road	54%	49%	41%

HISPANIC AMERICANS	Rarely	Frequently	Regularly
Presidential Vote			
Clinton	77%	*	64%
Dole	13%	*	28%
Perot	8%	*	8%
Congressional Vote			
Democratic	75%	*	62%
Republican	14%	*	29%
Political Self-Description			
Liberal	25%	*	22%
Conservative	21%	*	35%
Middle-of-the-road	54%	*	43%

AFRICAN AMERICANS	Rarely	Frequently	Regularly
Presidential Vote			
Clinton	87%	91%	89%
Dole	10%	5%	8%
Perot	3%	2%	3%
Congressional Vote			
Democratic	84%	89%	87%
Republican	11%	7%	9%
Political Self-Description			
Liberal	34%	25%	34%
Conservative	18%	21%	28%
Middle-of-the-road	49%	53%	39%

Note: Rarely = several times a year or less.
Frequently = once a month through several times a month.
Regularly = once a week or more.

Source: *Los Angeles Times* exit poll, November 5, 1996.

The Religious Factor: 1996 Vote and Liberalism/ Conservatism, By Denomination and Frequency of Church Attendance

ATTEND CHURCH WEEKLY OR MORE OFTEN	Protestant	Other Christian	Catholic
Presidential Vote			
Clinton	34%	31%	47%
Dole	**60%**	**59%**	**44%**
Perot	5%	9%	8%
Congressional Vote			
Democratic	33%	33%	51%
Republican	**64%**	**61%**	**43%**
Political Self-Description			
Liberal	10%	9%	14%
Conservative	**49%**	**61%**	**37%**
Middle-of-the-road	41%	30%	49%

ATTEND CHURCH LESS THAN WEEKLY	Protestant	Other Christian	Catholic
Presidential Vote			
Clinton	44%	46%	55%
Dole	**46%**	**41%**	**33%**
Perot	9%	11%	11%
Congressional Vote			
Democratic	45%	49%	56%
Republican	**51%**	**45%**	**38%**
Political Self-Description			
Liberal	14%	14%	19%
Conservative	**36%**	**34%**	**25%**
Middle-of-the-road	50%	52%	56%

Source: *Los Angeles Times* exit poll, November 5, 1996.

The Religious Factor: The Vote and Political Stands of Northeastern and Southern Whites, Compared Further by Their Income and Frequency of Church Attendance

	Vote for President/House				Self-Described Ideology/Party ID			
	Clinton %	Dole %	Democrat %	Republican %	Liberal %	Conservative %	Democrat %	Republican %
Whites, Northeast, households earning less than $40,000								
Church attendance								
Rarely	60	24	57	37	21	20	46	23
Frequently	45	47	42	52	9	42	36	43
Whites, South, households earning less than $40,000								
Church attendance								
Rarely	51	30	64	31	18	28	48	24
Frequently	31	64	34	62	11	46	32	54
Whites, Northeast, households earning $60,000 or more								
Church attendance								
Rarely	54	35	49	46	21	23	41	32
Frequently	45	49	37	56	12	43	40	42
Whites, South, household earning $60,000 or more								
Church attendance								
Rarely	43	51	43	55	21	39	30	53
Frequently	21	72	16	78	6	63	18	67

Note: Rarely = several times a year or less often
Frequently = once a week or more often

Source: *Los Angeles Times* exit poll, November 5, 1996.

1996 Votes and Party Identification of Whites, By Denomination and Region

NORTHEAST	Protestant	Other Christian	Catholic
Presidential Vote			
Clinton	47%	33%	50%
Dole	45%	54%	39%
Perot	7%	11%	10%
Congressional Vote			
Democratic	41%	38%	46%
Republican	56%	56%	49%
Party Identification			
Democrat	37%	24%	41%
Republican	41%	43%	33%
Independent	20%	33%	26%

MIDWEST	Protestant	Other Christian	Catholic
Presidential Vote			
Clinton	39%	32%	49%
Dole	50%	54%	39%
Perot	10%	14%	12%
Congressional Vote			
Democratic	40%	34%	55%
Republican	55%	62%	39%
Party Identification			
Democrat	32%	25%	41%
Republican	44%	48%	33%
Independent	24%	25%	25%

SOUTH	Protestant	Other Christian	Catholic
Presidential Vote			
Clinton	31%	20%	42%
Dole	63%	64%	48%
Perot	6%	15%	9%
Congressional Vote			
Democratic	32%	24%	48%
Republican	65%	69%	47%
Party Identification			
Democrat	27%	16%	39%
Republican	53%	61%	34%
Independent	19%	21%	27%

WEST	Protestant	Other Christian	Catholic
Presidential Vote			
Clinton	34%	22%	47%
Dole	55%	65%	42%
Perot	9%	11%	9%
Congressional Vote			
Democratic	35%	26%	55%
Republican	61%	67%	41%
Party Identification			
Democrat	29%	18%	46%
Republican	53%	62%	32%
Independent	18%	18%	19%

Source: *Los Angeles Times* exit poll, November 5, 1996.

1996 Vote by Age and Education

Age & Education	Presidential Vote			Congressional Vote	
18-29 years old	Clinton	Dole	Perot	Democrat	Republican
High School or less	51%	39%	11%	51%	40%
Some College	51%	35%	10%	53%	38%
College Degree	46%	42%	9%	44%	49%
Post College	50%	38%	8%	57%	39%
30-44 years old					
High School or less	50%	36%	14%	51%	41%
Some College	43%	45%	11%	47%	47%
College Degree	45%	46%	8%	45%	51%
Post College	47%	46%	5%	45%	51%
45-64 years old					
High School or less	57%	32%	10%	61%	34%
Some College	45%	45%	9%	47%	49%
College Degree	40%	51%	8%	42%	53%
Post College	49%	44%	6%	48%	49%
65+ years old					
High School or less	58%	35%	6%	60%	37%
Some College	49%	44%	5%	42%	55%
College Degree	39%	45%	12%	46%	49%
Post College	54%	38%	6%	56%	40%

Source: *Los Angeles Times* exit poll, November 5, 1996.

The Gender Story: Women as Voters and Candidates in the 1996 Elections
By Jody Newman

Despite the inflammatory rhetoric and misleading headlines, the gender gap in the recent elections was not a chasm, women did not flock back to the polls after staying home in 1994, and attempts by Bob Dole's campaign to close the gender gap may have hurt rather than helped him. Women's behavior and influence as voters, and the successes they achieved as candidates, were similar to those found in elections for the past 25 years. Women continued to make up slightly more than half of the electorate, to vote somewhat more Democratic than men, and to make slow, steady progress in increasing their numbers in elected office.

The Gender Gap in 1996

A rare convergence of the interests of the press, pundits and pollsters led to a rash of front page stories this past cycle about a political war between the sexes, portraying the gender gap as having reached such overwhelming proportions that it had become a veritable chasm. It may be hard to believe

> " *It may be hard to believe after all the hype and dramatic headlines, but the gender gap in 1996—although very real and certainly significant—was not a chasm.* "

after all the hype and dramatic headlines, but the gender gap in 1996—although very real and certainly significant—was not a chasm. In fact, it was exactly the same size as in the 1980 election between Ronald Reagan and Jimmy Carter and was much smaller than a number of other gaps which divide the electorate today. The simple, although perhaps less interesting, truth is that the gender gap has been a consistent and important factor in elections for at least the past 40 years. Although the gap in the presidential election in 1996 was as large as any that has been measured, it is an exaggeration to characterize it as a chasm, and there is no war looming between the sexes, at least politically.

The gender gap is nothing more and nothing less than a difference between the way men and women vote. This difference was first touted in the early 1980s by Democratic women leaders who used it to lobby for the ERA and for a woman vice presidential candidate, but the difference itself existed long before 1980. Although data by gender for elections before 1950 are scant, there is some evidence that a gap has existed ever since the day women were given the franchise.

In the 1950s and 1960s, women voted more Republican than men did. Adlai Stevenson and John Kennedy did substantially better among men than among women. Kennedy, in fact, won in 1960 by winning among men while

losing among women. And since 1980, women have consistently been voting somewhat more Democratic than men.

A gender gap is often confused with a lead among women, but the two are quite different and actually independent of one another. A candidate can finish with a huge lead among women, but if he does equally well among men, there will be no gender gap at all. If a candidate does better among women than among men, or better among men than among women, he will have a gender gap, whether or not he loses or wins among men or among women.

In the stampede in 1996 to make the gap appear as new and dramatic as possible, the definition used by the popular press to measure it was changed. In the past, the gender gap was defined as the difference between the *percentage of the vote* that a candidate received among women and the percentage of the vote he received among men. Over the last year, the pundits and press started defining it as the difference between the *margin of victory* that a candidate received among women and the margin of victory he received among men.

Although the newer definition is as valid to use as the old one when comparing one gap to another, it makes the size of the gap appear twice as large. Some of the false claims about record gender gaps and chasms may have stemmed from this change in definition. Either definition can correctly be used; what is important is that the same definition be used consistently when comparing various gender gaps over time, or when comparing the gender gap to other gaps; otherwise, one will be comparing apples and oranges.

In 1996 Bill Clinton won by 16 points among women but lost by one point among men, which the press defined as a gender gap of 17 points. Ronald Reagan beat Jimmy Carter by 19 points among men and

Table 1: The Gender Gap in Presidential Elections

	Men	Women	Gap
1996			
Clinton	43%	54%	11
Dole	<u>44</u>	<u>38</u>	<u>6</u>
	-1	16	17
1992			
Clinton	41	45	4
Bush	<u>38</u>	<u>38</u>	<u>0</u>
	3	7	4
1988			
Dukakis	41	49	8
Bush	<u>57</u>	<u>50</u>	<u>7</u>
	-16	-1	15
1984			
Mondale	37	44	7
Reagan	<u>62</u>	<u>56</u>	<u>6</u>
	-25	-12	13
1980			
Carter	36	45	9
Reagan	<u>55</u>	<u>47</u>	<u>8</u>
	-19	-2	17

Note: This table shows the gender gap according to both the traditional and new definitions.
Source: 1982-88 exit polls by CBS News/*New York Times*, 1990-92 exit polls by Voter Research & Surveys, and 1994-96 exit polls by Voter News Service.

by only 2 points among women, for an identical gender gap of 17 points. These gender gaps are as large as any that have been measured over the last 15 or 20 years, but are not out of line with other gaps in the period, as can be seen in Table 1.

As is obvious from the exit poll data in the table, it is not necessary for a Republican (or a Democrat) to "close the gender gap" in order to win an election. Ronald Reagan won handily in 1984 with the same gender gap Bob Dole had in 1996. In 1988 George Bush did 7 points worse among women than among men and won the election; in 1992 he did equally as well with women as with men, and he lost.

As the political adage goes, all that matters is winning 50% of the vote plus one, and this applies whether the votes come from women or from men. Bob Dole needed to do 10 points better among women *and* 10 points better among men, in which case he would have won the election with numbers like Ronald Reagan in 1980. Closing the gender gap would not necessarily have helped Dole; in fact, to the extent that his campaign targeted women over men, it may have been aiming at exactly those voters it was least likely to win over.

Women voters tend to vote more Democratic than men because fewer women are conservative; on average, women believe in a greater role for government than men, particularly on matters like education and Medicare and the disadvantaged. Dole's anti-government, lower-taxes message

> **Although data by gender for elections before 1950 are scant, there is some evidence that a gap has existed ever since the day women were given the franchise.**

was one that was more likely to attract men than women. No matter how many women he put on the podium at the convention in San Diego, or how well-liked his wife was, or how much he talked about his support of the Violence Against Women Act, he was not going to close the gender gap.

Table 2: The Gender Gap in US House Elections

(percent voting Democratic)

	Male	Female	Gap
1980	49%	55%	6
1982	55	58	3
1984	48	54	6
1986	51	54	3
1988	52	57	5
1990	52	55	3
1992	52	55	3
1994	42	53	11
1996	45	54	9

Note: This table shows the traditional definition of the gender gap. If the new definition were used, each gap would appear twice as large.
Source: 1982-88 exit polls by CBS News/*New York Times*, 1990-92 exit polls by Voter Research & Surveys, and 1994-96 exit polls by Voter News Service.

The gender gap has little to do with abortion or women's rights. It was the fact that Bob Dole was a Republican and that he was more conservative on social programs and government spending that caused him to do better among men than among women, and not his position on so-called "women's issues." Candidates who focus on abortion and breast cancer and spousal abuse as though women can't get beyond their own bodies have missed the point. In fact, men and women hold almost identical views on abortion and women's rights, and at least as many women as men consider themselves pro-life.

As was the case in the presidential campaign, the gender gap in congressional races in 1996 was real and significant but not a chasm; in fact it was smaller than in 1994. Table 2 shows the gender gap in US House elections since 1980, using the traditional definition of the gender gap (the percent of women who voted Democratic minus the percent of men who voted Democratic).

As can be seen, women have stayed remarkably consistent in their voting over the past 16 years, with between 53 and 58% voting Democratic each year. Men's voting behavior has been more erratic, ranging from 42 to 55% Democratic. In fact, this table shows quite clearly that it was men's dramatic shift to the right in 1994 that resulted in the victories of Newt Gingrich and the Republicans, rather than any apathy on the part of women.

The similarity between the way women and men vote is much larger than the difference. Most husbands vote the same way their wives do, despite the myth about couples going to the polls and canceling out each other's votes. However, although the gender gap is not a chasm, there are other gaps which do constitute chasms in the electorate today.

For example, whereas 54% of women voted for Clinton in 1996 and only 43% of men, 84% of blacks voted for him and only 44% of whites. This is a chasm. Clinton lost to Dole by 2 points among whites and won by 72 points among blacks, which would be a "race gap" of 74 points according to the new definition of a gap. Similarly, 41% of Protestants voted for Clinton,

> *Women voters tend to vote more Democratic than men because fewer women are conservative; on average, women believe in a greater role for government than men, particularly on matters like education and Medicare and the disadvantaged.*

compared with 80% of Jews (a gap of 73 points). Despite the current fascination with differences between men and women—the Mars/Venus phenomenon—it is more instructive to look at the income, education, race, religious and geographic differences that divide voters today than at differences between the sexes.

Women Voting for Women

A study I did analyzing US Senate races that was published in *Public Perspective* last year found that the sex of the candidate made a small difference in the size of the gender gap. No such relationship, however, was found in US Senate races in 1996. The gender gap—or difference between the way men and women voted—was related to the fact that women voters are more Democratic and less conservative than men, and not to whether the candidate was a woman. Putting a woman on the ticket did not necessarily win over women voters.

In 1996, the gender gap did not grow when the Democratic candidate was a woman nor shrink when a woman was the Republican candidate. The average gender gap in the 25 US Senate races in which a Democratic man faced a Republican man was 7.4 percentage points. In other words, on average the Democratic candidate did 7.4 points better with women voters than with men. The average gap in the five races in which the Democratic candidate was a woman and the Republican candidate a man was actually smaller—4.4 points. And in the four races in which the Democratic candidate was a man and the Republican candidate a woman, it was about

the same—7.0 points. The assumption that women will vote for a woman, and the coupling of women candidates and women voters that is often made by the press and pundits as though they are the same topic, are based on myths rather than reality.

> " *Once again, this election showed that the reason there aren't more women in elected office is not that women have a tougher time winning elections than men, but that there haven't been enough women running for winnable seats.* "

Women's Turnout

In the 1996 elections, women made up 52% of the electorate. Women have been the majority of voters in every election since 1964, and their turnout rate—or percent of those eligible who actually turned out to vote — has been higher than men's in every election since 1980.

In Table 3, a pattern emerges of women making up a slightly higher

proportion of the electorate in presidential than in non-presidential years. This pattern continued in 1996. It can also be seen that the myth that women "stayed home from the polls" in 1994 is just that—a myth. The statement that 16 million women who voted in 1992 did not vote in 1994, and the even more dramatic statement that 55 million eligible women did not vote in 1994, are both technically correct but misleading. Large numbers of women who voted in 1992 did not do so in 1994, just as large numbers of men who voted in 1992 did not do so in 1994, because 1992 was a presidential election year and 1994 was not. Turnout is routinely much higher—for men as well as women—in presidential than non-presidential elections.

According to the Census Bureau, women's turnout rate was 44.9% in 1994, compared with men's turnout rate of 44.4%. Any attempt to blame women for the Republican takeover of Congress in 1994, or to attribute Newt Gingrich's success in 1994 to women's apathy, is misinformed.

The number of women who voted in 1996 was higher than in 1994 because 1996 was a presidential election year. Despite the women's vote drives in 1996 and the push that was made to appeal to women and to encourage

Table 3: Percent of Voters Who Were Women

Presidential Elections		Non-Presidential Elections	
1984	51	1982	50
1988	52	1986	52
1992	52	1990	50
1996	52	1994	51

Source: 1982-88 exit polls by CBS News/*New York Times*, 1990-92 exit polls by Voter Research & Surveys, and 1994-96 exit polls by Voter News Service.

them to vote, women continued to make up the same 52% they did in 1988 and 1992.

Women as Candidates

Twenty-five years ago, there were 13 women in the US House of Representatives, one in the US Senate, and none in governors' mansions. This year there are almost four times as many in the House—a record 51 (up from 48 in the last Congress). A record nine were elected to the Senate, and there are now two women governors (double the lonely one who served last year). Although these increases are not as dramatic as those that occurred in 1992 (the so-called "year of the woman" when a record number of women ran for the open seats that resulted from redistricting and the check-kiting scandals that year), they represent the same kind of "slow, steady progress" that has been made in other elections since the early 70s and that has made it no longer an oddity to see a woman debating on the floor of the Senate or the House.

Once again, this election showed that the reason there aren't more women in elected office is not that women have a tougher time winning elections than men, but that there haven't been enough women running for winnable seats. Six of the 48 incumbent women in the US House chose not to run for reelection in 1996, and another was defeated in her primary, so the tally was down to 41 before the races even started. Women comprised only 14% of US House candidates in the general election, the same percentage as in 1994. Although they were 18% of the challengers (up from 13% in 1992 and 16% in 1994), challengers generally win their elections only 5% of the time. For open seats, which represent the level playing field where women have a real chance to make significant gains, only 15% of the candidates were women, down from 22% in 1992 and 16% in 1994.

In light of the small numbers who ran, women's progress was impressive. The 11 new women who won seats in the US House more than made up for the six who retired and the two who were defeated. The two new women elected to the US Senate made up for Nancy Kassebaum's retirement and the defeat of Sheila Frahm, who had been appointed to fill Bob Dole's seat. And Jeanne Shaheen joined Chris- tine Todd Whitman as the nation's only women governors. The conclusion is that "when women run, women win," but the impediment to progress remains the small number of women running.

Women Are Crucial in Modern Elections

Women are crucial in elections today not because they vote as a bloc, but because they make up more than half of the electorate. Misunderstanding the influence of women voters can only compound the problems caused by a misunderstanding of the gender gap.

Blacks and Jews are true voting blocs; women are not. Those who speak of "the women's vote" as though it represents a special interest group or a homogeneous segment of voters are in danger of underestimating the diverse, influential majority of voters that women comprise. No Democratic candidate can afford to take women's votes for granted; no Republican can afford to lose too many. A force this powerful should not be surrounded by hyperbole and spin, but rather carefully understood and accurately interpreted.

The Gender Story: Proportion of the 1996 Electorate that is Male and Female

State	Male	Female
Alabama	44%	56%
Alaska	50	50
Arizona	48	52
Arkansas	46	54
California	47	53
Colorado	48	52
Connecticut	48	52
Delaware	49	51
District of Columbia	40	60
Florida	48	52
Georgia	49	51
Hawaii	47	53
Idaho	50	50
Illinois	48	52
Indiana	48	52
Iowa	48	52
Kansas	47	53
Kentucky	47	53
Louisiana	44	56
Maine	49	51
Maryland	46	54
Massachusetts	49	51
Michigan	48	52
Minnesota	50	50
Mississippi	46	54
Missouri	48	52
Montana	49	51
Nebraska	49	51
Nevada	47	53
New Hampshire	51	49
New Jersey	45	55
New Mexico	47	53
New York	46	54
North Carolina	49	51
North Dakota	47	53
Ohio	48	52
Oklahoma	48	52
Oregon	47	53
Pennsylvania	48	52
Rhode Island	48	52
South Carolina	45	55
South Dakota	51	49
Tennessee	46	54
Texas	48	52
Utah	47	53
Vermont	48	52
Virginia	45	55
Washington	48	52
West Virginia	50	50
Wisconsin	47	53
Wyoming	48	52

Source: Survey by Voter News Service exit poll, November 5, 1996.

The Gender Story: Men's and Women's Presidential Vote, by State

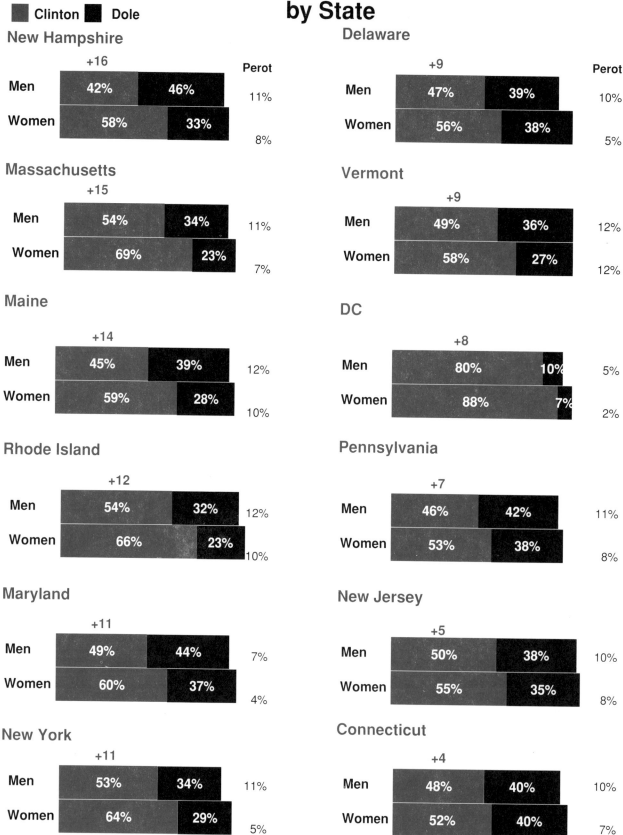

■ Clinton ■ Dole

New Hampshire
+16   Perot

Men 42% 46%   11%
Women 58% 33%   8%

Massachusetts
+15

Men 54% 34%   11%
Women 69% 23%   7%

Maine
+14

Men 45% 39%   12%
Women 59% 28%   10%

Rhode Island
+12

Men 54% 32%   12%
Women 66% 23%   10%

Maryland
+11

Men 49% 44%   7%
Women 60% 37%   4%

New York
+11

Men 53% 34%   11%
Women 64% 29%   5%

Delaware
+9   Perot

Men 47% 39%   10%
Women 56% 38%   5%

Vermont
+9

Men 49% 36%   12%
Women 58% 27%   12%

DC
+8

Men 80% 10%   5%
Women 88% 7%   2%

Pennsylvania
+7

Men 46% 42%   11%
Women 53% 38%   8%

New Jersey
+5

Men 50% 38%   10%
Women 55% 35%   8%

Connecticut
+4

Men 48% 40%   10%
Women 52% 40%   7%

Source for pp. 108-111: Voter News Service exit poll, November 5, 1996.

The Men-Women Gap was Largest in Northern New England, in Kentucky...

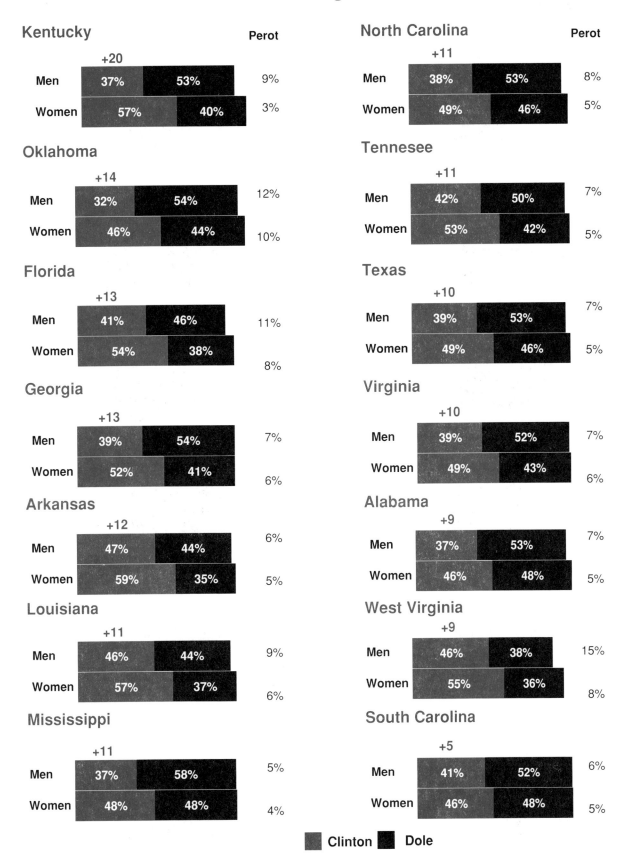

Kentucky
Perot

+20
- **Men** — 37% | 53% — 9%
- **Women** — 57% | 40% — 3%

Oklahoma

+14
- **Men** — 32% | 54% — 12%
- **Women** — 46% | 44% — 10%

Florida

+13
- **Men** — 41% | 46% — 11%
- **Women** — 54% | 38% — 8%

Georgia

+13
- **Men** — 39% | 54% — 7%
- **Women** — 52% | 41% — 6%

Arkansas

+12
- **Men** — 47% | 44% — 6%
- **Women** — 59% | 35% — 5%

Louisiana

+11
- **Men** — 46% | 44% — 9%
- **Women** — 57% | 37% — 6%

Mississippi

+11
- **Men** — 37% | 58% — 5%
- **Women** — 48% | 48% — 4%

North Carolina
Perot

+11
- **Men** — 38% | 53% — 8%
- **Women** — 49% | 46% — 5%

Tennesee

+11
- **Men** — 42% | 50% — 7%
- **Women** — 53% | 42% — 5%

Texas

+10
- **Men** — 39% | 53% — 7%
- **Women** — 49% | 46% — 5%

Virginia

+10
- **Men** — 39% | 52% — 7%
- **Women** — 49% | 43% — 6%

Alabama

+9
- **Men** — 37% | 53% — 7%
- **Women** — 46% | 48% — 5%

West Virginia

+9
- **Men** — 46% | 38% — 15%
- **Women** — 55% | 36% — 8%

South Carolina

+5
- **Men** — 41% | 52% — 6%
- **Women** — 46% | 48% — 5%

Clinton ■ Dole

...in Michigan in the Midwest...

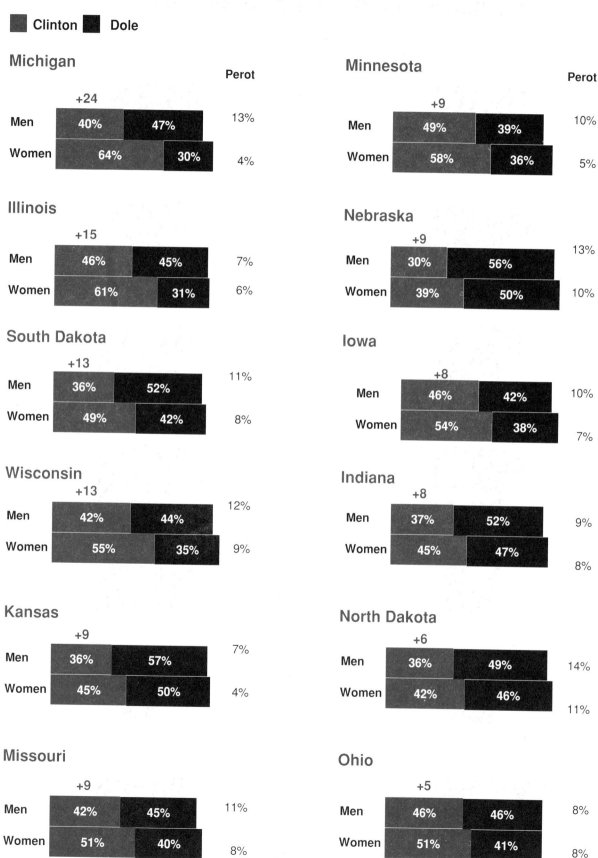

■ Clinton ■ Dole

Michigan
Perot

+24

Men 40% 47% 13%

Women 64% 30% 4%

Minnesota
Perot

+9

Men 49% 39% 10%

Women 58% 36% 5%

Illinois

+15

Men 46% 45% 7%

Women 61% 31% 6%

Nebraska

+9

Men 30% 56% 13%

Women 39% 50% 10%

South Dakota

+13

Men 36% 52% 11%

Women 49% 42% 8%

Iowa

+8

Men 46% 42% 10%

Women 54% 38% 7%

Wisconsin

+13

Men 42% 44% 12%

Women 55% 35% 9%

Indiana

+8

Men 37% 52% 9%

Women 45% 47% 8%

Kansas

+9

Men 36% 57% 7%

Women 45% 50% 4%

North Dakota

+6

Men 36% 49% 14%

Women 42% 46% 11%

Missouri

+9

Men 42% 45% 11%

Women 51% 40% 8%

Ohio

+5

Men 46% 46% 8%

Women 51% 41% 8%

...And in Colorado and Washington in the West

Colorado
Perot

+16

	Clinton	Dole	
Men	39%	52%	8%
Women	55%	36%	7%

Clinton ■ Dole

Washington

+15

Men	44%	41%	10%
Women	59%	32%	6%

California
Perot

+8

Men	46%	42%	7%
Women	54%	35%	6%

Alaska

+12

Men	30%	57%	10%
Women	42%	42%	2%

New Mexico

+8

Men	45%	45%	7%
Women	53%	39%	6%

Hawaii

+12

Men	51%	36%	9%
Women	63%	27%	7%

Oregon

+8

Men	43%	42%	11%
Women	51%	34%	9%

Nevada

+12

Men	38%	48%	10%
Women	50%	39%	10%

Montana

+7

Men	37%	48%	13%
Women	44%	41%	14%

Utah

+12

Men	27%	57%	12%
Women	39%	51%	9%

Arizona

+4

Men	44%	43%	10%
Women	48%	44%	7%

Idaho

+11

Men	30%	54%	16%
Women	41%	53%	6%

Wyoming

+3

Men	35%	49%	14%
Women	38%	50%	10%

How Key Demographic Groups Voted for the US House of Representatives 1984-1996

		1996 D	1996 R	1994 D	1994 R	1992 D	1992 R
Total		48.6%	48.9%	45.5%	52.5%	50.9%	45.5%
By Gender							
Men		49%	51%	43%	57%	51%	47%
Women		57%	43%	54%	46%	54%	44%
By Gender/Age							
Women	18-29	62%	38%	58%	42%	57%	41%
	30-44	52%	48%	52%	48%	53%	44%
(1996=45-64)	45-59	56%	45%	53%	47%	53%	45%
(1996=65+)	60+	58%	42%	54%	46%	55%	42%
Men	18-29	47%	53%	43%	57%	50%	46%
	30-44	47%	53%	42%	58%	50%	47%
(1996=45-64)	45-59	48%	52%	42%	58%	49%	49%
(1996=65+)	60+	52%	48%	45%	55%	55%	43%
By Gender/Education							
Women	H.S.	60%	40%	52%	48%	57%	40%
	College	53%	47%	58%	42%	53%	45%
Men	H.S.	54%	46%	49%	51%	59%	38%
	College	45%	55%	42%	58%	45%	53%
By Race/Ethnicity							
Whites		46%	54%	42%	58%	49%	49%
Blacks		86%	14%	92%	8%	87%	11%
Hispanics		75%	25%	60%	40%	70%	27%
Asians		44%	56%	55%	45%	48%	49%
By Race/Region							
Whites	North	48%	52%	45%	55%	49%	48%
	South	41%	59%	35%	65%	46%	52%
Blacks	North	91%	9%	89%	11%	88%	10%
	South	77%	23%	94%	6%	87%	11%
By Age							
18-29		55%	45%	51%	49%	54%	44%
30-44		50%	50%	47%	53%	51%	46%
45-59 (1996=45-64)		52%	48%	48%	52%	51%	47%
60+ (1996=65+)		55%	45%	50%	50%	55%	43%
By Age/Education							
18-29	H.S.	54%	46%	55%	45%	62%	36%
30-44		53%	47%	42%	58%	52%	45%
45-59 (1996=45-64)		62%	38%	51%	49%	60%	37%
60+ (1996=65+)		58%	42%	54%	46%	61%	37%
18-29	College	51%	49%	51%	49%	50%	49%
30-44		47%	53%	53%	47%	49%	48%
45-59 (1996=45-64)		47%	53%	51%	49%	46%	52%
60+ (1996=65+)		53%	47%	42%	58%	48%	50%

Note: N/A = data not available.

Source for pp. 112-115: The 1996 aggregate vote totals are from the *Congressional Quarterly Weekly Report*, November 23, 1996. All other aggregate vote totals are from *Statistical Abstract of the United States, 1990* and *1993-94*. Surveys by the *Los Angeles Times*, November 5, 1996; Voter News Service, November 8, 1994; Voter Research & Surveys, for 1990 and 1992; CBS News and *New York Times* for 1984 and 1988.

Gender Gap in House Vote Same in '96 as '94

		1990		1988		1984	
		D	R	D	R	D	R
Total		52.9%	44.9	53.4%	45.5%	52.3%	46.8%
By Gender							
Men		50%	46%	49%	46%	46%	53%
Women		54%	43%	54%	41%	51%	48%
By Gender/Age							
Women	18-29	55%	43%	52%	43%	51%	47%
	30-44	53%	43%	54%	41%	53%	46%
	45-59	53%	44%	55%	40%	50%	50%
	60+	54%	44%	54%	42%	48%	52%
Men	18-29	48%	49%	50%	45%	43%	54%
	30-44	52%	45%	48%	47%	49%	49%
	45-59	48%	49%	47%	48%	45%	54%
	60+	52%	45%	52%	45%	44%	55%
By Gender/Education							
Women	H.S.	57%	40%	56%	39%	51%	48%
	College	55%	42%	52%	44%	52%	47%
Men	H.S.	57%	40%	54%	40%	47%	51%
	College	48%	50%	44%	52%	45%	53%
By Race/Ethnicity							
Whites		50%	47%	47%	48%	43%	56%
Blacks		78%	20%	81%	14%	91%	8%
Hispanics		71%	27%	73%	23%	66%	32%
Asians		62%	36%				
By Race/Region							
Whites	North	50%	46%	46%	49%	44%	55%
	South	49%	50%	50%	46%	42%	57%
Blacks	North	77%	21%	80%	14%	90%	9%
	South	80%	19%	84%	13%	96%	4%
By Age							
18-29		52%	46%	51%	44%	47%	50%
30-44		53%	44%	51%	44%	51%	48%
45-59		51%	46%	51%	44%	48%	52%
60+		53%	45%	53%	43%	46%	54%
By Age/Education							
18-29	H.S.	60%	37%	52%	43%	43%	54%
30-44		59%	38%	54%	41%	50%	48%
45-59		54%	43%	56%	39%	53%	46%
60+		56%	41%	57%	38%	49%	50%
18-29	College	52%	45%	49%	46%	50%	48%
30-44		52%	45%	49%	46%	52%	46%
45-59		50%	47%	44%	52%	41%	58%
60+		48%	50%	48%	48%	39%	60%

Income Differences in House Voting Constant Over Time

	1996 D	1996 R	1994 D	1994 R	1992 D	1992 R
By Education						
Less than H.S.	72%	28%	60%	40%	65%	32%
H.S. Grad	57%	43%	48%	52%	57%	41%
Some College	50%	50%	42%	58%	51%	46%
College Grad	48%	52%	50%	50%	48%	49%
By Income (see note)						
Less than $15,000	68%	32%	63%	37%	67%	30%
$15,000-29,999	56%	44%	53%	47%	56%	42%
$30,000-49,999	50%	50%	46%	54%	51%	47%
$50,000-74,999	49%	51%	45%	55%	46%	52%
$75,000-100,000	41%	59%	N/A	N/A	N/A	N/A
Over $100,000	41%	59%	N/A	N/A	N/A	N/A
By Denomination						
Protestant	42%	58%	40%	60%	45%	53%
Catholic	57%	43%	48%	52%	55%	42%
Other Christian	45%	55%	50%	50%	49%	48%
Jewish	79%	21%	78%	22%	77%	21%
None	69%	31%	63%	37%	66%	29%
Union Household	64%	36%	61%	39%	66%	32%
Not checked	52%	48%	46%	54%	49%	48%
Married	48%	52%	43%	57%	49%	49%
Not Married	60%	40%	56%	44%	59%	38%
Attend Religious Services						
Once a week/month	45%	55%	N/A	N/A	46%	52%
Less than once a month	60%	40%	N/A	N/A	57%	40%
By Party ID						
Democrat	92%	8%	89%	11%	87%	11%
Republican	8%	92%	8%	92%	15%	83%
Independent	50%	50%	42%	58%	52%	43%
By Ideology						
Liberal	89%	11%	82%	18%	77%	18%
Moderate	60%	40%	58%	42%	56%	42%
Conservative	23%	77%	20%	80%	27%	71%

Note: For 1996, the income categories are: Less than $20,000; $20,000-$39,999; $40,000-$59,999; $60,000-$74,999; $75,000-$100,000; $100,000+. For 1994 and 1992, the highest income category available was $50,000+.

In 1996 Union Households Gave Democratic Candidates Their Familiar Margin

	1990 D	1990 R		1988 D	1988 R		1984 D	1984 R
By Education								
Less than H.S.	59%	38%		59%	34%		56%	43%
H.S. Grad	56%	41%		54%	41%		48%	51%
Some College	51%	45%		50%	45%		46%	53%
College Grad	51%	46%		48%	48%		48%	51%
By Income								
Less than $15,000	63%	34%		63%	31%		59%	39%
$15,000-29,999	54%	42%		53%	43%		49%	50%
$30,9000-49,999	52%	45%		50%	45%		45%	54%
$50,000+	49%	48%		43%	52%		37%	61%
By Denomination								
Protestant	47%	51%		45%	50%		40%	60%
Catholic	55%	41%		53%	43%		55%	43%
Other Christian	56%	42%		52%	42%		44%	54%
Jewish	73%	25%		66%	31%		70%	28%
None	56%	37%		61%	33%		65%	33%
Union Household	63%	34%		60%	35%		61%	38%
Not checked	52%	45%		48%	47%		43%	56%
Married	50%	47%		49%	46%		46%	53%
Not Married	58%	39%		56%	38%		53%	45%
Attend Religious Services								
Once a week/month	49%	49%		N/A	N/A		N/A	N/A
Not checked	57%	40%		N/A	N/A		N/A	N/A
By Party ID								
Democrat	78%	19%		80%	16%		83%	16%
Republican	25%	73%		20%	75%		13%	86%
Independent	51%	45%		51%	43%		45%	52%
By Ideology								
Liberal	71%	25%		76%	19%		73%	24%
Moderate	56%	41%		55%	41%		54%	45%
Conservative	38%	59%		32%	62%		28%	71%

How Key Demographic Groups Voted in Selected '96 Senate Races

Democrat   Republican

	Maine		New Hampshire		Massachusetts		New Jersey	
	Brennan	Collins	Swett	Smith	Kerry	Weld	Torricelli	Zimmer
By Race								
White	44%	49%	46%	49%	51%	46%	47%	48%
African American	*	*	*	*	NA	NA	85	13
Hispanic	*	*	*	*	*	*	NA	NA
Asian	*	*	*	*	*	*	*	*
Other	*	*	*	*	*	*	*	*
By Religion								
Protestant	38	54	41	58	39	56	51	46
Catholic	52	45	46	46	53	43	45	50
Other Christian	31	55	31	69	45	51	63	37
Jewish	*	*	*	*	69	30	71	26
Other	*	*	*	*	80	19	66	29
None	47	47	72	28	64	32	NA	NA
By Age								
18-29	42	50	42	47	55	39	57	38
30-44	44	47	47	48	52	45	49	46
45-59	42	53	48	49	50	46	56	39
60+	47	48	45	54	50	46	53	42
By Income								
Under $15,000	49	38	52	38	55	40	65	30
$15,000-$30,000	48	47	39	52	62	33	61	38
$30,000-$50,000	43	52	44	53	52	43	53	40
$50,000-$75,000	37	55	53	42	52	45	52	43
$75,000-$100,000	NA	NA	44	52	51	48	46	50
Over $100,000	NA	NA	NA	NA	42	55	47	47
By Education								
No High School	60	37	NA	NA	63	29	69	29
High School Grad.	45	47	36	57	52	43	53	40
Some College	44	49	46	50	45	50	53	43
College Grad.	38	55	44	54	49	48	50	46
Post Grad.	41	50	57	35	60	38	50	45

Note: See page 121 for notes/source for this page and pp. 117-121.

	Maine		New Hampshire		Massachusetts		New Jersey	
	Brennan	Collins	Swett	Smith	Kerry	Weld	Torricelli	Zimmer
By Party ID								
Democrat	76%	22%	89%	9%	80%	17%	86%	12%
Republican	13	79	16	83	15	79	16	79
Independent/Other	38	51	46	43	45	51	50	42
By Ideology								
Liberal	66	28	81	15	77	21	79	19
Moderate	45	49	52	39	52	45	55	38
Conservative	26	65	15	85	24	71	26	70
Republicans in Congress in last 2 years[1]								
Approve	15	76	19	80	15	79	18	78
Disapprove	66	29	69	23	75	22	82	15
How much should government do?[2]								
More	64	32	68	24	69	28	70	27
Less	31	60	32	64	35	60	32	62
By '92 Presidential vote								
Clinton	69	26	81	13	76	22	81	15
Bush	17	74	19	80	16	78	16	80
Perot	29	65	25	65	35	60	38	48
Other	*	*	*	*	*	*	*	*
No Vote	43	49	47	43	58	40	65	31

Voting in Selected '96 Senate Races

	North Carolina		South Carolina		Georgia		Arkansas		Louisiana	
	Gantt	Helms	Close	Thurmond	Cleland	Millner	Bryant	Hutchinson	Landrieu	Jenkins
By Race										
White	36%	63%	32%	65%	37%	59%	43%	56%	32%	68%
African American	89	10	78	20	47	47	NA	NA	91	9
Hispanic	*	*	*	*	*	*	*	*	*	*
Asian	*	*	*	*	*	*	*	*	*	*
Other	*	*	*	*	*	*	*	*	*	*
By Religion										
Protestant	42	57	NA	NA	39	59	NA	NA	NA	NA
Catholic	42	58	NA	NA	48	47	NA	NA	NA	NA
Other Christian	45	55	NA	NA	54	40	NA	NA	NA	NA
Jewish	*	*	NA	NA	*	*	NA	NA	NA	NA
Other	67	30	NA	NA	57	31	NA	NA	NA	NA
None	NA	NA	NA	NA	NA	NA	NA	NA	NA	NA
By Age										
18-29	51	48	43	54	49	47	41	59	53	47
30-44	46	53	43	51	47	47	43	57	50	50
45-59	43	56	43	55	48	49	49	51	50	50
60+	46	53	46	54	52	47	56	43	48	51
By Income										
Under $15,000	56	43	63	29	60	36	57	43	71	29
$15,000-$30,000	50	49	50	48	55	39	43	57	60	40
$30,000-$50,000	46	53	40	58	53	43	46	53	44	56
$50,000-$75,000	41	59	40	56	44	51	48	52	38	61
$75,000-$100,000	44	56	47	52	38	62	NA	NA	30	70
Over $100,000	42	58	26	68	28	70	NA	NA	33	65
By Education										
No High School	50	50	NA	NA	NA	NA	NA	NA	NA	NA
High School Grad.	41	58	NA	NA	53	41	NA	NA	NA	NA
Some College	46	54	NA	NA	48	47	NA	NA	NA	NA
College Grad.	43	56	NA	NA	41	58	NA	NA	NA	NA
Post Grad.	58	41	NA	NA	53	43	NA	NA	NA	NA

	North Carolina		South Carolina		Georgia		Arkansas		Louisiana	
	Gantt	Helms	Close	Thurmond	Cleland	Millner	Bryant	Hutchinson	Landrieu	Jenkins
By Party ID										
Democrat	78%	22%	79%	19%	81%	14%	78%	22%	74%	26%
Republican	13	86	12	87	13	87	6	94	15	84
Independent/Other	45	53	41	53	47	46	38	62	38	62
By Ideology										
Liberal	82	17	68	26	76	17	76	23	78	21
Moderate	56	44	55	42	57	38	59	41	66	34
Conservative	18	81	23	74	26	73	24	76	25	74
Republicans in Congress in last 2 years[1]										
Approve	17	83	59	38	17	80	12	88	21	79
Disapprove	80	19	22	77	84	12	76	24	75	25
How much should government do?[2]										
More	64	35	NA	NA	72	25	NA	NA	NA	NA
Less	32	67	NA	NA	32	63	NA	NA	NA	NA
By '92 Presidential vote										
Clinton	81	19	80	18	80	15	74	25	80	19
Bush	13	87	14	85	17	82	10	90	15	85
Perot	30	66	NA	NA	34	54	NA	NA	32	68
Other	*	*	*	*	*	*	*	*	*	*
No Vote	48	51	40	52	52	43	NA	NA	51	49

Voting in Selected '96 Senate Races

	Democrat		Democrat		Republican					
	Kansas		**Kansas**		**South Dakota**		**Colorado**		**Oregon**	
	Thompson	Roberts	Docking	Brownback	Johnson	Pressler	Strickland	Allard	Bruggere	Smith
By Race										
White	33%	64%	42%	54%	52%	48%	42%	55%	46%	51%
African American	NA	NA	NA	NA	*	*	NA	NA	*	*
Hispanic	*	*	*	*	*	*	80	18	*	*
Asian	*	*	*	*	*	*	*	*	*	*
Other	*	*	*	*	*	*	*	*	*	*
By Religion										
Protestant	NA	NA	NA	NA	NA	NA	34	62	39	60
Catholic	NA	NA	NA	NA	NA	NA	53	46	54	43
Other Christian	NA	NA	NA	NA	NA	NA	36	63	28	66
Jewish	NA	NA	NA	NA	NA	NA	*	*	*	*
Other	NA	NA	NA	NA	NA	NA	62	29	75	19
None	NA	NA	NA	NA	NA	NA	77	17	62	34
By Age										
18-29	38	58	44	54	51	49	52	46	45	50
30-44	35	63	40	55	50	50	49	46	44	52
45-59	36	59	44	53	49	50	45	53	48	50
60+	31	68	45	53	56	43	37	61	47	49
By Income										
Under $15,000	NA	NA	49	46	55	44	46	44	57	38
$15,000-$30,000	42	51	46	49	53	47	50	48	42	55
$30,000-$50,000	39	57	44	55	55	44	45	52	45	51
$50,000-$75,000	30	67	37	59	53	46	49	48	48	51
$75,000-$100,000	32	68	51	49	NA	NA	48	52	50	49
Over $100,000	23	77	40	60	NA	NA	32	64	NA	NA
By Education										
No High School	NA	NA	NA	NA	NA	NA	NA	NA	56	38
High School Grad.	NA	NA	NA	NA	NA	NA	42	55	43	55
Some College	NA	NA	NA	NA	NA	NA	47	51	39	57
College Grad.	NA	NA	NA	NA	NA	NA	41	54	48	50
Post-Grad.	NA	NA	NA	NA	NA	NA	55	45	56	39

	Kansas	Kansas		South Dakota		Colorado		Oregon	
	Thompson	Roberts	Docking	Brownback	Johnson	Pressler	Strickland	Allard	Bruggere	Smith
By Party ID										
Democrat	80%	20%	84%	16%	87%	13%	83%	16%	76%	21%
Republican	9	90	18	80	25	75	15	84	12	87
Independent/Other	40	50	51	40	52	47	51	41	50	42
By Ideology										
Liberal	73	25	77	21	81	19	80	18	83	13
Moderate	43	54	56	42	70	30	52	44	54	43
Conservative	14	83	18	79	26	74	14	84	11	87
Republicans in Congress in last 2 years[1]										
Approve	13	86	20	79	28	72	16	83	13	86
Disapprove	63	31	74	22	76	23	78	17	75	19
How much should government do?[2]										
More	NA	NA	NA	NA	NA	NA	NA	NA	70	26
Less	NA	NA	NA	NA	NA	NA	NA	NA	32	65
By '92 Presidential vote										
Clinton	70	28	83	17	83	17	80	16	80	18
Bush	8	91	17	82	25	75	14	86	11	89
Perot	28	63	40	53	47	52	37	54	34	61
Other	*	*	*	*	*	*	*	*	*	*
No Vote	NA	NA	39	59	46	54	51	47	38	51

*= 0-2% No respondents or too few to accurately report.
NA= Not available.
[1] "In general, do you approve or disapprove of what the Republicans in Congress have done in the last two years?"
[2] "Which comes closer to your view?
    1.Government should do more to solve problems.
    2.Government is doing too many things better left to businesses and individuals."
Source: Survey by Voter News Service exit poll, November 5, 1996.

How the Contest for Control of the House Looked in Pre-Election Polls

Question: If the elections for Congress were being held today, which party's candidate would you vote for in your Congressional district—the Democratic Party's candidate or the Republican Party's candidate? (If undecided or other) As of today, do you lean more to the Democratic Party's candidate or to the Republican Party's candidate?

Dem.	Rep.	Und./Other	Date (Sample)	Survey Organization
48	45	7	11/3-4 (LV)	Gallup/CNN/USA Today
48	45	7	11/2-4	PSRA/Newsweek
51	43	6	11/2-3 (LV)	Gallup/CNN/USA Today
43	41	8	11/2-3	NBC/WSJ
52	40	8	11/2-3	ABC News
43	43	14	11/2-3	US News/Tarrance
40	39	*21	11/1-3	Reuters/Zogby
51	41	6	10/31-11/1	ABC News
51	41	8	10/31-11/2	ABC News
47	41	*12	10/30-11/2	CBS/NYT
44	41	16	10/30-31 (LV)	Opinion Dynamics
50	42	7	10/30-31	ABC News
39	38	*23	10/29-31 (LV)	Reuters/Zogby
50	42	8	10/29-30	ABC News
50	45	5	10/29-30 (LV)	Gallup/CNN/USA Today
40	38	*22	10/28-30 (LV)	Reuters/Zogby
48	45	7	10/28-29 (LV)	Gallup/CNN/USA Today
45	42	*13	10/27-29 (LV)	CBS News
39	37	*24	10/27-29 (LV)	Reuters/Zogby
54	39	7	10/27-28	ABC News
50	42	8	10/27-28 (LV)	Gallup/CNN/USA Today
39	37	*24	10/26-28 (LV)	Reuters/Zogby
53	39	8	10/26-27	ABC News
49	44	7	10/26-27 (LV)	Gallup/CNN/USA Today
43	37	*21	10/25-29 (NA)	Washington Post
46	39	15	10/25-29 (NA)	Washington Post
39	35	*26	10/25-27 (LV)	Reuters/Zogby
50	43	7	10/25-26 (LV)	Gallup/CNN/USA Today
50	41	*9	10/24-26	ABC News
50	41	*9	10/24-25	ABC News
49	38	*13	10/23-27 (LV)	CBS News
45	36	*19	10/23-27	Washington Post
47	40	13	10/23-27	Washington Post
49	41	10	10/23-24	ABC News
48	44	8	10/23-24 (LV)	Gallup/CNN/USA Today
37	38	*25	10/22-24 (L)	Reuters/Zogby
51	42	7	10/22-23 (LV)	Gallup/CNN/USA Today
49	42	9	10/22-23	ABC News
36	37	*27	10/21-23 (LV)	Reuters/Zogby
48	43	9	10/21-22	ABC News
36	37	*27	10/20-22 (LV)	Reuters/Zogby
50	42	8	10/20-21	ABC News
39	38	23	10/19-22	NBC/WSJ
37	35	*28	10/19-21 (LV)	Reuters/Zogby
52	42	6	10/19-20 (LV)	Gallup/CNN/USA Today
50	41	9	10/19-20	ABC News
38	36	*26	10/18-20 (LV)	Reuters/Zogby
47	37	*16	10/17-20	CBS/NYT
50	43	7	10/17-19	ABC News
50	36	14	10/17-18	PSRA
50	44	6	10/16-18	ABC News
39	34	*27	10/15-17 (LV)	Reuters/Zogby
53	40	7	10/15-16	ABC News
49	42	9	10/14-20	PSRA/Pew
39	33	*28	10/14-16 (LV)	Reuters/Zogby
53	40	7	10/14-15	ABC News
39	33	*28	10/13-15 (LV)	Reuters/Zogby
53	40	7	10/13-14	ABC News
38	33	*29	10/12-14 (LV)	Reuters/Zogby
52	42	6	10/12-13 (LV)	Gallup/CNN/USA Today
39	34	*27	10/11-13 (LV)	Reuters/Zogby
53	41	6	10/11-12 (LV)	Gallup/CNN/USA Today
47	41	*12	10/10-13 (LV)	CBS/NYT
52	38	10	10/10-11	Yankelovich/Time/CNN
48	36	*16	10/10-11	Yankelovich/Time/CNN
36	35	29*	10/8-10 (LV)	Reuters/Zogby
35	36	*29	10/7-9 (LV)	Reuters/Zogby
51	41	8	10/7-8	ABC News
36	36	*28	10/6-8 (LV)	Reuters/Zogby
37	37	*26	10/5-7 (LV)	Reuters/Zogby
38	36	*26	10/4-6 (LV)	Reuters/Zogby
51	43	6	10/1-2	Gallup/CNN/USA Today

Most Polls Showed a Democratic Lead Most of the Time

Dem.	Rep.	Und./Other	Date (Sample)	Survey Organization	Dem.	Rep.	Und./Other	Date (Sample)	Survey Organization
34	35	*31	9/30-10/3 (LV)	Reuters/Zogby	51	41	8	8/25-26	ABC News
36	35	*29	9/28-30 (LV)	Reuters/Zogby	48	43	10	8/24-25	ABC News
49	43	8	9/25-29	PSRA/Pew	47	43	9	8/22-24	ABC News
48	41	11	9/25-29	ABC News	39	39	23	8/20-22	Public Opinion Strategies
41	40	19	9/24-26, 29	Hotline/Battleground	38	37	25	8/20-21	NBC/WSJ
48	45	7	9/20-22 (LV)	Gallup/CNN/USA Today	41	38	*21	8/18-20 (LV)	Reuters/Zogby
40	39	21	9/19, 22-24	Hotline/Battleground	49	42	9	8/18-19	ABC News
48	43	9	9/19-20	PSRA/Newsweek	49	42	9	8/17-18	ABC News
50	43	7	9/18-22	ABC News	49	43	8	8/17-20	American Viewpoint
38	42	20	9/15-18	Hotline/Battleground	39	39	*22	8/16-18	Wirthlin Worldwide
52	42	6	9/13-15 (LV)	Gallup/CNN/USA Today	49	45	6	8/16-18	Gallup/CNN/USA Today
42	36	22	9/12-17	NBC/WSJ	43	41	*16	8/16-18	CBS/NYT
49	45	6	9/11-15	ABC News	45	46	9	8/15-18	ABC News
41	38	21	9/9-12	Hotline/Battleground	46	43	10	8/14-15	ABC News
50	40	10	9/7-10	Los Angeles Times	48	42	10	8/13-14	ABC News
42	39	19	9/6-11	Roper Center	41	38	*21	8/12-14	CBS News
42	36	*23	9/6-8	Wirthlin Worldwide	49	43	8	8/12-13	ABC News
50	40	10	9/6-8	Gallup/CNN/USA Today	49	42	9	8/11-12	ABC News
51	43	6	9/5-8	PSRA/Pew Center	49	40	11	8/10-11	ABC News
48	42	10	9/4-5	Yankelovich/Time/CNN	44	47	9	8/8-9	PSRA/Newsweek
40	37	23	9/3-5,8	Hotline/Battleground	42	39	19	8/7-8 (LV)	Fox News/Opinion Dynamics
48	44	8	9/3-4	ABC/WP	51	39	10	8/7-8	Yankelovich/Time/CNN
48	43	9	9/2-5	American Viewpoint	49	41	10	8/6-10	ABC News
42	41	*17	9/2-4 (LV)	Reuters/Zogby	47	43	10	8/6-8	American Viewpoint
44	40	*16	9/2-4	CBS/NYT	48	44	8	8/5-7	Gallup/CNN/USA Today
51	41	8	8/30-9/1	Gallup/CNN/USA Today	47	43	10	8/3-6	Los Angeles Times
53	39	9	8/28-29	ABC News	46	39	*15	8/3-5	CBS/NYT
51	40	9	8/27-28	ABC News	38	38	*24	8/2-6	NBC/WSJ
45	36	*19	8/26-28	CBS News	39	41	*20	8/2-4	Wirthlin Worldwide
51	41	8	8/26-27	ABC News	49	43	8	8/1-5 (NA)	ABC/WP
38	41	21	8/26-27	Hotline/C. Tribune/Battleground					

Note: Question wording varies slightly from organization to organization. Asked of registered voters except where noted. LV = Likely Voters; NA = National Adults. * = Respondents who replied "other" or "undecided" were not asked toward which party they were leaning. All other items include leaners.

Chapter 5

Citizen-Initiated Ballot Measures

In addition to electing officeholders in 1996, voters in 20 states also determined the outcome of 90 citizen-initiated ballot measures. Although ballot items varied among states, policy areas such as term limits, campaign finance reform and gambling were frequently addressed. Term limits, as in the 1994 elections, found significant support, passing in 10 of 15 states. Measures dealing with campaign finance reform passed in every state in which they were considered. Gambling initiatives, however, encountered considerable resistance, failing in four out of six states.

As Mark DiCamillo of the Field Institute points out in the following article, California's 1996 initiatives stirred up national controversy when voters were asked to decide the future of the state's affirmative action programs and whether the medical use of marijuana should be allowed. Other issues relating to state regulation of health maintenance organizations and legal matters were also on the California ballot. Additionally, DiCamillo touches on Californians' opinions about the initiative process, maintaining that citizens perceive a failure by their legislature to address the often complex and controversial issues that appear on the ballot. In spite of this criticism, voters nonetheless prize direct democracy.

Following DiCamillo, Tom Smith of the National Opinion Research Center discusses (in an article previously published in *The Public Perspective*) the clash, created by affirmative action programs, between our society's ideals of individualism and equality. According to Smith, affirmative action's mission to address societal inequalities conflicts with our commitment to individual rights.

The Chapter concludes with an overview by policy area of 1996 ballot measures that passed and failed.

—Pamela Hunter

Californians End Affirmative Action and Legalize Medical Use of Marijuana

By Mark DiCamillo

The 15 propositions that appeared on California's general election ballot in 1996 provided much of the drama in an otherwise unsuspenseful presidential election year. The diverse array of topics spanned such issues as the highly controversial initiative to prohibit race and gender-based affirmative action programs, the medical use of marijuana, the minimum wage, increased regulations on health maintenance organizations and campaign financing, tort reform, taxes, jail construction, veterans' assistance and state water projects.

A review of the election returns shows that the electorate was highly discriminating, approving eight propositions and rejecting seven. Voters backed the controversial anti-affirmative action initiative as well as the medical marijuana initiative. Two tort reform measures were defeated, but an initiative limiting auto insurance liability in certain cases was passed. Californians approved one campaign finance reform initiative but rejected another. While voters rejected both health maintenance reform initiatives, they approved an increase in the state minimum wage. Changes that make increasing property taxes and fees by local governments more difficult were approved, but an extension of a higher tax rate on the state's top earners was rejected. Voters passed two state bonds, one to finance water projects and another for veterans assistance, but rejected a third bond measure that would have provided additional moneys for jail construction.

The following analysis reviews some of the most salient initiatives in this year's elections as covered by the California-based Field Institute's *Field Poll*.

Proposition 209, the California Civil Rights Initiative

The closely watched campaign to qualify for the ballot the California Civil Rights Initiative, which deals with affirmative action, began in early 1995. In the ensuing months it evolved into one of the state's most controversial initiatives in recent years.

The official wording of Proposition 209 was itself an issue in the campaign. The exact ballot title and summary of Prop. 209 which voters saw when they went to the polls read as follows:

Prohibition Against Discrimination or Preferential Treatment by State and other Public Entities. Initiative Constitutional Amendment. *Generally prohibits discrimination or preferential treatment based on race, sex, color, ethnicity or national origin in public employment, education and contracting. Fiscal impact: Could affect state and local programs that currently cost well in excess of $125 million annually. Actual savings would depend on various factors (such as future court decisions and implementation actions by government entities).*

Salient Propositions on the California Ballot

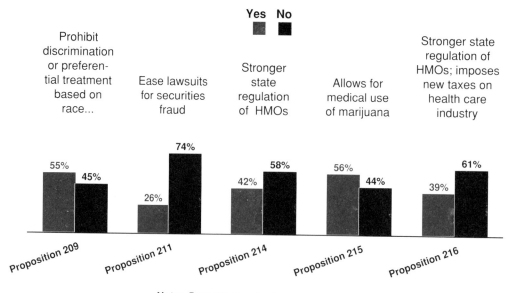

Yes No

| Prohibit discrimination or preferential treatment based on race... | Ease lawsuits for securities fraud | Stronger state regulation of HMOs | Allows for medical use of marijuana | Stronger state regulation of HMOs; imposes new taxes on health care industry |

55% 45% | 26% 74% | 42% 58% | 56% 44% | 39% 61%

Proposition 209   Proposition 211   Proposition 214   Proposition 215   Proposition 216

Note: Data are actual vote percentages.

Two Hotly Contested Propositions on the California Ballot Cut Sharply Across Party Lines

California Proposition 209— Abolish Affirmative Action

California Proposition 215— Medical use of Marijuana

Yes   No

	Prop 209 Yes	Prop 209 No
Total	55%	45%
Gender		
Men	59%	41%
Women	52%	48%
Race		
White	62%	38%
Black	27%	73%
Hispanic	30%	70%
Asian	44%	56%
Age		
18-29	48%	52%
30-44	52%	48%
45-59	57%	43%
60+	59%	41%
Income		
Less than $15,000	39%	61%
$15,000-$30,000	47%	53%
$30,000-$50,000	59%	41%
$50,000-$75,000	57%	43%
$75,000-$100,000	57%	43%
Over $100,000	64%	36%
Party ID		
Democrat	32%	68%
Republican	80%	20%
Independent/Other	53%	47%
Legal Immigrants to US		
Increase	50%	50%
Decrease	64%	36%
Stay the same	52%	48%

	Prop 215 Yes	Prop 215 No
Total	56%	44%
Gender		
Men	54%	46%
Women	57%	43%
Race		
White	55%	45%
Black	72%	28%
Hispanic	56%	44%
Asian	41%	59%
Age		
18-29	62%	38%
30-44	60%	40%
45-59	55%	45%
60+	42%	58%
Income		
Less than $15,000	59%	41%
$15,000-$30,000	62%	38%
$30,000-$50,000	51%	49%
$50,000-$75,000	58%	42%
$75,000-$100,000	52%	48%
Over $100,000	58%	42%
Party ID		
Democrat	70%	30%
Republican	36%	64%
Independent/Other	62%	38%
Religion		
Protestant	48%	52%
Catholic	48%	52%
Other Christian	52%	48%
Jewish	75%	25%
Other	76%	24%
None	78%	22%

Source: Survey by VNS, California Exit Poll, November 5, 1996.

The words "affirmative action" were not mentioned in the ballot description, yet implementation of the initiative requires dismantling existing race and gender-based affirmative action programs in the state's university systems as well as in public employment and contracting.

In six successive Field Polls conducted throughout 1995 and during the first six months of 1996, voters were inclined to support the initiative by margins ranging from 21 to 25 points. However, in the final weeks of the campaign as the controversy about the issue intensified, support for the measure dropped—to single digits at one point—but was finally approved by a 55% to 45% margin.

Prop. 209 became salient early in the campaign as a result of heavy and almost continuous free media play and with virtually no campaign advertising. All major newspapers, TV and radio properties featured the pros and cons of Prop. 209 regularly in their news coverage in 1995 and 1996. Only during the final weeks of the campaign was paid advertising visible.

Prior to the final fortnight of the campaign, voter reaction to Prop. 209 was not highly partisan. Republicans were heavily supportive and Democrats mildly supportive of the measure. However, in the closing weeks of the campaign, GOP leaders, notably California Governor Pete Wilson and Republican presidential nominee Bob Dole, supported the initiative. It was widely reported that Wilson, Dole and many GOP congressional candidates believed advocacy of Prop. 209 was a winning issue that would attract swing voters to their party. Campaign ads for Dole and some Republican congressional candidates featured them backing Prop. 209 and President Clinton opposing it.

Whereas Prop. 209 had originally appeared as only marginally partisan, Republican leaders made the differ-

ences between the two parties on this issue clear late in the campaign. So much so that Ward Connerly, the leader of the Prop. 209 campaign, publicly questioned Republican leaders in the campaign's final week about their decision to emphasize party differences on the initiative.

As a result, a pronounced partisan split in the vote on Prop. 209 began to appear in the final two Field surveys, the first completed 10 days prior and the last completed two days prior to the election. And, according to the Voter News Service exit poll, the final vote on Prop. 209 showed that 80% of Republicans supported the initiative while 68% of Democrats opposed it.

A post-election survey of voters completed by the Field Poll found that Prop. 209 supporters were clear about the impact of their vote on existing affirmative action programs. According to the survey, 91% of "Yes" voters agreed with the statement, "a Yes vote on Proposition 209 was a vote to end race and gender-based affirmative action programs in public employment, education and contracting." Only 5% disagreed while 4% weren't sure.

"No" voters, however, were less clear about their voting intent. Three out of four "No" voters (74%) agreed with the statement, "a No vote on Proposition 209 was a vote to continue race and gender-based affirmative action programs in public employment, education and contracting" while 18% disagreed and 8% weren't sure.

The same post-election study found that while more than eight in 10 voters (84%) agreed that discrimination was still common in society, two in three (69%) said they supported at least some relaxation in affirmative action policies. Yet there were wide differences of opinion between "Yes" and "No" voters regarding the extent of the changes they would support. The dominant mood among "Yes" voters was that affirmative action pro-

grams should be completely eliminated because such laws are fundamentally flawed. In contrast, half of the "No" voters said they supported some change in affirmative action laws while only a few supported their complete elimination.

Proposition 215, Medical Use of Marijuana

Proposition 215 sought to exempt from criminal laws patients and caregivers who possess or cultivate marijuana for medical treatments as recommended by a doctor. The results of four pre-election Field surveys showed the measure consistently ahead in the fall election campaign; voters eventually approved Prop. 215 by a comfortable 56% to 44% margin.

The Prop. 215 campaign was distinctive compared to other prominent statewide propositions because there was little paid political advertising for or against the initiative. Yet large majorities of the public were aware of and seemed interested in its fate. Field polls conducted as early as September showed a majority of voters aware of Prop. 215, ranking it among the most prominent state initiatives in terms of voter awareness in this election cycle.

Prop. 215's popularity appeared to result from the combination of two somewhat different voting constituencies including one group supportive of the relaxation of all state laws relating to marijuana. According to previous Field surveys, Californians who support the outright legalization of marijuana included about a quarter to a third of the state's electorate, and they tended to be more politically liberal. These voters were joined by a pivotal segment of middle-of-the-road voters who were drawn to Prop. 215 for its perceived potential medical benefits to relieve pain and nausea among the afflicted.

This combination ultimately gave Prop. 215 supporters a broad-based profile crossing most voter subgroups. According to the Field pre-election surveys and the VNS exit poll, majorities of men, women, whites, Latinos, blacks, as well as voters of all income and education groups favored its passage.

State Attorney General Dan Lungren and other law enforcement officials led the fight against Prop. 215. They were concerned about its apparent vagueness in defining who could prescribe the medical use of marijuana. They also believed that Prop. 215's passage would cause enforcement problems of other state and federal marijuana laws. Despite these warnings, most voters seemed to view the initiative as more benign and limited in scope than as a radical or wholesale shift in state laws and policies regarding marijuana.

Propositions 214 and 216, HMO Regulation and Reform

Propositions 214 and 216 were two similarly worded initiatives aimed at providing greater protections to patients enrolled in managed care health plans. The initiatives came at a time when increasing reports of a managed care "backlash" were spreading across the state and the nation. Compared to other states, California appeared to be a particularly ripe locale for such a backlash since an estimated two-thirds of California's insured population are in managed care plans.

Two separate initiatives were placed on the ballot rather than one largely because consumer groups could not agree on the extent of state regulation. Both initiatives included stronger state regulation of HMOs and staffing standards, banned gag orders which restricted physicians from telling patients about all of their potential treatment options, prohibited incentives to physicians for withholding certain types of care, required second opinions before withholding such treatments, and prohibited physicians from disclosing patient information to oth-

ers without their consent. However, Prop. 216 went further and included some regulations not covered by Prop. 214 such as the levying of taxes or fees on health care businesses to finance health care reforms.

Opponents of the initiatives included most of the state's leading health maintenance organizations and insurance companies, although the influential California Medical Association remained neutral. The "No" side campaign portrayed Props. 214 and 216 as being poorly drafted and potentially adding to health care costs and increasing government's role in the health care system.

Field Poll pre-election surveys of voters on these two initiatives showed that relatively few Californians were aroused by them and that support never achieved a critical mass. In five statewide pre-election surveys conducted between August and late October, fewer than half of the electorate reported any awareness of the initiatives and few could distinguish between the two. Ultimately, Prop. 214 was defeated by a 58% to 42% margin, while Prop. 216 failed by a somewhat larger 61% to 39% margin.

The main reason behind the general lack of enthusiasm for the patient protection initiatives was probably voters' self-described contentment with their own health insurance plans. Field surveys showed that relatively few voters, including those covered by managed care plans, reported overall dissatisfaction with their health plans. According to a post-election survey, voter opposition to both Props. 214 and 216 echoed the "No" side's main advertising claims that the measures would create unnecessary government regulations and increase health care costs.

Proposition 211, Securities Fraud

The campaigns for and against Proposition 211, the securities fraud measure, established new state records both for overall spending on a single initiative and for spending by one side against another. Estimates place the total expenditures for this initiative at about $50 million, with roughly 80% raised and spent by its opponents.

Opponents of Prop. 211 were motivated to spend such huge amounts because of the potentially dire consequences they felt the measure would have on many of the state's and nation's largest and most profitable businesses, particularly those

> *Field surveys have found that the public is becoming increasingly critical of the initiative process. They wish the legislature would make a greater effort to do its job and deal with many of the highly complex issues that voters are now asked to decide.*

in the high technology sector. Prop. 211's provisions allowed stockholders to claim fraud and sue a corporation simply because of wide swings in a company's stock price, and individual officers of these corporations could be held personally liable in these cases. Moreover, any company doing business in California, no matter where the location of its headquarters, could potentially become a target of lawsuits from a disgruntled shareholder. Under Prop. 211, virtually all major US corporations would be vulnerable to such suits in California's courts.

The major sponsors of the measure were a group of well-financed securities lawyers who were joined by consumers groups, labor unions, and the state Democratic Party, despite President Bill Clinton's opposition. Early Field polls showed initial support for Prop. 211 primarily due to the inherent appeal of its ballot description. However, support was considered soft, and large portions of voters remained undecided. Amid a torrent of "No" side advertising that primarily played off of public distrust of lawyers and their claims, opinions dramatically changed in the final month of the campaign. A Field Poll conducted about two

> *Each of these trends—multiple propositions on the same topic, the strong ideological cast of so many of the initiatives, and initiatives sponsored by highly parochial special interest groups—may be contributing to another broader political trend in California: increasing voter alienation and disinterest. 1996 voter turnout in California was the lowest for a presidential election in 72 years.*

weeks prior to the election showed the "No" side vaulting ahead of the "Yes" side by an almost two-to-one margin, a reversal from earlier voter sentiment. This margin expanded further in the Field Poll's final pre-election survey, and ultimately voters rejected the initiative overwhelmingly 74% to 26%.

Opponents were so confident of Prop. 211's defeat that in the campaign's final two weeks they transferred millions of dollars from their huge campaign war chest to help defeat two other statewide initiatives on the ballot—Proposition 207, relating to attorney fees, and Proposition 217, which sought to reinstate a higher income tax rate on the state's top earners. Both measures were defeated at the polls. Prop. 217, however, was only narrowly defeated—51% to 49%—suggesting that the late-injection of "No" side campaign advertising dollars was largely responsible for its ultimate defeat.

Summary

As California voters are being called upon to decide an increasingly diverse set of ballot initiatives in recent years, a number of generalizations can be cited. First, multiple initiatives on the same topic and on the same ballot are

becoming more common. For example, in 1988 five different measures qualified for the general election ballot, all dealing with automobile insurance reform with some in opposition to each other. In contrast, the 1996 ballot listed two very competitive initiatives on campaign finance reform (Propositions 208 and 212), two tort reform initiatives relating to attorneys fees and securities fraud (Props. 207 and 211), two others (Props. 214 and 216) which attempted to reform the abuses of managed care health plans, and two tax measures (Props. 217 and 218).

Over the years California ballots have featured numerous initiatives dealing with social policy (e.g. higher education, fair housing, homosexual teachers in the public schools, English as the state's official language, welfare policy, and euthanasia). Recent examples of propositions sponsored by conservative advocates were the 1994 anti-illegal immigration initiative and this year's anti-affirmative action initiative. On the liberal side, the medical marijuana initiative and the two HMO health care reform measures were this year's notable illustrations.

While it is too early to know the public policy impact of the passage of some of California's more ideologically driven initiatives, they are affecting, although sometimes unintentionally, the underlying dynamic of this state's election politics. The popular 1994 anti-illegal immigration initiative struck a visceral chord with large portions of the electorate and significantly impacted other candidate races up and down the election ballot. Yet efforts to replicate this effect through the 1996 anti-affirmative action initiative were not as successful and, if anything, achieved the opposite effect of drawing minorities who might not have otherwise voted.

In 1996, California voters were again asked to decide among some highly expensive turf battles involving the state's well-heeled special interests. This year's proposition line-up featured wealthy lawyers vs. wealthy corporations, labor union vs. labor union, and even consumer group vs. consumer group. Big business interests alone set a record for initiative spending by one side against another, raising an estimated $40 million to defeat Proposition 211. Including efforts to defeat a second tort reform initiative, Prop. 207, and three other measures included in this year's March primary election, the final spending tally on the five tort-reform battles voted on in California in 1996 exceeded $90 million. Ironically, the net effect of all this spending was to leave the existing status quo intact since all five initiatives were ultimately defeated.

Each of these trends—voters increasingly sorting their way through multiple propositions on the same topic, the strong ideological cast of so many of the initiatives, and the task of deciding between the relative merits of initiatives sponsored by highly parochial special interest groups—may be contributing to another broader political trend in California: increasing voter alienation and disinterest. 1996 voter turnout in California was the lowest for a presidential election in 72 years. While certainly not solely attributable to California's proposition elections, a case can be made that voter turnout this year was not positively influenced by them, as none of them either singly or together stimulated voter interest.

Field surveys have found that the public is becoming increasingly critical of the initiative process. They wish the legislature would make a greater effort to do its job and deal with many of the highly complex issues that voters are now asked to decide. In many cases, the public is unable to understand all of the elements contained in the ballot propositions whose summary descriptions are typically highly legalistic or technical.

Voters also decry the way many of the more complicated ballot propositions are reduced to simplistic and often misleading advertising slogans featured in repetitive 30-second television commercials in the campaign's final months.

Yet Californians remain highly supportive of the privilege of voting on propositions. A September 1996 Field Poll found that 70% of the public felt proposition elections were good for California while only 7% said they were bad. While the proportion giving a positive response about proposition elections is down somewhat from the 83% who felt this way in 1979, the public is not ready to give up its option of deciding for themselves some of the important government policies that are affecting their lives.

The Dilemma of the American Ideology
By Tom W. Smith

If Russia is "a riddle wrapped in a mystery inside an enigma" as Churchill observed, then America is a dilemma encased in a contradiction inside a paradox. At the core of the American ideology are a series of noble, inspirational ideals that are inherently at odds with themselves. At best,

> " *The ideological progeny of the pioneers view government warily, seeing every government handout as a hand on their liberties. The descendants of the small-town society of equals see government as the tool for solving problems of poverty and the undemocratic concentration of wealth.* "

this creates a synergy that spurs America to greatness and helps maintain a balance that keeps the nation from veering too far off-course. At worst, this generates a schizophrenia that blurs our collective vision and debilitates the national will. A central contradiction revolves around the ideals of freedom and equality. We usually see these two values as

easily in tandem as when Lincoln described America as "born in liberty and dedicated to the proposition that all men are created equal." But the pursuit of freedom and equality leads in opposite directions. Our pursuit of freedom is epitomized by the rugged individualism of the pioneer, free of government and social conformity, engaged in a one-on-one struggle with the wilderness. Our search for equality lives in our populist distrust of great wealth and power, centering around an idealized society of small farmers, artisans, and shopkeepers.

Individualism vs. Equality

Perhaps no contemporary social issue captures the conflict between these two ideals more so than affirmative action. The spirit of individualism calls for equality of opportunity, even if this results in a meritocracy of talents and efforts. The principle of egalitarianism says that disparities between races, genders, and other groups would not naturally occur and that steps must be taken to remove their unjustifiable existence.

To its opponents, affirmative action policies based on group rights and implemented by quotas and special prefer-

Lower Our Taxes... But Spend More on Education, Health, and Environment

Question: Do you consider the amount of federal income tax which you pay as too high, about right, or too low?

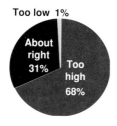

Too low 1%
About right 31%
Too high 68%

Question: ...for those with middle incomes, are taxes...?

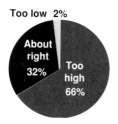

Too low 2%
About right 32%
Too high 66%

Question: We are faced with many problems in this country, none of which can be solved easily or inexpensively. I'm going to name some of these problems, and for each one I'd like you to tell me whether you think we're spending too much money on it, too little money, or about the right amount...?

	Too Little	About Right	Too Much
Education	73%	22%	6%
Health	66%	25%	9%
Environment	62%	28%	10%

Source: Survey by the National Opinion Research Center-General Social Survey, 1996.

---

ences are at best anathema to individual rights and Horatio Algerism and at worst reverse discrimination. To its proponents, affirmative action is essential for overcoming inequalities created by racism, sexism, and other bigotries.

Siding with the foes of affirmative action, the public opposes special preferences and quotas. On the 1996 General Social Survey (GSS) conducted by the National Opinion Research Center at the University of Chicago, only 16% backed giving African Americans preference in hiring and promotion, and on a related item just another 16% said that "Blacks have been discriminated against for so long that the government has a special obligation to help improve their living standards." But the public also shares Bob Dole's sentiment that "This is America. No discrimination. Discrimination ought to be punished...". In a Yankelovich survey conducted in 1995, 64% fa-

vored "affirmative action programs that promote black employment, but do not contain quotas."

President Clinton has tried to finesse the dilemma with his "mend it, don't end it" review of current federal policies, but voters in California decided instead just to end it. They passed with 55% of the vote the California Civil Rights Initiative (Proposition 209) which says that "(t)he state shall not discriminate against, or grant preferential treatment to, any individual or group on the basis of race, sex, color, ethnicity, or national origin." Of course that will hardly end the debate. Already the ACLU has challenged the constitutionality of the CCRI and civil rights activists have met with White House and Justice Department officials to urge Clinton to lead the fight for affirmative action.

While race alone makes this a divisive issue, the difficulties it raises

are ultimately philosophical and ideological. They involve serious conflicts over individual vs. group rights, between equality of opportunity and equality of outcome, and over the role of race in opposing racism. Only by facing up to the contradictory ideals that are tapped by affirmative action can American society decide on what its appropriate role should be.

Role of Government

This same tension between maximizing individual liberty and furthering social equality extends to the very purpose of government itself. The ideological progeny of the pioneers view government warily, seeing every government handout as a hand on their liberties. The descendants of the small-town society of equals see government as the tool for solving problems of poverty and the undemocratic concentration of wealth.

These and other divisions ensconced in the American soul lead to great tensions within American public opinion. On one hand, the public wants the government to improve education, reduce poverty, and solve other social problems. Large majorities endorse more governmental spending for the poor, the environment, schools, and other programs. For example, in the 1996 GSS, 55% said the government was spending too little on assistance to the poor while only 19% thought it was spending too much. Likewise, the pro-spending balance was 62% to 10% for the environment and 73% to 6% for education.

But on the other hand, the public wants lower taxes, fewer government regulations, and less meddling in people's lives. The 1996 GSS found that 66% think taxes on the middle class are too high and 68% declare that their own federal income tax is too high.

Also, 64% think the federal government has too much power and 69% believe that the information that the government keeps on people is a threat to individual privacy. The public endorses New Deal goals and Reaganite means!

Crisis of Confidence

Moreover, these and other policy contradictions are, perhaps, becoming greater and less tractable. Confidence in both the executive and legislative branches of the federal government fell to a 23-year low in 1996. Asking about confidence in 13 institutions, the 1996 GSS found Congress and the executive branch of the federal government battling for bottom place with 44% of the public having "hardly any" confidence in both branches of government. In the case of Congress the non-confidence vote rose from only 16% in 1973 to being over 40% since 1993. For the executive branch the 1996 figure topped

even the 1974 Watergate level of 43% and is up from 22% in 1991. The crisis in confidence is also reflected in the little trust that people place in their government. Only 25% agree that the "people we elect to Congress try to keep the promises they have made during the election" and just 19% think that "most government administrators can be trusted to do what is best for the country."

Unable to resolve the deep-seated uncertainties over who should do what, the electorate swings between electing a Democratic president and a Republican Congress, while third parties have gained a greater percent of the presidential vote in two successive elections than at any time since before the Civil War. Unless some candidate or party understands the foundational conflicts within American culture and rallies the citizenry behind a new balance of these competing ideals, public dissatisfaction will rise and our paralysis of values and policies will worsen.

Citizen-Initiated Ballot Measures—
Term Limits and Campaign Finance Reform
Find Wide Support

Campaign Finance Reform

	Yes	No
Nevada	71%	29%
Arkansas	67%	33%
Colorado	66%	34%
California[a]	61%	39%
Maine	56%	44%
California[b]	49%	51%

[a]Measure involves disclosure of campaign contributions.
[b]Measure involves restrictions on lobbyists.

Congressional Term Limits

	Yes	No
South Dakota	68%	32%
Arkansas	61%	39%
Maine	59%	41%
Nebraska	58%	42%
Missouri	58%	42%
Idaho	56%	44%
Colorado	55%	45%
Alaska	54%	46%
Wyoming	54%	46%
Nevada	53%	47%
Oregon	48%	52%
North Dakota	47%	53%
Washington	45%	55%
Montana	44%	56%

Measures to Allow or Expand Gambling

	Yes	No
Arizona	64%	36%
Michigan	52%	48%
Washington	43%	57%
Arkansas	39%	61%
Ohio	38%	62%
Colorado	31%	69%

ELECTION RESULTS:
Citizen-Initiated Measures that Passed

Electoral Process

State	Subject Matter Covered on the Ballot	Percent Yes	No
Alaska	Instructs elected officials to support congressional term limits	55%	45%
Arkansas	Instructs elected officials to support congressional term limits	61	39
Arkansas	Campaign contribution limits and disclosures; specifies requirements for small donor political action committees and independent expenditure committees	67	33
California	Disclosure of campaign contributions and spending limits	61	39
Colorado	Instructs elected officials to support congressional term limits	54	46
Colorado	Limits individual contributions to legislators, statewide candidates, and political parties and committees	66	34
Idaho	Instructs elected officials to support congressional term limits	56	44
Maine	Instructs elected officials to support congressional term limits	59	41
Maine	Campaign finance limits	56	44
Missouri	Instructs elected officials to support congressional term limits	58	42
Montana	Limits contributions from corporations for initiatives	52	48
Nebraska	Instructs elected officials to support congressional term limits	58	42
Nevada	Term limits for state and local officers in executive and legislative branches	54	46
Nevada	Establishes, limits, and defines campaign contributions	71	29
Nevada	Instructs elected officials to support congressional term limits	53	47
South Dakota	Instructs elected officials to support congressional term limits	68	32
Wyoming	Repeals 1995 legislative act which extended legislative service from 6 to 12 years	54	46
Wyoming	Instructs elected officials to support congressional term limits	54	46

Crime/Legal System

Arizona	Requires juveniles ages 15 and older to be tried as adults for murder, rape, or armed robbery; all juvenile proceedings open to the public	63	37
Arizona	Statute revisions for controlled substances; allows medical use of marijuana	65	35
California	Denies recovery of all damages to convicted felons for crime-related injury, and damages for pain and suffering to convicted drunk drivers and most uninsured drivers	77	23
California	Allows medical use of marijuana	56	44
Montana	Allows lawsuits for harassing and intimidating behavior by extremists	53	47
Oregon	Establishes rights for crime victims; expands admissible evidence; limits pretrial release; allows murder conviction on 11-1 vote	59	41

Government

State	Subject Matter Covered on the Ballot	Percent	
		Yes	No
California	Prohibits discrimination or preferential treatment by state and other public entities	55%	45%

Financial/Taxes

State	Subject Matter Covered on the Ballot	Yes	No
California	Minimum wage increase	62	38
California	Voter approval for local government taxes; limitations on fees, assessments, and charges	57	43
Colorado	Investment of state education funds	52	48
Florida	Two-thirds vote required for new state taxes/fees	69	31
Missouri	Increases sales and use tax for land, water conservation, state parks	67	33
Nevada	Two-thirds majority of legislature necessary to increase any tax or revenue	70	30
North Dakota	Transfers administrative authority for Veterans' Postwar Trust Fund from legislature to board established by governor	76	24
Oregon	Increases cigarette and tobacco taxes	56	44
Oregon	Minimum wage increase	57	43
Oregon	Reduces and limits property taxes; limits local revenue; replacement fees	52	48

Health Care

State	Subject Matter Covered on the Ballot	Yes	No
Arizona	Allocates lottery revenues for health programs	72	28

Environment

State	Subject Matter Covered on the Ballot	Yes	No
Alaska	Prohibits same-day airborne hunting	59	41
Colorado	Prohibits use of leghold traps, body-gripping traps, poison or snares to take wildlife	52	48
Florida	Requires polluters to pay for cleaning up the Everglades	68	32
Florida	Creates trust fund to protect and clean up the Everglades	57	43
Massachusetts	Prohibits use of traps for hunting bear and bobcat	64	36
Washington	Prohibits hunting of black bear with bait, and cougar, bobcat and lynx with dogs	63	37

Gambling

State	Subject Matter Covered on the Ballot	Yes	No
Arizona	Allows five additional tribes to operate gambling facilities	64	36
Michigan	Permits casino gambling in qualified cities	52	48

ELECTION RESULTS:
Citizen-Initiated Measures that Failed

Electoral Process

		Percent	
State	**Subject Matter Covered on the Ballot**	**Yes**	**No**
California	Spending limits and campaign contributions; lobbyist restrictions	49%	51%
Colorado	Changes initiative and referendum laws	31	69
Montana	Instructs elected officials to support congressional term limits	44	56
Nebraska	Requirements for collection of signatures for initiative and referendum laws	42	58
Nevada	Term limits for justices and judges	41	59
North Dakota	Instructs elected officials to support congressional term limits	47	53
North Dakota	Allows citizens to call a constitutional convention to adopt term limits for federal office holders	44	56
Oregon	Instructs elected officials to support congressional term limits	48	52
Oregon	Counts non-voters as "no" votes on tax measures	12	88
Washington	Instructs elected officials to support congressional term limits	45	55

Crime/Legal System

California	Attorney's fees; right to negotiate; frivolous lawsuits	34	66
California	Changes state laws relating to fraudulent behavior by corporations in dealing with investors; bans legislated limits on attorney fees	26	74
Colorado	Reaffirms parental rights; specifies that parents have right to direct and control upbringing of their children	43	57

Government

Oregon	Limits legislative change to statutes passed by voters	49	51
Oregon	Requires public employee earnings be expressed as employer's cost for employee per hour worked	35	65
Oregon	Amends collective bargaining law for public safety employees	44	56
Oregon	Raises public employees' normal retirement age; reduces benefits	35	65

Financial/Taxes

California	Reinstates top income tax brackets	49	51
Colorado	Eliminates property tax exemptions for nonprofits	17	83
Idaho	Limits property taxes to 1%	37	63
Missouri	Minimum wage increase	29	71
Montana	Minimum wage increase	38	62
Nebraska	Creates property tax limits for various government subdivisions; tax increases require voter approval.	25	75
Oregon	Authorizes bonds for Portland area light rail	47	53

Education

State	Subject Matter Covered on the Ballot	Percent Yes	No
Nebraska	Makes "Quality Education" a fundamental right	22%	78%
Oregon	Requires testing of public school students and a public report	35	65
Washington	Provides vouchers for K-12 students to attend schools of their choice	35	65
Washington	Authorizes charter schools funded by state	36	64

Health Care

State	Subject Matter	Yes	No
California	Stronger regulation of health maintenance organizations; provides consumer protection such as prohibiting incentives to physicians for withholding certain types of care	42	58
California	Stronger regulation of HMOs including more consumer protection; levies taxes and fees on health care businesses to finance reforms	39	61
Oregon	Restricts bases for providers to receive pay for health care	35	65
Oregon	Forbids discrimination among health care provider categories	44	56

Environment

State	Subject Matter	Yes	No
Florida	Imposes fee on sugar production in the Everglades to combat water pollution there	46	54
Idaho	Prohibits use of dogs and bait for hunting bear, and shortens season	40	60
Idaho	Requires legislative and voter approval for agreement on receipt and storage of radioactive waste	37	63
Maine	Bans clearcutting in logging	*	*
Michigan	Limits bear hunting season; prohibits use of bait and dogs to hunt	38	62
Montana	Increases requirements for water treatment	47	53
Oregon	Gives Oregon Fish and Wildlife Commission exclusive wildlife management authority; repeals 1994 bear and cougar hunting ban	43	57
Oregon	Broadens types of beverage containers requiring deposit	40	60
Oregon	Prohibits livestock in certain polluted waters or on adjacent lands	36	64

Gambling

State	Subject Matter Covered on the Ballot	Percent Yes	No
Arkansas	State lottery; permits nonprofits to conduct charitable games and raffles	39%	61%
Colorado	Permits gambling in city of Trinidad if approved by local vote	31	69
Michigan	Amends Bingo Act	44	56
Ohio	Provides for state gambling to support education; allows charitable bingo	38	62
Washington	Allows limited electronic gaming on Indian lands	43	57

* This initiative was divided into three parts. Part A, the original petition from citizens to ban clear cutting, received 29% of the vote. Part B, from the governor and legislature, would limit clear cutting without banning it. This portion of the initiative received 47% of the vote and will be voted on again at the next statewide election. Part C, which allowed citizens to reject both Parts A and B, failed.

Note: Initiatives are proposed changes in state law or proposed state constitutional amendments placed on the ballot by citizen petition. In the 24 states that have a citizen initiation process, an individual, group, or organization that gathers and submits a sufficient number of valid petition signatures has its measure placed on the ballot. There are three types of citizen-initiated ballot measures: 1) Direct initiative goes directly to a vote of the people; 2) Indirect initiative goes first to a vote of the state legislature and if the legislature passes it, the measure becomes law. If the legislature does not pass it, the measure is placed on the ballot for the voters to decide; 3) Referendum is similar to the initiative process but refers a bill passed by the legislature to the ballot for voter approval.

Source: Data compiled by the Public Affairs Research Institute of New Jersey.

Chapter 6

The Money Story

While stories about money in politics have long been a staple in the media's coverage of election campaigns, they stole the spotlight in the waning days of the 1996 race (and continued to hold it in early 1997). From the questionable donations of foreign interests to the rewards national parties offered their biggest contributors, much attention has been paid to the dramatic increase in the amount of money that was raised and spent. If 1992 was the year of the woman, then 1996 was certainly the year of the dollar. Herbert Alexander estimates total political costs of the election to be somewhere in the range of $4 billion, making it the most expensive in American history.

According to the Citizens' Research Foundation, a total of $700 million was spent on the presidential selection process alone, over 20% more than what was spent in 1992 (see p. 143). One of the most publicized aspects of the 1996 money story—the increased importance of "soft money" in the financing of the presidential election campaign—goes a long way in explaining this jump.

Soft money refers to funds raised by the national party committees which fall outside the restraints imposed by federal campaign finance law. Although fairly strict limits have been placed on the amount of money that individuals and PACs can contribute to political candidates, the FEC allows the parties to raise unlimited amounts for general "party building" purposes—like registration and get-out-the-vote efforts. While not meant for the benefit of federal campaigns, this money is increasingly being used to support indirectly the parties' presidential candidates through polls, advertising and other activities.

Together, the Republicans and Democrats took in an unprecedented $263 million in soft money in 1996, a 200% increase from 1992—the first time that the FEC required detailed reporting (see p. 154). Because the giving of soft money is not subject to limits, it was quite common in this past cycle for individuals, unions and corporations to write checks for $50,000 or $100,000 and to contribute to both parties in an effort to expand their political access (see p. 155).

Spending in Congressional races reached new levels as well, climbing to over $650 million in 1996. This is an increase of $37 million from the previous high set two years ago (see p.149). As was true in the previous election, the average House incumbent in 1996 spent more than twice as much as the average House challenger (see p. 150).

But it is sufficiency and not parity that is needed to wage a successful House challenge, and in 1996, twenty-one incumbents were defeated in general election contests. As Michael Malbin has previously argued, challengers must spend enough to become known to their constituencies, but they need not spend as much as their incumbent opponents to win. (See Michael Malbin, "The Money Story" in *America at the Polls 1994*.)

Because these figures represent only direct spending by the candidate's campaigns, they do not even begin to tell the whole tale. Indeed, in the 1996 elections, "independent expenditures" played an important role. Independent expenditures are funds that individuals and groups are permitted to spend in unlimited amounts to advocate the election or defeat of a particular candidate, provided these expenditures are made without consultation or collaboration with the candidates or their campaigns.

According to the FEC, almost $5 million was spent independently, but on behalf of House candidates, and almost $16 million was spent in Senate races through November 25. Although the legitimacy of these expenditures has been challenged by campaign finance reform advocates, the Supreme Court, in equating the right to spend money in elections with the right of free speech, has opened the door to the prospect of virtually unlimited sums being spent on behalf of candidates for federal office.

Finally, while independent expenditures and soft money contributions are required by law to be disclosed, millions of dollars spent in the 1996 elections were not. The substantial sums spent by various organizations in states and districts around the country on "issue advocacy" campaigns need not be reported to the FEC, although they are an important part of the overall campaign finance picture. The most visible example of this type of expenditure in the 1996 cycle was the estimated $35 million that the AFL-CIO spent on "voter education"—aimed at ousting dozens of Republican House candidates.

—Regina Dougherty

Financing the 1996 Election
By Herbert E. Alexander

Many years ago a British campaign agent adopted a principle that appears to have guided American politicians in 1996. It went: Win the election; never mind the expense; a defeat is the most expensive of all contests. If that dictum characterized spending by parties and candidates in 1996, it applied as well to spending by interest and issue groups on behalf of, or opposed to, candidates.

The numerous political committees operating at the national level spent about $1.5 billion in 1996, resulting in the most expensive presidential and congressional elections in American history. If we add to that other monies spent at the national, state and local levels, on the maintenance of the political party system, by political action committees, and on ballot issues in more than 20 states, the total of all political campaign costs comes to $4 billion. This high mark in political spending is up 25% from the $3.2 billion spent in the equivalent 1991-92 election cycle.

From 1952, the first year for which total campaign costs in the United States were calculated, to 1996, spending in presidential election cycles has steadily increased (see Table 1).

Patterns in Political Giving

Although the total costs of television (about $400 million at all levels), campaigning, and the general availability of funding have risen dramatically over recent decades, the percentage of those who donate to candidates and parties has

Table 1: Total US Political Costs, 1952-1996

1952	$140,000,000
1956	155,000,000
1960	175,000,000
1964	200,000,000
1968	300,000,000
1972	425,000,000
1976	540,000,000
1980	1,200,000,000
1984	1,800,000,000
1988	2,700,000,000
1992	3,220,000,000
1996	4,000,000,000

Source: Data provided by the Citizens' Research Foundation.

Table 2: Political Contributions from the Public Have Remained Low

Those who contributed to:

	Republican	Democrat	Total
1952	3%	1%	4%
1956	5	5	10
1960	7	4	12
1964	5	4	10
1968	3	3	8
1972	4	5	10
1976	4	4	9
1980	3	1	4
1984	2	2	4
1988	4	2	6
1992	2	2	4
1996	NA	NA	NA

NA = Not Available
Note: In some instances, Democratic and Republican contributors may not add to the total because of individuals contributing to both major parties, to candidates of both major parties, to non-major parties, or not specifying what party they contributed to.
Source: Surveys by the American National Election Study, Center for Political Studies, University of Michigan.

not changed much since 1952. An overview of responses to National Election Study surveys on political contributions from 1952 to 1992 indicates that only about 4% of adults nationwide say they made campaign contributions (see Table 2). Although these figures are subject to a polling error of up to 4%, their replication over the years gives confidence that the parameters of giving are accurate. Yet campaign spending has increased because those individuals who give are giving more, and institutional giving by corporations, labor unions, trade associations, and others, has increased greatly.

Presidential Elections

A combined total of $700 million was spent on the three phases of the presidential selection process which is a 21% increase from the equivalent 1991-92 period cost of $550 million (see Table 3). Public funds provided the basic monies in each phase of the presidential election process. Election laws provided for public matching funds for qualified candidates in the prenomination period, public grants to pay for the two major parties' national nominating conventions, and public grants for the major party general election candidates.

Spending limits, however, applied to each phase of the election process (see Table 4). The laws also established criteria whereby minor parties and new parties could qualify

Table 3: Costs of Electing a President, 1996
(in millions of dollars)

Prenomination (as of October 31, 1996)

Spending by major party candidates	$227.3
Spending by minor party candidates	11.3
Independent expenditures	1.2
Communication costs	1.0
Compliance costs	10.0
Subtotal	$250.8

Conventions (including host cities and committees)

Republicans	$31.0
Democrats	30.0
Subtotal	$61.0

General Election

Spending by major party candidates[a]	$123.6
Parties coordinated expenditures[b]	24.0
Compliance	12.0
Spending by minor parties	30.4
Independent expenditures	2.0
Labor, corporate, association spending	20.0
Parties soft money[c]	101.7
Communication costs	3.0
Subtotal	$316.7
Miscellaneous expenses[d]	$71.5
Grand total	$700.0

[a]Includes $61.8 million in public funds spent by each major party ticket.
[b]Includes $12.0 million in hard money coordinated expenditures for each major party ticket.
[c]Includes "soft money" expenditures related to the presidential campaigns by the Democratic National Committee and the Republican National Committee.
[d]Includes a reasonable portion of funds spent by nonpartisan organizations to conduct voter registration and get-out-the-vote drives that benefitted presidential candidates; and miscellaneous out-of-pocket expenses.

Source: Data provided by the Citizens' Research Foundation.

for public funds to pay nominating convention and general election campaign costs. In fact, the general election campaign of the Reform Party's ticket, Ross Perot and Pat Choate, was mainly publicly financed because Perot had become eligible for public funds based on his 1992 showing.

The feasibility of public financing has depended on taxpayers' willingness to earmark a small portion of their tax liabilities to the Presidential Election Campaign Fund by using the federal income-tax checkoff. But, the checkoff rates have been declining, from a high of 28.7% in 1981 to the 1995 rate of 12.8%. However, in 1993, the checkoff amount tripled, from $1 to $3 per taxpayer, which provided sufficient monies to cover public funding costs. About $234 million, or approximately 35% of total spending on the presidential selection process, consisted of public funding provided by the US Treasury based on certifications of the Federal Election Commission. As a comparison, $175.4 million was paid out in the 1991-92 election cycle which represented a 45% increase from previous totals (see Table 5). These increases have strained the presidential public funding system, and have left about $3 million for presidential elections in 2000.

While 1996 spending was high, the long-term trends are not so alarming (see Table 6). When adjusted for inflation, the costs of presidential campaigns since 1960 have increased only by a factor of four and one-half, whereas aggregate unadjusted costs have risen almost twenty-four fold from 1960 to 1996.

Prenomination Campaigns

In the presidential prenomination period, $238.6 million was spent by Democratic, Republican, Reform Party, Libertarian Party and other candidates. Eleven candidates received federal matching funds, accounting for $56.8 million or 23% of the total.

Three candidates spent large amounts of their own money:

* Ross Perot spent $8.5 million on the Reform Party which, if added to his $64 million self-contribution in 1992, makes him the largest contributor in American history;

* Most of the $41.6 million spent by Steven Forbes seeking the Republican nomination was his own money;

* Morris Taylor, an industrialist who also sought the Republican nomination, spent $6.5 million, mostly his own money.

Two other candidates, largely dependent on contributions from others, did not seek matching funds: Richard

Both President Clinton, and the eventual Republican nominee, Robert Dole, accepted public funds and spent up to the $37.1 million limit in seeking nomination, yet the two campaigns could not have been more different. Clinton, who had no competition for the Democratic nomination, spent the maximum. Some of the money was spent in primary and caucus states, but much of it was used in ways that would be helpful in the November election, thus giving the Clinton-Gore ticket an advantage.

the ante, forcing Dole to spend even more to remain competitive.

The Republican nominee was, therefore, dangerously close not only to the overall prenomination spending limit of $37.1 million but also to individual state limits in areas especially important in the general election. After clinching the nomination in March, Dole was forced to resort to various subterfuges, including campaign forays thinly disguised as book tours and "generic" issue advertising on television paid for by Republican state and

Table 4: Major Party Presidential Expenditure Limits and Public Funding, 1976-1996 (in millions of dollars)

| | Prenomination Campaign | | | | | General Election Campaign | | | |
	National Spending Limit[a]		Exempt Fund Raising[b]		Overall Spending Limit[c]	Nominating Convention	Public Treasury Grant[d]		National Party Spending[e]		Overall Spending Limit[c]
1976	$10.9	+	$2.2	=	$13.1	2.2[f]	$21.8	+	$3.2	=	$25.0
1980	14.7	+	2.9	=	17.7	4.4	29.4	+	4.6	=	34.0
1984	20.2	+	4.0	=	24.2	8.1	40.4	+	6.9	=	47.3
1988	23.1	+	4.6	=	27.7	9.2	46.1	+	8.3	=	54.4
1992	27.6	+	5.5	=	33.1	11.0	55.2	+	10.3	=	65.5
1996	30.9	+	6.2	=	37.1	12.4	61.8	+	12.0	=	73.8

Source: Data provided by the Citizens' Research Foundation.

[a]Based on $10 million plus cost-of-living increases (COLA) using 1974 as the base year. Eligible candidates may receive no more than one-half the national spending limit in public matching funds. To become eligible, candidates must raise $5,000 in private contributions of $250 or less in each of twenty states. The federal government matches each contribution to qualified candidates up to $250. Publicly funded candidates also must observe spending limits in the individual states equal to the greater of $200,000+ COLA (base year 1974), or 16 cents x the voting-age population (VAP) of the state + COLA.

[b]Candidates may spend up to 20 percent of the national spending limit for fund raising.

[c]Legal and accounting expenses to ensure compliance with the law are exempt from the spending limit.

[d]Based on $20 million + COLA (base year 1974).

[e]Based on 2 cents x VAP of the United States + COLA.

[f]Based on $2 million + COLA (base year 1974). Under the 1979 FECA Amendments, the basic grant was raised to $3 million. In 1984, Congress raised the basic grant to $4 million.

Lamm spent $289,500 contesting the Reform Party nomination won by Ross Perot; Harry Browne, the Libertarian Party candidate, spent $1.3 million.

Because they did not draw on public funds, these five candidacies reduced the matching fund component of the total $238.6 million spent, compared with earlier years.

On the other hand, Dole's spending was in a highly competitive field of candidates. Early in the campaign season, front-runner Dole was forced to spend money to fend off vigorous and sometimes well-financed challengers such as Senator Phil Gramm and commentator Patrick Buchanan. When the independently wealthy Steve Forbes later joined the fray, he upped

local party committees. His ability to present his message directly to voters was curtailed by his legal inability to spend money in his own way. The spending limit reduced Dole's flexibility and rigidified the campaign process.

Table 5
Payouts From the Presidential Election Campaign Fund, 1976-1996

Year	Amount
	(in millions)
1976	$71.4
1980	101.6
1984	132.6
1988	176.9
1992	175.4
1996	234.0

Source: Data provided by the Federal Election Commission.

Conventions

The second phase of the presidential selection process consisted of the national nominating conventions. The major party conventions were financed in part by public funds; in 1996 the Republicans and Democrats each received $12.4 million in public funds which was the legal limit for convention expenses. But the actual costs of the conventions were twice as much. Other resources from the convention cities' municipal host committees, tourist bureaus, and corporate and labor sponsors paid for the additional amounts beyond the spending limits. Again, the expenditure limits did not control spending.

General Election

In the 1996 general election period, three distinct but parallel campaigns were conducted, either by the major-party candidates or on their behalf. Only one of them operated under legally-imposed spending limits. The three campaigns broke down as follows: In the *first campaign*, spending was limited by law to the $61.8 million provided in public funding. This money was supplemented by allowable national party coordinated expenditures of $12 million, making the official spending limit $73.8 million for each of the major party tickets.

In the *second campaign*, however, spending was not limited under the law. A small portion represents funds raised under the law to pay compliance costs to ensure that candidates do not violate the law. A much larger portion paid direct and indirect campaign costs, beyond the limits. Much was "soft money" raised by the parties outside federal limits from wealthy individuals, corporations and labor unions. It also represented money spent on the nominees' behalf by labor unions, trade associations and membership groups on partisan communications with their constituencies and on nominally nonpartisan activities directed to the general public but clearly intended to benefit the nominees.

In the *third campaign*, independent spending was conducted by individuals and groups legally permitted to spend unlimited amounts to advocate the election or defeat of selected candidates, as long as there is no consultation or collaboration with candidates and their campaigns.

Adding together the amounts spent on these three aspects of the presidential campaigns in 1996, as seen in Table 7, a total of $156.7 million was spent by or on behalf of the Clinton-Gore ticket, and $130.6 million by or on behalf of the Dole-Kemp ticket.

Thus all three phases of the presidential selection process provided evidence that the overall spending limits were not effective.

Important components of these amounts were both hard and soft monies. Hard money is raised and spent within the limitations and restraints imposed by federal law. Soft money is raised and spent on a variety of party-building activities outside the limits of federal law but spent in accordance with state laws on activities that may benefit federal candidates.

In 1996 there was a marked increase in spending on behalf of, or against, candidates by political parties, labor unions, businesses, the Christian

Table 6: Presidential Spending, 1960-1996 (in millions of dollars)

	Actual Spending	Adjusted Spending
1960	$30.0	$30.0
1964	60.0	57.3
1968	100.0	85.1
1972	138.0	97.7
1976	160.0	83.2
1980	275.0	98.9
1984	325.0	93.7
1988	500.0	126.5
1992	550.0	117.8
1996	$700.0	$132.1

Note: Spending figures include prenomination, convention, and general election costs. Adjusted spending figures are based on 1960 dollars.
Source: Data provided by the Citizens' Research Foundation.

Table 7: Sources of Funds, Major Party presidential Candidates, 1996 General Election (in millions of dollars)

Sources of Funds		Clinton	Dole
Limited campaign funds			
Candidate controlled			
	Federal grant	$61.8	$61.8
	National party	$12.0	$12.0
Unlimited campaign funds			
Candidate may coordinate			
	Party soft money	$53.9	$47.8
	Labor, Corporate/association	$20.0	$2.0
	Compliance	$8.0	$6.0
Independent of candidate			
	Independent expenditures	$1.0	$1.0
Total		$156.7	$130.6

Source: Data provided by the Citizens' Research Foundation, based on Federal Election Commission and other data.

Table 8: Gross Receipts and Disbursements for Third Party Presidential Campaigns 1995-96 (through October 1996)

	Receipts	Disbursements
Ross Perot	$40,059,383	$27,036,535
Harry Browne	$1,462,142	$1,453,170
John Samuel Hagelin	$1,359,852	$1,353,486
Richard D. Lamm	$214,779	$197,608
James Edward Harris, Jr.	$86,891	$83,494
Howard Phillips	$68,634	$66,983
Jo Anne Jorgensen	$64,149	$64,148
Robert P. Casey	$47,188	$47,188
David L. Drye	$21,253	$21,217
Mary Cal Hollis	$18,394	$16,665
Richard Tompkins	$15,787	$15,194
Janka Cvorovic	$10,186	$9,001
Monica Gail Moorehead	$8,059	$6,627
Diane Beall Templin	$3,125	$6,609
Lenora B. Fulani	$4,290	$5,745
Robert Adgate Congdon	$5,004	$5,004
Burgess Glenn Dillard	$34,763	$475
Nick Didominicus	$5,245	$0
Total	$43,489,274	$30,389,299

Note: Includes only candidates who have reported receipts or disbursements of $5,000 or more. For those involved in both primary and general elections, includes all activity reported for both campaigns.

Source: Data provided by the Federal Election Commission.

Coalition and others, some disclosed and some not disclosed.

One curiosity in spending occurred as the result of a Supreme Court decision in a Colorado case. This decision opened a new avenue for political party spending and independent expenditures. The National Republican Senatorial Committee spent about $10 million in this category, and the Democratic Senatorial Campaign Committee about $4 million.

Minor Parties and Independent Presidential Candidates

Ross Perot was the most important and influential minor party candidate in 1996, but there were others. Table 8 shows that $30.4 million was spent by Perot and others. Perot, however, spent about $27 million of it.

The federal law established criteria whereby minor and new parties and independent candidates can qualify for public funds to help pay general election campaign costs. Ross Perot qualified in 1996 for public funds based on his independent candidacy in 1992, in which he gained 19% of the vote; this made his newly-organized Reform Party eligible to receive $29.2 million for Perot's 1996 general election campaign.

Campaign Reform

An unremarkable presidential selection process was highlighted in the last month before the election by extraordinary attention paid to campaign financing, including calls for federal reforms. Of special interest were revelations that the Democratic National Committee returned some $1.5 million in contributions mainly from foreign sources; some contributors had been invited to the White House, to meetings and seminars with the president and vice president, and to golf, the convention and other outings. The Republicans received smaller amounts of money from dubious sources.

1996 Congressional Elections

The costs of electing a Congress totaled nearly $770 million. This amount is divided into three portions: (1) direct spending by general election candidates including their primary expenses ($653 million); (2) candidate spending in special elections ($16 million); and (3) spending by candidates who lost in the primaries ($100 million). The Federal Election Commission has reported that $421.8 million was spent on campaigns for the House of Representatives and $230.8 million was spent on campaigns for the Senate. These amounts were for the period from January 1, 1995, through December 31, 1996, and are almost $45 million higher than for the 1993-94 election cycle.

Spending on congressional campaigns reached its peak late in the election season even though polling results throughout 1996 consistently showed President Clinton ahead of Senator Dole in the presidential campaigns. By October, significant party funds were diverted from the presidential to the congressional campaigns. Party control of both the Senate and House was in doubt, and excess spending, particularly for House campaigns, was thought perhaps to influence party control.

Spending in Senate campaigns was down from 1994 for two reasons: (1) There were no Senate campaigns in the two largest and most costly states, California and New York; and (2) fewer wealthy candidates spent large amounts of their own money as in 1994, when Michael Huffington spent $28 million of his own money in a losing Senate campaign in California. For this latter reason, the index of self-spending candidates was down from 1994 as in the presidential campaigns, but these amounts tell only part of the story. In addition to candidate spending, as noted, there was party spending ($881 million of both hard and soft money, and independent expenditures during the election cycle), PAC operations (not counting funds given to presidential or congressional candidates), independent expenditures (over $15 million in Senate campaigns, and almost $5 million in House campaigns), and issue advocacy (variously estimated at $100 million or more)—much of it intended to affect the outcome of Senate and House contests as well.

The Federal Election Campaign Act (FECA) dramatically changed federal campaign financing in this country. The law was enacted in 1971 and amended in 1974, 1976, and 1979; however, it has not been altered since that latter date. Regardless, many changes have occurred in campaign financing. We have more fragmented and diffused spending opportunities for a variety of political actors—some spending on the books and required to be disclosed (candidates, political parties, PACs, and independent expenditures), and some off the books and not required to be disclosed (certain labor and business spending, issue organizations such as environmental groups, and others).

The 1995-96 election cycle raised serious doubts about the ability of the 1970s laws and the Federal Election Commission, to cope with, or regulate, campaigns in the mid-1990s.

Conclusions

The 1996 elections cost more than any other previous contest yet produced the lowest voter turnout since 1924. Combining presidential and congressional expenditures with those at the state and local levels, an estimated $4 billion was spent on politics in the 1995-96 election cycle.

The FECA found itself outdated in 1996. There was a great diversity of spending by the many actors in our expanding political arena. And the infusion of money from foreign sources raised doubts about the effectiveness of the regulatory system.

Spending limits in the publicly-funded presidential campaigns failed to control amounts spent in all three phases of the presidential selection process—the prenomination campaigns, the national nominating conventions, and the general election campaigns. One may ask: why enact spending limits that only give the illusion they are effective but actually fail to control spending?

Congressional Campaign Spending: A Roper Center Review of the Federal Election Commission Data

The data on pages 149-155 were obtained from published Federal Election Commission (FEC) reports and, in some instances, derived from an on-line FEC computer database, by the Rockefeller Institute of Government at the State University of New York and from the Center for Responsive Politics. Where averages are reported herein it is important to consider that in some cases the number of candidates may have been small, particularly in the Senate, and thus distort measures of central tendency including means.

For the data contained herein we have used the following definitions regarding challenger and open-seat elections. Cases in which an incumbent lost in the primary have been classified as open-seat elections. In FEC publications, only if the incumbent does not run are the seats classified as open. The FEC classifies elections where an incumbent loses in the primary as challenger seats in the general election. Here challengers are only those running against an incumbent in the general election.

The Roper Center would like to express appreciation to the American Enterprise Institute for much of the 1986-94 FEC data which was published in AEI's *Vital Statistics on Congress 1995-1996*, editors: Norman J. Ornstein; Thomas E. Mann; and Michael J. Malbin. Special thanks to Michael Malbin, director of the Rockefeller Institute of Government, for his assistance in gathering and calculating the 1996 congressional figures.

Total Campaign Expenditures for Congressional Candidates, 1986-1996

(in millions of dollars)

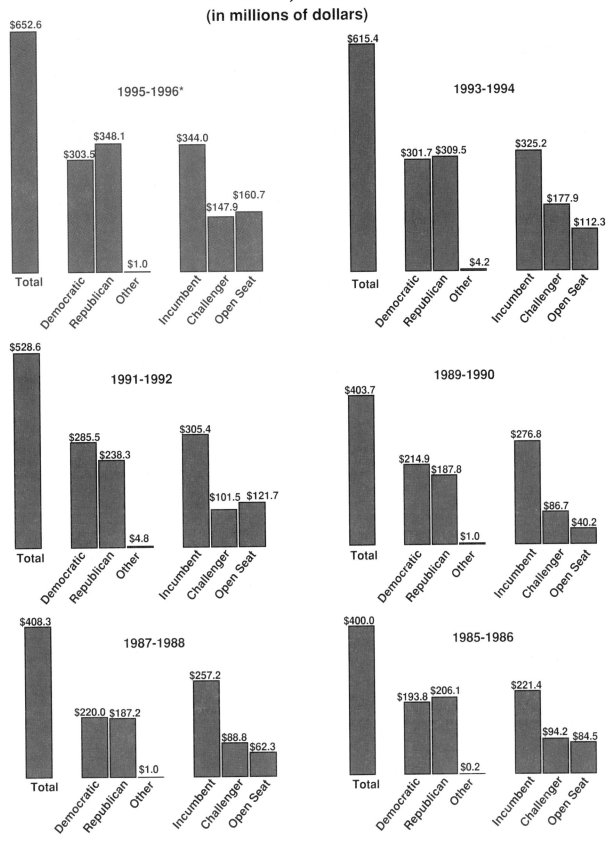

1995-1996*

$652.6 — Total
$303.5 — Democratic
$348.1 — Republican
$1.0 — Other
$344.0 — Incumbent
$147.9 — Challenger
$160.7 — Open Seat

1993-1994

$615.4 — Total
$301.7 — Democratic
$309.5 — Republican
$4.2 — Other
$325.2 — Incumbent
$177.9 — Challenger
$112.3 — Open Seat

1991-1992

$528.6 — Total
$285.5 — Democratic
$238.3 — Republican
$4.8 — Other
$305.4 — Incumbent
$101.5 — Challenger
$121.7 — Open Seat

1989-1990

$403.7 — Total
$214.9 — Democratic
$187.8 — Republican
$1.0 — Other
$276.8 — Incumbent
$86.7 — Challenger
$40.2 — Open Seat

1987-1988

$408.3 — Total
$220.0 — Democratic
$187.2 — Republican
$1.0 — Other
$257.2 — Incumbent
$88.8 — Challenger
$62.3 — Open Seat

1985-1986

$400.0 — Total
$193.8 — Democratic
$206.1 — Republican
$0.2 — Other
$221.4 — Incumbent
$94.2 — Challenger
$84.5 — Open Seat

*Reflects campaign expenditures for major party candidates and independent Bernard Sanders (VT).
Note: Includes expenditures for the primary and general election by general election candidates.

Campaign Expenditures for Congressional Candidates, 1986-1996

(net dollars)

House:	1996	1994	1992	1990	1988	1986
All House Candidates						
Total expenditures	$421,750,905[a]	$343,268,389	$332,689,465	$231,309,131	$223,067,265	$210,331,695
Average expenditure[b]	516,219[c]	441,632[c]	408,240[c]	325,145	305,665	295,602
Democratic average	472,313	487,493	462,897	355,862	319,389	301,955
Republican average	559,914	396,799	352,351	290,910	289,798	290,092
Incumbents						
Incumbent average[b]	678,556[c]	561,441[c]	594,699[c]	422,124	394,779	362,103
Democratic average	590,814	622,937	621,890	427,178	380,386	349,918
Republican average	746,474	473,281	552,952	414,222	416,413	379,917
Challengers						
Challenger average[b]	286,582	240,183	167,411	134,465[c]	136,851	155,607
Democratic average	319,472	177,136	143,935	131,194	164,483	170,562
Republican average	241,389	276,493	275,867	133,889	114,815	141,356
Open Seats						
Open-seat average[b]	647,336	585,991	588,722	443,129	532,817	430,484
Democratic average	647,490	560,569	561,258	547,541	495,513	420,138
Republican average	647,179	611,911	616,724	538,037	581,844	440,830
Senate:						
All Senate Candidates						
Total expenditure	230,806,273[b]	272,120,863	195,901,342	172,394,972	185,208,933	189,724,088
Average expenditure[b]	3,550,866	4,000,274	2,876,627	2,592,163	2,814,650	2,737,798
Democratic average	3,402,098	3,395,629	2,815,826	2,468,527	2,951,549	2,260,415
Republican average	3,695,126	4,604,919	2,939,218	2,719,546	2,677,752	3,201,141
Incumbents						
Incumbent average[b]	4,236,694	4,691,617	3,852,428	3,582,136	3,772,558	3,374,602
Democratic average	5,205,263	5,154,744	2,851,102	3,618,244	3,480,898	2,712,796
Republican average	3,715,156	3,950,616	5,104,086	3,541,212	4,137,133	3,688,089
Challengers						
Challenger average[b]	3,139,479	3,997,104	1,824,993	1,705,098	1,822,852	1,899,417
Democratic average	2,958,889	1,266,445	2,551,654	1,401,259	2,166,874	1,911,693
Republican average	3,470,562	5,703,766	1,202,141	1,988,680	1,547,635	1,874,864
Open Seats						
Open-seat average[b]	3,310,759	3,006,247	2,938,871	1,599,792	2,890,904	3,138,282
Democratic average	2,848,751	2,634,075	3,145,940	934,046	3,197,528	2,628,009
Republican average	3,772,767	3,378,419	2,731,801	2,265,538	2,584,280	3,648,555

[a]Reflects campaign expenditures for major party candidates and independent Bernard Sanders (VT).
[b]Major party candidates only.
[c]Includes independent Bernard Sanders (VT).

Note: Averages calculated using a mean. Includes expenditures for the primary and general election by general election candidates who filed reports with the Federal Election Commission.

1996 House Candidate Expenditures
by the total proportion of the vote they received
(average net dollars)

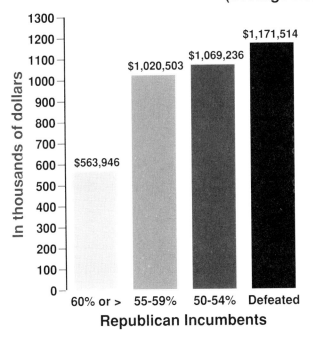

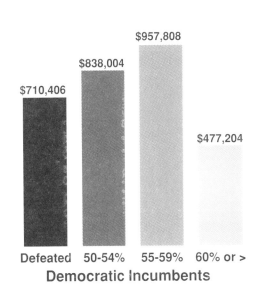

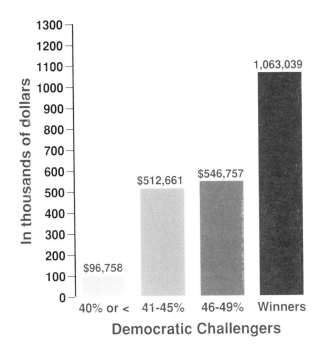

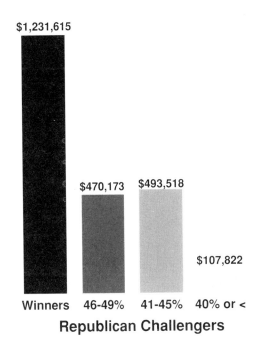

Note: Averages calculated using a mean. Includes expenditures for the primary and general election by general election candidates.
Source: Data provided by the Rockefeller Institute of Government.

Expenditures of House Challengers Who Won, 1986-1996
(average net dollars)

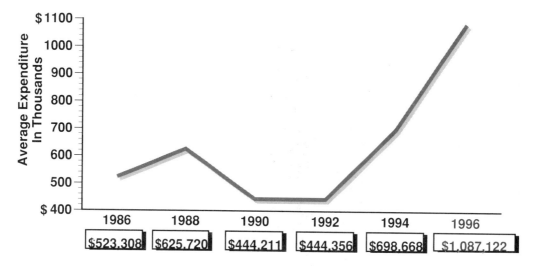

1986	1988	1990	1992	1994	1996
$523,308	$625,720	$444,211	$444,356	$698,668	$1,087,122

Note: Averages calculated using a mean. Includes expenditures for the primary and general election by general election candidates.

Candidates Spending $1 Million or More on House Campaigns

	Incumbents	Challengers	Open Seats	Total
1979-80	2	0	0	2
1981-82	2	1	2	5
1983-84	2	2	0	4
1985-86	10	2	6	18
1987-88	13	4	5	22
1989-90	9	1	4	14
1991-92	44	3	7	54
1993-94	34	10	4	48
1995-96	72	17	13	102

Note: Includes expenditures for the primary and general election by general election candidates.

Top Spenders in the House and Senate, 1996

Top Ten Senate Spenders	Amount Spent	Lost/Won?	Top Ten House Spenders	Amount Spent	Lost/Won?
Mark Warner (D-VA)	$11.5	lost	Newt Gingrich (R-GA)	$5.6	won
John Kerry (D-MA)	$10.7	won	Michael Coles (D-GA)	$3.3	lost
Guy Millner (R-GA)	$9.2	lost	Richard Gephardt (D-MO)	$3.1	won
Robert Torricelli (D-NJ)	$9.1	won	Ellen Tauscher (D-CA)	$2.6	won
Dick Zimmer (R-NJ)	$8.2	lost	Greg Ganske (R-IA)	$2.3	won
Harvey Gantt (D-NC)	$7.9	lost	Vic Fazio (D-CA)	$2.3	won
Bill Weld (R-MA)	$7.8	lost	Martin Frost (D-TX)	$2.0	won
Jesse Helms (R-NC)	$7.7	won	Joe Kennedy (D-MA)	$2.0	won
Phil Gramm (R-TX)	$6.2	won	Ron Paul (R-TX)	$1.9	won
Paul Wellstone (D-MN)	$6.0	won	John Ensign (R-NV)	$1.9	won

Money Raised and Where It Came From

	Net Receipts (in millions)	Individual Contributions	PAC/Other Committee Contributions	Candidate Loans and Contributions
	1992	1992	1992	1992
House:	309.8	49%	38%	9%
Democratic	174.7	44	45	6
Incumbents	117.9	41	52	1
Challengers	22.0	52	29	14
Open Seats	34.8	50	31	16
Republican	135.1	54	29	12
Incumbents	72.0	53	41	1
Challengers	39.3	52	10	33
Open Seats	23.8	60	24	11
Senate:	181.1	66	25	5
Democratic	91.2	66	27	2
Incumbents	41.1	55	38	2
Challengers	31.6	79	15	3
Open Seats	18.6	70	22	3
Republican	90.0	65	22	8
Incumbents	51.7	66	27	0
Challengers	18.8	68	12	18
Open Seats	19.5	57	18	22

Note: Major party candidates only. The percentages do not sum to 100 because not all receipts are listed. These include such items as contributions from parties, transfers from other candidate committees, interest earned on campaign funds and deposits on items including phone banks where deposits are returned to the candidate when services are canceled. Data are through 20 days after the general election.

Political Party Support for Congress, 1986-1996
Contributions and Coordinated Expenditures

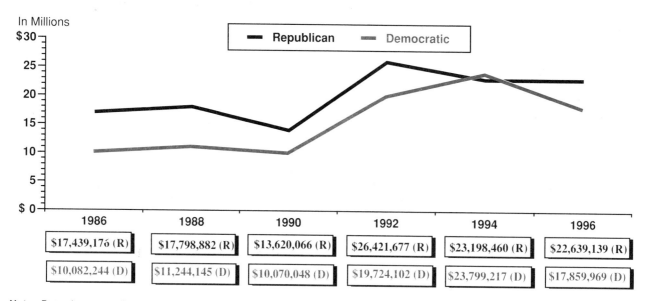

1986	1988	1990	1992	1994	1996
$17,439,176 (R)	$17,798,882 (R)	$13,620,066 (R)	$26,421,677 (R)	$23,198,460 (R)	$22,639,139 (R)
$10,082,244 (D)	$11,244,145 (D)	$10,070,048 (D)	$19,724,102 (D)	$23,799,217 (D)	$17,859,969 (D)

Note: Data shown are direct support (contributions and coordinated expenditures) for congressional candidates only.

Party Receipts Reported to the Federal Election Commission
(through 20 days after the general election)

(in millions of dollars)

	1996	1994	1992
Democrats			
Hard Money	$210.0	$121.1	$155.5
Soft Money	122.3	49.1	36.3
Total	332.3	170.2	191.8
Republicans			
Hard Money	407.5	223.7	266.3
Soft Money	141.2	52.5	49.8
Total	548.7	276.2	316.1
Total	**$881.0**	**$446.4**	**$507.9**

1996 Campaign Contributions:
Many Corporate PACs Spread Them Around

	Republicans	Democrats
AT&T	$552,340	$422,184
American International Group	$213,500	$245,000
Anheuser-Busch	$359,950	$401,107
Bechtel	$150,450	$166,300
Ernest & Young	$156,600	$193,235
Freddie Mac	$270,000	$287,500
Occidental Petroleum	$225,600	$260,750
Textron	$373,300	$274,700
Sprint	$172,923	$183,823
Time Warner	$325,000	$401,250
United Technologies	$239,350	$231,400

Source: Data provided by Center for Responsive Politics.

Since the Early 1980s the Number of PACs Has Remained Steady

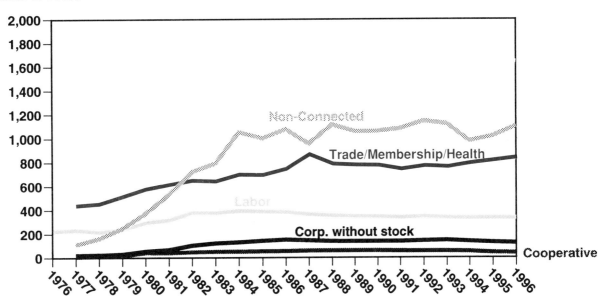

Chapter 7
The Polling Story

Pre-election polls have become an essential part of the media's coverage and the public's understanding of the election process. Undertaken on a systematic basis by George Gallup and Elmo Roper in the 1930s, such polling until recently played but a small role in the conduct of campaigns in the United States. The Roper Center's archives hold only 10 askings of the presidential "trial heat" question from Labor Day through Election Day in 1968—but we have more than ten times that number for 1996. And the political community's appetite for election polls is still growing. Some would argue that the elections themselves are increasingly framed in terms of these survey results.

In the final months of the1996 campaign, four media-sponsored tracking polls measured the ups and downs of the presidential race. Beginning on the first of September, the Gallup/CNN/*USA Today* poll and the Tarrance Group/Lake Research's Battleground/ *Hotline* poll, supplied the pols, the pundits, and the public with daily vote choice numbers. The Zogby/ Reuters poll initiated its daily tracking at the beginning of October, with ABC News following in the middle of that month. In all, the Roper Center estimates that the question, "How would you vote if the election were being held *today*?," was asked more than 125 times between September 1st and November 5th.

To say that there was some controversy surrounding the use and interpretation of the polls in 1996 would be to put it mildly. Certainly part of the debate had to do with the sheer number of pre-election polls conducted.[1] To be sure, no prior election compares in terms of just how many individual readings were taken.

In the December/January issue of *The Public Perspective* , Jeffrey Alderman, director of polling for ABC News, Peter Feld, vice president of Lake Research, Lori Gundermuth, vice president of The Tarrance Group, Frank Newport, editor-in-chief of The Gallup Poll, John Zogby, president and CEO of The Zogby Group, Larry McGill, director of research for the Media Studies Center, and Glenn Roberts of Glenn Roberts Research participated in a round-table on the tracking polls' methodologies, their reporting in the media, and their impact on the outcome of the election. We reprint their discussion here.

Finally, while Congressional races tend to be somewhat overshadowed in a presidential election year, there was certainly no dearth of polling data on this front. The same four polling organizations tracking the presidential race followed the parties' fortunes in the House as well, with two of them showing the Democrats with a five to ten point advantage over their Republican counterparts right up until the end. Late Congressional vote trial heats have, since the 1950s, consistently overestimated the Democrats' proportion of the actual vote.

Endnotes
[1]See, for example, Everett Ladd's "The Election Polls: An American Waterloo" in *The Chronicle of Higher Education*, November 22, 1996, and Kathleen Frankovic's and Frank Newport's respective responses in the December/January issue of *The Public Perspective.*

—Regina Dougherty

Tracking Polls: How We Did Them

A Roper Center Symposium with Jeffrey Alderman, Peter Feld, Lori Gudermuth, Larry McGill, Frank Newport, Glenn Roberts, and John Zogby

Public Perspective: Describe for our readers the survey methodology employed in your tracking polls.

John Zogby: I suspect that our methods are different because we do not use random-digit dialing (RDD). Instead, we use a CD-ROM of listed telephone numbers throughout the contiguous 48 states. But we insure that our sampling frames are representative of every household, area code and three-digit exchange we draw from.

Over the years, both personal experience and research I have examined suggests that there is no advantage to RDD. First, there has been a significant democratization of unlisted telephone numbers. Second, in tracking polls you may run into caller fatigue or caller discretion that may involve skipping sampling frames that have not been productive. Third, in our follow-up studies and comparisons of RDD samples to the samples we draw, we have found no difference in our demographic groups.

Frank Newport: Our basic methodology in our tracking surveys is the same and hopefully even enhanced over what we would do for any national Gallup poll. Our fundamental assumption is an equal probability of selection. We want every household in America to have an equal chance of falling into the sample. For that reason we use random-digit dialing procedures.

In comparison to our routine Gallup polls we enhanced our call-back procedure for our tracking survey. We employed a five call-back design throughout our tracking which allowed for more call-backs than is possible for many of our non-tracking Gallup polls. Further, we did a complete within-household selection where we asked the respondent to list by age and gender every adult in the household. We randomly selected one adult and then proceeded to employ the five call-backs designed for the individual who was selected. The tracking actually allows us to do that better than we could do in a normal two or three-day poll, because we can actually come back to that same number over the course of several days.

Our data were derived from two days of completed interviews, so, for example, Monday and Tuesday night's completed interviews were rolled together. But for an individual who was in Tuesday night's sample, our first approach to that individual—once that number fell into the sample and once he or she was selected randomly within the

household—could have been initiated two to five days before.

Jeffrey Alderman: Essentially, we used the same method we use for all of our other polling as well. Our method is pretty consistent with the methods Frank has described with one major exception—we do not use a call-back procedure (in the traditional sense). Instead we do an at-home sample.

If someone picks up the phone we make every effort to get an interview among those at home. We will call back later that night if it will be more convenient for the respondent we have selected, but after that we move on to a new phone number. We have found that call-backs beyond the same evening are a waste of time and money.

For our tracking survey, we introduced a "live sample" method. About 20% of each night's sample was left over from a previous night where the phone rang but no one answered. Some will find that to be a major difference between ABC's practices and the more traditional methods used at CBS and Gallup in terms of call-backs but we save ourselves a great deal of money, time and effort. We're able to process a lot more of the sample by not making appointments to talk to people three days later.

Lori Gudermuth: For our tracking research we used RDD with a minimum of three callbacks. After examining our unlisted versus our listed numbers we found large concentrations of unlisted numbers, especially in California. This, coupled with the mobility among younger voters, minority voters, and anyone more likely to rent rather than own a home, has led us to stay with RDD.

One thing we did differently than the other pollsters doing a daily tracking was that we only interviewed Sunday through Thursday. We have found that in certain areas of the country Friday and Saturday calling has extreme problems—we tend to get much older and more liberal samples. We did a separate poll on the Saturday and Sunday before the election and, actually, found that our numbers for Monday-Thursday of the previous week had been more accurate.

Peter Feld: When we have done tracking for political clients, we have avoided Fridays and Saturdays for the same reason. It's an assumption that needs to be periodically reexamined, but for now we just feel more confident avoiding those days.

JA: We've noticed this Friday-Saturday phenomenon too.

FN: We did not find a significant day of the week effect.

JZ: Just for the record, we do at least three call-backs on our sample and we call all day long, 9 am to 9 pm local time. Then we start with an entirely new sample the next day.

> *The idea of reporting two-day results was based on our hopes that we could monitor fairly quick changes and get a feel for how much impact events such as a new ad, or Dole falling off the podium, or Clinton's Middle East Summit could have on the electorate. The trade off is that you get more short-term volatility.*
>
> **—Frank Newport**

Glenn Roberts: Don't you find that those you call in the morning tend to be disproportionately women?

JZ: Only slightly. America has changed; there are people who work swing shifts and people who are unemployed. We average about 30% of our calls before 5 pm local time, 70% of our calls afterward.

PP: If you do 70% of your calls after five and you're doing three same day call-backs, what is your success rate on those call-backs?

JZ: It's not very high, but we do have the opportunity to reach people not previously or otherwise available.

PP: Do each of you calculate response rates for any of the tracking polls you conduct? And how seriously do you promote achieving a high response rate?

FN: We take promoting high response rates seriously. Our assumption is that the higher the response rate, the better off we are.

JZ: We average a response rate of 60 to 65%. These numbers reflect those who complete the interview versus those who don't complete the survey or refuse to participate. This figure does not include respondents who were repeatedly not at home.

On a different subject, if I may, Jeff, I have read interviews where you have called party identification a dependent variable and I don't see it that way. I see it

fundamentally as an independent variable. Most people still get their party identification through inheritance or through experience and in most instances they carry it with them for their adult lives. In that sense, I see party identification as a variable to be weighted similar to other demographic variables.

JA: I agree with you that for some people party ID is a demographic as much as race is, but for some people, they go to bed a Republican and wake up a Democrat, and that's not a good weight to use.

FN: Look at 1994 as an example. Had we gone in with preconceived notions about party identification, we would have been significantly off the mark. Our final allocated likely-voter model was very accurate in 1994 and there was a considerably higher number of people calling themselves Republicans.

PP: Do each of you have a sense that your organization does a good job communicating to the press and to viewers the level of precision that's associated with your survey findings? For example, the Zogby/Reuters results represent the vote distribution to a decimal place. John, do you think that connotes more precision than is really the case?

JZ: We do it only because it sets us apart.

GR: There are a lot of races—local and state races—where a half-percentage point may be very important in an extremely close race. You should report it that way to show the closeness. Otherwise, I wouldn't report by half-percentage points.

> *One thing we did differently than the other pollsters doing a daily tracking was that we only interviewed Sunday through Thursday. We have found that in certain areas of the country Friday and Saturday calling has extreme problems— we tend to get much older and more liberal samples.*
>
> **—Lori Gudermuth**

JA: We all know that the margin of error is the least likely source of error in our work—that's what we ought to be telling the public, not pretending that we're physicists. I think we could do a lot better to point that out to the public.

FN: Do the American people understand that you're not, in September or early October, saying this is the way the election will come out on November 5th, but you're saying that this is an estimate based on where the race stands in the minds of the people as of today? I have quite a bit of faith in the public that they understand that we're giving them an estimate for that point in time.

PP: The point spread between the candidates is often used as a litmus test for whether there's a change in the race. In a number of reports a change in the margin of five points was reported by the media as a real shift in the race. Clearly, the change could have been due to sampling error.

PF: The gap is a valid and legitimate thing to look at and it's definitely of interest, but it's twice as volatile as the actual percentages; the margin of error effectively doubles for the gap.

JA: I think the gap is problematic. It doubles the spread, exaggerates change.

PP: It has been suggested that taken as a body, the polls made the Democrats look stronger and Republicans weaker than they turned out to be on Election Day. Do you agree or disagree?

FN: I think the changes during the fall represented reality. That's the whole reason we continued to do polling. I don't think it's appropriate to say that the polls were inaccurate because, earlier on in the race, polls were showing Clinton with higher numbers than he ended up getting.

JZ: In some instances, the wider gap did tend to influence how the campaign was covered. Dole was portrayed often as being behind by as much as 23 points, and I didn't think enough was said to show the range of that gap.

PF: If consumers of our polls followed the results day-to-day, the data could create the illusion of a much more volatile race than if they examined only the average for our four-day samples. Looking at the data in this manner, there wasn't a lot of change during the months of September and October. However, we did find a narrowing toward the end of the race.

FN: The idea of reporting two-day results was based on our hopes that we could monitor fairly quick changes and get a feel for how much impact events such as a new ad, or Dole falling off the podium, or Clinton's Middle East Summit could have on the electorate. The trade off is that you get more short-term volatility.

GR: I'm not convinced that the public knows the difference between a two-day poll or a five to six-day poll. Why not publish the data weekly rather than daily? This would eliminate all this bounce and public misunderstanding.

PP: Do you think the daily bounce is real? Is the electorate

that volatile or is the movement an artifact of sampling? If it is an artifact are we misleading people by suggesting that the movement is real?

JZ: It's a result of the sampling and in some instances external events. We tried to caution in our releases that one day does not make a trend. In some instances where there did appear to be a change from one day to the next, we reported the one-day result with all the necessary caveats to suggest that somebody had a good day, or perhaps for this reason or that reason change occurred, but "stay tuned tomorrow or the next day."

> *The public's perception that Dole was going to lose was not just based on the media's reporting of the latest poll results. Nothing Dole did seemed to get him any kind of traction—choosing Kemp, announcing the tax cut, giving a speech, or resigning from the Senate.*
>
> **—Peter Feld**

FN: Yes. I think that, day-to-day, there were changes. A significant percent of the electorate were uncommitted. People's minds were changed as the campaign events began to hit them.

GR: Frank, on October 10th, you showed a 13-point spread followed by a 23-point spread on the 11th, 21 points on the 12th, 18, 13, 9, 12, 15, then back up to 23 points on October 18th. Do you think those numbers are real?

JA: You're doing exactly what I warned against. You're using the gap.

GR: That's because the media promote the daily gap and frequently the "bounce." I oppose using the gap, but daily tracking polls tend to encourage this kind of reporting.

FN: I have every confidence that the public was able to look at the numbers and interpret them correctly. I have confidence in the public, and that more information is better than less. The public was able to consume it.

PP: Putting the individual day-to-day bounce aside, the clear message of the polls up until the election was that Clinton was somewhere in the low-50s and Dole in the mid-30s. That suggests a much bigger difference between the two and a much clearer likelihood of a Clinton victory than, in fact, the final margin showed. There was some evidence that there was a narrowing at the end or, at the very least, the picture in mid-October was not quite as close as the picture on November 5th. How much of that perception got across to the public?

PF: The public's perception that Dole was going to lose was not just based on the media's reporting of the latest poll results. Nothing Dole did seemed to get him any kind of traction—choosing Kemp, announcing the tax cut, giving a speech, or resigning from the Senate.

Larry McGill: Are we getting too much of a fluctuation in the gap because we're trying to push undecideds too hard? Don't these undecideds more or less want to remain undecided until the last minute?

> **One of the reasons we started tracking remains true today. Do what the politicians are doing to keep them honest. It's called scrutiny of the press and that's what I do. I'm a reporter of public opinion—that's my beat. We're not in market research, but news.**
> **—Jeffrey Alderman**

JZ: That's a part of it. It's not reported enough that 25 to 28% of those who identify themselves as supporters of Clinton or Dole are basically "soft" supporters right up to the last week before the election.

FN: The whole reason the campaigns are spending millions of dollars from Labor Day to the election is to change people's minds. So it's not surprising that from day-to-day, people would be changing their minds.

PP: We had four tracking polls in 1996. Have we reached a saturation point?

JZ: No, the more, the merrier. Voters are consumers. Let them see what's out there and make their own judgments.

FN: The same question could be asked about news in general: Do we have too much news? And the answer to both questions is no.

PP: A recent Media Studies Center/Roper Center study shows that people think there's too much made about the horse race in the media. Clearly, the tracking polls promote horse race reporting.

FN: First, I don't think it's just tracking polls that emphasize the horse race. Second, we also asked the public (not specifically mentioning the horse race), "Do you think there are too many polls?" and we didn't find the same result.

Third, I saw a study quoted in *US News and World Report* analyzing the content of ABC, CBS and NBC news, and they said there was significantly less coverage this year of the horse race than in 1992.

JZ: I think the expansion of the daily tracking polls in a very important sense has driven issues analysis and coverage. The more tracking polls, the more attempts by the networks and by the major print media to explain the changes.

The public has got so much going on in their lives they don't worry about whether there's an extra tracking poll or two. That's not going to have any impact on how they vote.

Concluding Thoughts

LG: At the national level this was a lackluster election. There was, however, some genuine excitement further down the ballot. Republicans were not enthused about their national ticket but people paid attention to Senate and congressional races, especially in the last two weeks of the campaign.

PF: It's fair to say that there may have been some impact on Democratic voter turnout by the expectation that this race was a lock, but there were a combination of other factors at work. You had two candidates, both of whom were regarded with ambivalence by their base, and at the same time, you had an outcome that was considered not to be in doubt—that contributed to the tightening at the end of the race.

I don't think it's unfair that we reported 15-point races when that was probably reality at the time. Anyone who tuned in to the election the last weekend could hear whispers that a narrowing was taking place.

JA: One of the reasons we started tracking remains true today. Do what the politicians are doing to keep them honest. It's called scrutiny of the press and that's what I do. I'm a reporter of public opinion—that's my beat. We're not in market research, but news.

We need to have some tool to bring the public into the broadcast. There are plenty of other means of doing it beyond polling, but there's certainly no better way. Sure, the horse race may become repetitive. You may get tired of it and you may think it's stealing the election, but it's also providing a wealth of information about other issues that are on the American agenda.

FN: If you don't do accurate independent polling, people

Chapter 7

will look for it in other sources. George Gallup used to say that reporters would go into the bars and ask people whom they supported, and arrive at some guess anyhow. Or perhaps worse, they'd look for leaks from the campaign—from people who would be more than happy to selectively give out information.

People also are guided by the need for social comparison. They sometimes like to make their choices based on how other people stand. They ask their friends, "Who are you going to vote for?" Polling gives them a mechanism for doing that.

GR: This has been a valuable discussion on the important issue of daily tracking polls. We now know more about the daily tracking methodologies. We have learned there are some differences in sample design, weighting and reporting data.

With all these differences, one wonders why tracking polls are published and compared without clearly pointing out the differences and approaches to election polling each polling organization employs. It's no surprise that they frequently come up with different results.

Daily tracking polls should not be published. Leave tracking for the campaign strategists. Tracking polls were

designed for internal use—as a strategy tool for candidates with private pollsters—not to be released unless the findings were favorable to their candidates. Then they were usually "leaked" to reporters.

districts, state senate districts and so on.

We were able to suggest why the race tightened. The Indonesian campaign contribution and all of that business, in a very important respect, chis-

> 66
>
> *In some instances, the wider gap did tend to influence how the campaign was covered. Dole was portrayed often as being behind by as much as 23 points, and I didn't think enough was said to show the range of the gap.*
>
> —John Zogby
> 99

Public opinion researchers have allowed the "private pollster" to take over the process and turn it into a "public poll" by publishing the daily tracking. Now it's the common thing, and I think it's bad for the public and for public opinion research.

JZ: This was not a 20-point race. While no chance was given to Dole, polling certainly didn't suggest that there was one. There was enough action in congressional, state and local elections to suggest a substantial Republican turnout and at least the potential for a bottom-up impact in a narrowed race. We watched that closely as we polled nationally, and in states, congressional

eled away at Bill Clinton's support. And in the final analysis, the undecideds broke towards Dole whom they considered to be the real challenger and not Perot.

Daily tracking is a good thing. The only problem is that this race was not a blockbuster. So we can congratulate ourselves that we survived a boring election intact. Ultimately, daily tracking as well as the other polling that we do serves a very useful purpose. People want to be connected and know where they fit into the mainstream, and we're offering them a bridge, and with our bridge, they don't have to wait until the 21st century. They can have it right now.

Reprinted from The Public Perspective,
December/January 1997,
Vol. 8, No. 1, pp. 44-48.

Tracking the Tracking Polls: Clinton's Margin Greatest in Gallup and ABC News Surveys

Gallup

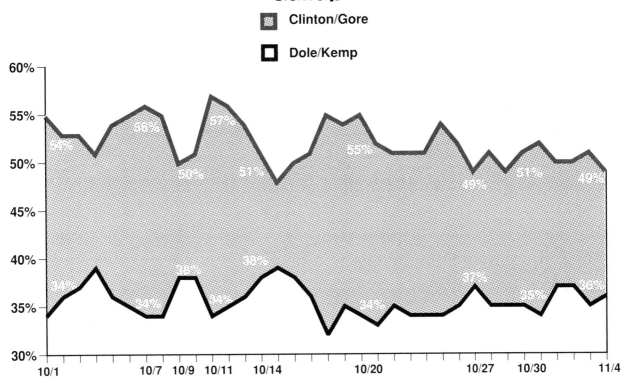

Note: Survey of likely voters .
Source: Surveys by the Gallup Organization for CNN/*USA Today*, October-November 1996.

ABC News

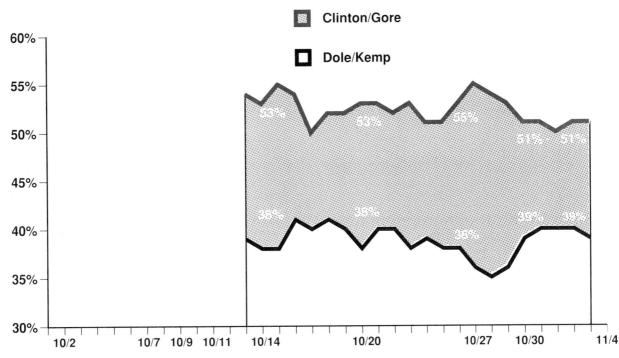

Note: Survey of likely voters.
Source: Surveys by ABC News, October-November 1996.

Clinton's Margin Smallest in Hotline and Zogby Surveys

Tarrance/Lake

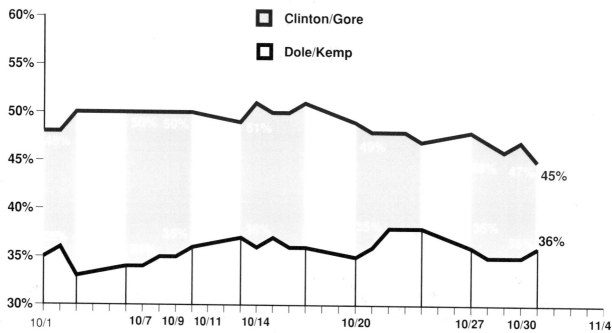

Note: Survey of likely voters. White spaces indicate the two days per week when no polling was done.
Source: Surveys by The Tarrance Group and Lake Research for the *Hotline*, October-November 1996.

Zogby

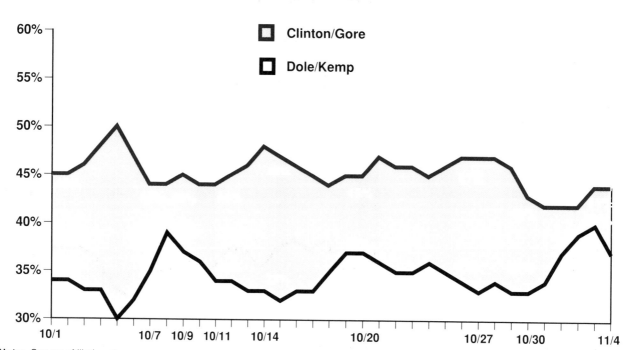

Note: Survey of likely voters.
Source: Surveys by the Zogby Group for Reuters, October-November 1996.

In the "generic congressional vote" trackings, the Democrats averaged in the 5 to 10 point range in the Gallup and ABC surveys...

ABC News

DATE	DEMOCRATIC	REPUBLICAN	MARGIN
No regular tracking polls done between 10/1 -10/10			
10/11-10/13	51%	43%	8%
10/12-10/14	50%	44%	6%
10/13-10/15	51%	43%	8%
10/14-10/16	52%	44%	8%
10/15-10/17	50%	45%	5%
10/16-10/18	50%	46%	4%
10/17-10/19	50%	45%	5%
10/18-10/20	50%	43%	7%
10/19-10/21	50%	45%	5%
10/20-10/22	49%	47%	2%
10/21-10/23	48%	47%	1%
10/22-10/24	47%	47%	0%
10/23-10/25	50%	45%	5%
10/24-10/26	50%	44%	6%
10/25-10/27	53%	41%	12%
10/26-10/28	54%	41%	13%
10/27-10/29	51%	42%	9%
10/28-10/30	50%	45%	5%
10/29-10/31	52%	44%	8%
10/30-11/1	53%	43%	10%
10/31-11/2	53%	42%	11%
11/1-11/3	53%	42%	9%

Note: Survey of likely voters.
Source: Surveys by ABC News, October-November 1996.

Gallup

DATE	DEMOCRATIC	REPUBLICAN	MARGIN
No regular tracking polls done between 10/1 - 10/21			
10/22-10/23	51%	42%	9%
10/23-10/24	48%	44%	4%
10/24-10/25	51%	42%	9%
10/25-10/26	50%	43%	7%
10/26-10/27	49%	44%	5%
10/27-10/28	50%	42%	8%
10/28-10/29	48%	45%	3%
10/29-10/30	50%	45%	5%
10/30-10/31	51%	44%	7%
10/31-11/1	49%	46%	3%
11/1-11/2	50%	44%	6%
11/2-11/3	51%	43%	8%
11/3-11/4	48%	45%	3%

Note: Survey of likely voters.
Source: Surveys by the Gallup Organization for CNN/*USA Today*, October-November 1996.

...while the 2 parties are shown running neck and neck in the Tarrance/Lake and Zogby trackings.

Tarrance/Lake

DATE	DEMOCRATIC	REPUBLICAN	MARGIN
9/26,9/29-10/1	42%	39%	3%
9/29-10/2	40%	39%	1%
9/30-10/3	40%	39%	1%
10/1-3, 6	41%	39%	2%
10/2-3, 6-7	41%	39%	2%
10/3, 6-8	42%	40%	2%
10/6-9	41%	40%	1%
10/7-10	41%	40%	1%
10/8-10, 13	41%	39%	2%
10/9-10, 13-14	42%	39%	3%
10/10, 13-15	42%	39%	3%
10/13-16	41%	39%	2%
10/14-17	41%	39%	2%
10/15-17, 20	40%	38%	2%
10/16-17, 20-21	41%	39%	2%
10/17, 20-22	41%	40%	1%
10/20-23	40%	40%	0%
10/21-24	40%	39%	1%
10/22-24, 27	40%	39%	1%
10/23-24, 27-28	39%	38%	1%
10/24, 27-29	40%	39%	1%
10/27-30	39%	40%	-1%
10/28-31	38%	41%	-3%
No tracking polls done after 10/31/96			

Note: Survey of likely voters.
Source: Surveys by The Tarrance Group and Lake Research for the *Hotline*, September-October 1996.

Zogby

DATE	DEMOCRATIC	REPUBLICAN	MARGIN
9/29-10/1	36%	35%	1%
9/30-10/2	35%	34%	1%
10/1-10/3	35%	35%	0%
10/2-10/4	34%	35%	-1%
10/3-10/5	37%	35%	2%
10/4-10/6	36%	35%	1%
10/5-10/7	38%	36%	2%
10/6-10/8	37%	37%	0%
10/7-10/9	36%	36%	0%
10/8-10/10	35%	36%	-1%
10/9-10/11	36%	35%	1%
10/10-10/12	39%	35%	4%
10/11-10/13	39%	34%	5%
10/12-10/14	36%	35%	1%
10/13-10/15	38%	33%	5%
10/14-10/16	39%	33%	6%
10/15-10/17	39%	33%	6%
10/16-10/18	39%	34%	5%
10/17-10/19	37%	36%	1%
10/18-10/20	38%	35%	3%
10/19-10/21	38%	36%	2%
10/20-10/22	37%	35%	2%
10/21-10/23	36%	37%	-1%
10/22-10/24	36%	37%	-1%
10/23-10/25	37%	38%	-1%
10/24-10/26	39%	37%	2%
10/25-10/27	39%	36%	3%
10/26-10/28	39%	35%	4%
10/27-10/29	39%	37%	2%
10/28-10/30	39%	37%	2%
10/29-10/31	40%	38%	2%
10/30-11/1	39%	38%	1%
10/31-11/2	39%	39%	0%
11/1-11/3	38%	41%	-1%
11/2-11/4	40%	39%	1%

Note: Survey of likely voters.
Source: Surveys by the Zogby Group for Reuters, September-November 1996.

Congressional Vote Intentions:

Since the 1950s, the late congressional vote trial heats have consistently overestimated the Democrats' proportion of the actual vote

In early May 1950, Gallup asked its national adult sample, "If the 1950 elections for Congress were being held today, which party would you like to see win in this state—the Republican Party or the Democratic Party?": Those saying they were "undecided" were then pushed as to how they leaned. Forty-seven percent declared themselves inclined to the Democratic Party, 31% to the Republican Party. Numerous variations of this "generic congressional vote intent" question have been posed by many different survey firms over the ensuing 45 years.

For much of the span Gallup asked,"Which party would you **like to see win** in this congressional district...?" Now, Gallup asks, "Which party's candidate would you **vote for** in your congressional district...?" Most other polling organizations ask variants of the "vote for" question in their surveys. The switch over from "like to see win" to "vote for" occurred after the 1992 elections. The figure on this page and the two that follow show all "like to see win" askings. Page 170 is entirely "vote for" questions. For each year shown, all askings by national survey organizations that the Roper Center has been able to locate are included in the graphs.

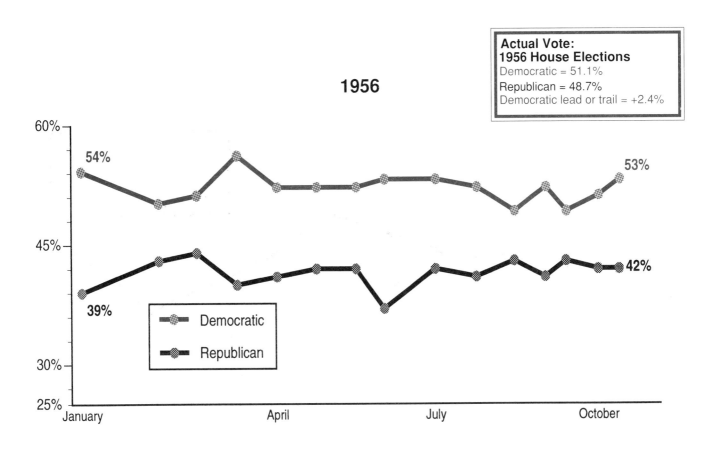

1956

Actual Vote:
1956 House Elections
Democratic = 51.1%
Republican = 48.7%
Democratic lead or trail = +2.4%

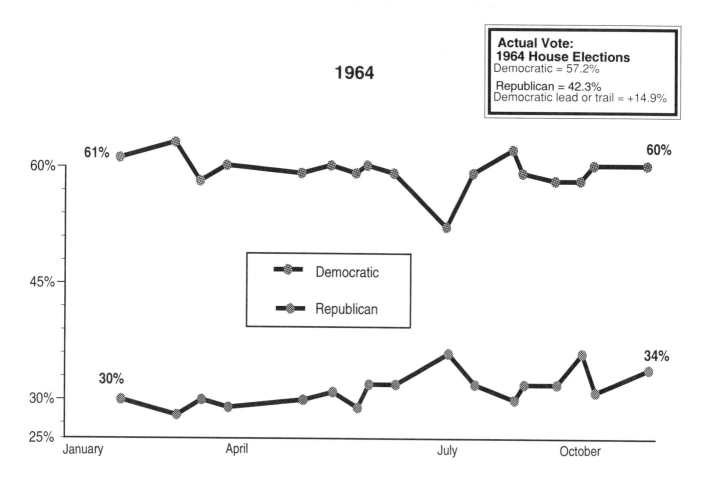

1964

Actual Vote:
1964 House Elections
Democratic = 57.2%

Republican = 42.3%
Democratic lead or trail = +14.9%

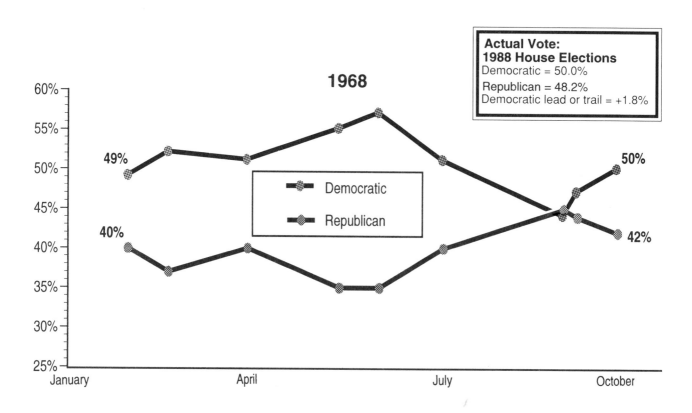

1968

Actual Vote:
1988 House Elections
Democratic = 50.0%

Republican = 48.2%
Democratic lead or trail = +1.8%

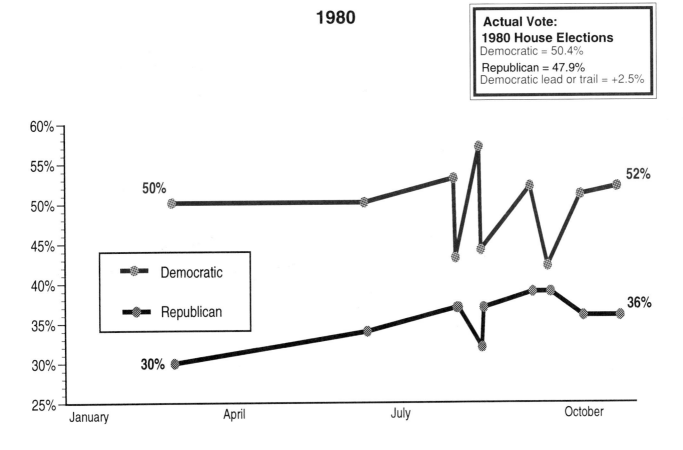

1980

Actual Vote:
1980 House Elections
Democratic = 50.4%
Republican = 47.9%
Democratic lead or trail = +2.5%

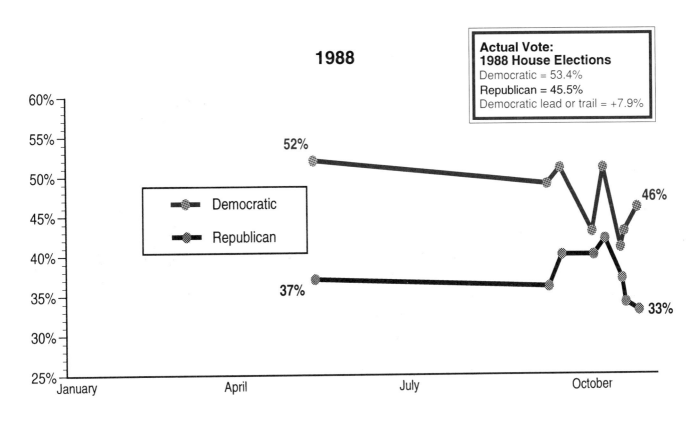

1988

Actual Vote:
1988 House Elections
Democratic = 53.4%
Republican = 45.5%
Democratic lead or trail = +7.9%

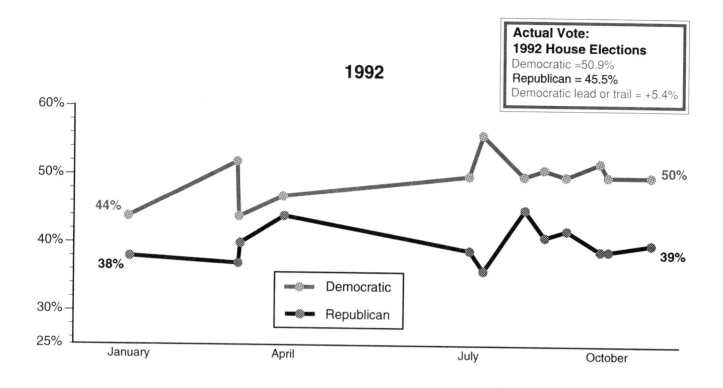

1992

Actual Vote:
1992 House Elections
Democratic =50.9%
Republican = 45.5%
Democratic lead or trail = +5.4%

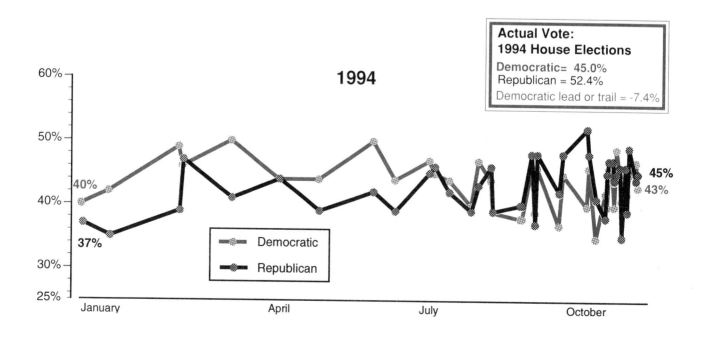

1994

Actual Vote:
1994 House Elections
Democratic= 45.0%
Republican = 52.4%
Democratic lead or trail = -7.4%

Chapter 8

The Electorate Assesses Media Performance in Campaign '96

By Kenneth Dautrich

The mass media have a pervasive presence in American life. By age 18, the typical American has spent more time watching television than attending school. On average, Americans spend about seven hours every day watching TV, reading a newspaper or magazine, or listening to the radio.[1]

Americans' affinity for the mass media extends to electoral politics, particularly in presidential campaigns. The electorate in 1996 unequivocally reported the media as their dominant source for learning about the campaign. For example, when asked where they got most of their information on the election, as many as 79% of those surveyed identified the news media while only 7% mentioned conversations with others. On a daily basis, many voters reportedly used a variety of news media sources to learn about the campaign—72% watched TV news, 61% read newspapers, and 50% routinely listened to the radio.[2]

> " *The media's trivializing effect on candidate discourse is one of the sharpest criticisms leveled by respondents. For example, 83% of those surveyed agreed that media coverage led candidates to avoid issues and instead perform for the cameras.* "

With this omnipresent role of the mass media in the eyes and ears of the electorate, it is not surprising that contemporary American presidential campaigns have become candidate-centered and media-driven—and 1996 is no exception. The great presence of the mass media in American life, including voters' reliance on the media for news, highlights its importance to the American electoral process. This chapter, therefore, evaluates the media's performance in the 1996 campaign from the perspective of the American voter.

Polling data from four organizations on the media's performance during and shortly after the 1996 campaign are reviewed, and results of a four-phased national voter panel study conducted by the Media Studies Center/Roper Center (MSC/RC) are closely examined. These four panels were conducted in January/February, early September, mid-October and immediately after the election.[3] Also, the Pew Center for the People and the Press' post-election survey is used in this analysis, as are Fox News/Opinion Dynamics surveys conducted in October and November.[4] Additionally, a post-election poll conducted by Louis Harris & Associates is examined.[5]

News Media as a Source of Campaign Information

Changes in the news media are at least partially responsible for the changes in political campaigns and voting behavior over the past 30 to 40 years. By the 1960s, television had become an important and readily accessible source of news for many voters.[6] Direct exposure to candidates through TV provided information and images outside the confines of voters' partisanship. Also, by this time many print journalists had begun advocating "objective" news reporting rather than a particular partisan viewpoint as most newspapers and magazines had done during the 1800s and early 1900s.[7]

Voters in 1996 relied heavily on the news media to learn about the campaign. From February through Election Day, 70% to 80% of voters identified the news media as their main source of information about the campaign (see Figure 1). Television continued to be the primary source of election news for most voters (56%), according to the MSC/RC surveys (see Figure 2). About 1-in-5 Americans identified newspapers as their main source of campaign news, while 1-in-10 mentioned radio. Harris' post-election survey also shows that local TV news, by a 2-to-1 margin, is more important to voters than network news.

Even though television was the primary news source for most voters, evidence from the Pew Center's research suggests that TV's dominance has leveled-off, if not declined, compared to recent presidential elections. For example, in comparing the top two news sources for voters in 1992 and 1996, the Pew Center found television use declined by 10 points, from 82% to 72% (see Figure 3).

The Internet

The latest entry in the host of information sources for presidential campaign politics is on-line news via the Internet. By Election Day, 8% of all voters said they used the Internet to obtain news about the campaign (see Table 1). While this repre-

Figure 1
Sources of Information about
the 1996 Presidential Campaign

Question: Would you say you got most of your information about the campaign from news media, from conversations you had with others, from paid political advertisements, or from some other source?

Figure 2
TV's Dominance in Media Use

Question: From which news medium would you say you got most of your information about the campaign?

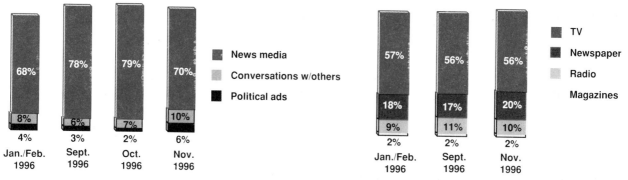

■ News media
■ Conversations w/others
■ Political ads

■ TV
■ Newspaper
■ Radio
   Magazines

Source: Surveys by the Media Studies Center/Roper Center (MSC/RC).

Figure 3
Dominant News Sources in the 1992 and 1996 Campaigns

Question: How did you get most of your news about the presidential election campaign?

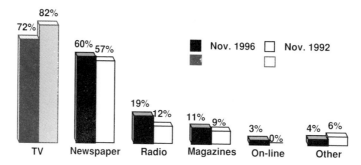

■ Nov. 1996   □ Nov. 1992
■   □

Note: Data include the top two mentions.
Source: Surveys by the Pew Center.

Table 1
Use of the Internet for Political Information

Questions: Do you currently use a computer, either at work or home?... Do you have access to the Internet?...Have you visited any politically-oriented Internet sites?

	Jan./Feb. '96	Sept. '96	Nov. '96
Use computer home/work	60%	59%	56%
Have access to internet	26%	28%	28%
Visited political sites	4%	6%	8%

Source: Surveys by the MSC/RC.

sents a small portion of the electorate, two factors suggest the Internet has the potential to be an important source of campaign information. First, throughout the campaign, only slightly more that one-quarter of all voters had access to the Internet. Among those with access, nearly one-third reported visiting political sites before Election Day. Continued expansion of Internet access will likely result in its greater utilization as a source of political information.

Second, even though the overall numbers are small, use of the Internet for political information doubled during the 1996 campaign from 4% in February to 8% by Election Day. This trend toward significantly greater use of the Internet as the campaign progressed, coupled with the likelihood that access to the Internet will increase, suggests that on-line sources will become more important to voters in the future.

Voters' Evaluations of the News Media

Voter evaluations of the news media's performance from the early primary season through Election Day were neither high nor low. What is clear, however, is that as November 5 drew closer and coverage became more focused on the campaign, voters' assessments of the media's performance improved. Figure 4 shows the clear trend toward improved ratings of the media over the course of the campaign from a 40% positive rating prior to the New Hampshire primary to a nearly 60% positive rating from mid-October through Election Day.

These increasingly favorable evaluations in part reflect voter perceptions of having sufficient information with which to chose candidates. Figure 5 shows that by Election Day 87% of voters felt they could make an informed choice. Three-quarters said they had learned enough about the candidates by the time they cast their ballots which suggests that considerable learning took place during the campaign. Because the media is the main source of news for most voters, most learning was probably a result of news coverage (see Figure 6).

By Election Day, a majority of voters in the MSC/RC survey gave the news media an overall grade of either "A" (14%) or "B" (40%) for their coverage of the campaign. Only 15% offered grades of "D" (9%) or "F" (6%) (see Table 2).

A Pew Center study utilizing the same sampling methodology, however, found significantly lower grades for the media when focusing on "how the press conducted themselves" during the campaign. Less than 3-in-10 offered a higher grade of "A" (6%) or "B" (22%), while nearly 4-in-10 gave the grade of "D" (19%) or "F" (18%).

The difference between the grades of the news media's overall job and the conduct of the press suggests that voters distinguish between the news product on the one hand, and the news-gathering process on the other hand. Clearly, voters were more enthusiastic about the news product than they were with the conduct of the press in covering the presidential election.[8]

Other survey data conducted during the campaign further sheds light on voter criticisms of the news-gathering process (see Figure 7). The media's trivializing effect on candidate discourse is one of the sharpest criticisms leveled by respondents. For example, 83% of those surveyed agreed that media coverage led candidates to avoid issues and instead perform for the cameras. A large majority (76%) also said the media gave undue advantage to election front-runners.

Figure 4
Ratings of the Media during Campaign 1996

Question: Overall, how would you rate the job the news media did in covering the presidential campaign?

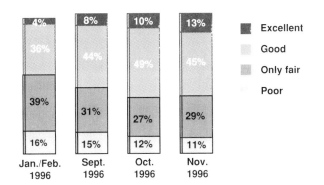

Source: Surveys by the MSC/RC.

Figure 5
Voters Say They Get Adequate Information to Make Their Vote Choice

Question: Did you feel you had received enough information about the presidential candidates to make an informed decision about whom to vote for?

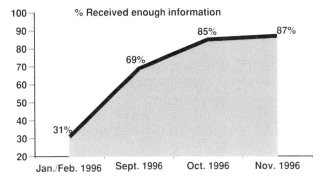

Source: Surveys by the MSC/RC.

Figure 6
Voters Say They Had Learned Enough About Candidates

Question: Do you feel you learned enough about the candidates and issues to make an informed choice?

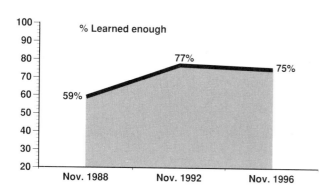

Source: Surveys by the Pew Center.

Table 2
Grading the Media and the Press

Question on press conduct: What grade would you give the press for the way they conducted themselves during the campaign? **Source:** The Pew Center

Question on media overall: If you had to give the media a grade for their coverage, would you give an A, B, C, D or F? **Source:** MSC/RC

	A	B	C	D	F
Nov. 1988--Press Conduct	8%	22%	33%	19%	16%
Nov. 1992--Press Conduct	11%	25%	29%	16%	15%
Nov. 1996--Press Conduct	6%	22%	33%	19%	18%
Nov. 1996--Media Overall	14%	40%	28%	9%	6%

Figure 7
News Media Coverage—What's Wrong, and Right?

Question: Please tell me if you agree or disagree with each of the following statements...

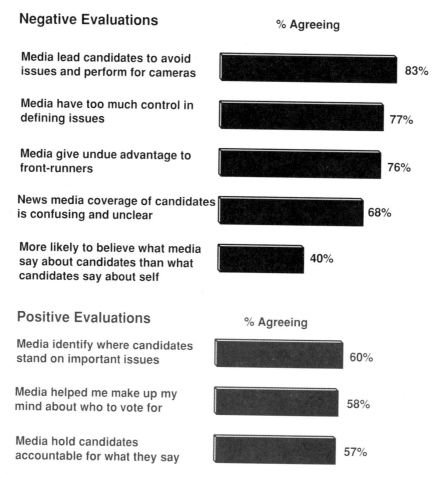

Negative Evaluations

% Agreeing

Statement	%
Media lead candidates to avoid issues and perform for cameras	83%
Media have too much control in defining issues	77%
Media give undue advantage to front-runners	76%
News media coverage of candidates is confusing and unclear	68%
More likely to believe what media say about candidates than what candidates say about self	40%

Positive Evaluations

% Agreeing

Statement	%
Media identify where candidates stand on important issues	60%
Media helped me make up my mind about who to vote for	58%
Media hold candidates accountable for what they say	57%

Source: Survey by the MSC/RC, January-February, 1996.

Voters in the MSC/RC survey were also critical of the news media's agenda-setting role in the campaign, with 77% agreeing that they have too much control in defining the issues. A Fox News poll also found that two-thirds of voters believed TV news had too much power. The Harris post-election survey corroborates these findings by showing that 58% thought the news media had too much influence and that 63% considered the media swayed by "powerful people and organizations."

The Harris survey also highlights other criticisms of the news gatherers' conduct. For example, 42% say that journalists are more arrogant than most people, 31% say they are more cynical, and 33% feel they are less compassionate.

Even with these criticisms of the media's conduct, many voters seemed satisfied that the news provided a satisfactory information source about the campaign. Figure 7 shows that almost 6-in-10 voters agreed that the news helped them decide how to vote, identified candidates' positions on important issues, and kept candidates accountable.

The Media's Usefulness

As mentioned previously, the vast majority of the electorate felt they could make an informed choice on Election Day. And despite their objections to some aspects of the news gathering process, their primary source of campaign information was the media. Survey respondents also specified which news sources they preferred.

Among 11 types of media coverage, voters in 1996 said live coverage of the presidential debates (see Table 3) was the single most valuable information source with 45% indicating they learned "a lot" from such coverage.

While viewing the debates live is clearly preferred, about 30% mention that "a lot" can be learned from TV news and the newspaper. About 2-in-10 also found useful information about the campaign from magazine articles, TV journalists' commentary, and debate-format political shows.

It's telling that live debate coverage, which involves direct, unmediated exposure to candidates, ranked high above the other categories of media information. Nine of the other 10 items involved information mediated by a journalist (the one exception is paid political ads which are viewed by voters as the least useful information source). Other survey data suggest that while direct exposure to the debates was valuable, journalistic accounts and commentary on the debates were problematic.

For example, Fox News found voters complaining that coverage was trying to influence opinions about who won the debates rather than putting debate content into context (see Figure 8). When asked whether they prefer watching debates with or without journalistic analysis and commentary, 6-in-10 preferred no commentary (see Figure 9). A MSC/RC survey also found a majority of voters preferred watching coverage of the national party conventions *without* journalists offering analysis and commentary.

Likewise, newspaper endorsements of candidates appeared to matter little to voters. Less than one-third were aware of a newspaper's endorsement of a candidate, 18% read the editorial in which the endorsement was made, and only 3% considered the endorsement to have influenced their opinions about the candidates.

Political Bias

Despite the news media's self-described goal of "objectivity" in reporting, a recurring question in presidential campaigns involves the issue of partisan or ideological bias by the news media. Throughout the 1996 campaign, Bob Dole frequently raised questions about a liberal/Democratic

bias in media coverage; Republican congressional candidates made similar claims. Interestingly, a 1995 Media Studies Center/Roper Center survey found that 89% of Washington-based political journalists voted for Bill Clinton in 1992.[9] This finding helped refuel the debate on political bias in news media coverage during the 1996 campaign.

Accusations of media bias are not new to American political campaigns. Some research documents a bias while many studies suggest that campaign coverage tends to be evenly balanced. While proving a bias in the 1996 news coverage awaits thorough and systematic content analysis, the perceptions of bias from the electorate's perspective is instructive.

Surveys conducted during the 1996 presidential campaign suggest that voters are quite skeptical that the news media is a fair and unbiased source of election information. As Figure 10 shows, a September MSC/RC survey found that only one-third of voters agreed that "news media stories about the campaign provide unbiased accounts of what is happening in the campaign."

Other surveys indicated similar conclusions. When asked if the media goes to great lengths to make sure coverage is fair and balanced, only 32% answered "yes" (see Figure 11). Another survey revealed a strong tendency for voters to believe that television news coverage goes beyond providing information and actually tries to influence which candidate wins the election (Figure 12). Also, the Harris survey found that only one-third of voters felt the media deals fairly with all sides in political reporting, and 74% said a fair amount or a great deal of political bias exists in the news.

The MSC/RC election surveys also provide insight on perceptions of ideological bias in campaign coverage. When asked about ideological biases in news reporting, about half

(48%) of voters claimed coverage was evenly balanced at the outset of the presidential primaries (see Figure 14). The percentage of voters saying coverage was evenly balanced increased to 52% after the national party conventions, and then to 59% immediately after the election.[10]

Throughout the campaign, then, half to three-in-five voters opined that news reporting was not ideologically biased. However, those who detected an ideological slant were more likely to say that it favored a liberal viewpoint rather than a conservative one. Also, the percentage identifying a liberal bias in campaign coverage remained at about 30%. The smaller number (13%) who said the coverage was conservatively biased in the pre-primary stage of the campaign dropped to 4% by Election Day.[11]

Responses to the ideological bias question, however, vary significantly among self-professed liberals, conservatives, and moderates. The conservative voter was disproportionately more likely to perceive an ideological bias to news reporting in 1996. By Election Day, 37% of conservatives said coverage was balanced, compared to 68% of moderates and 73% of liberals. And, not surprisingly, conservatives who sensed a bias were much more likely to see a liberal bias (55%) than a conservative one (4%).

Table 3: What Works?

Question: Generally, how much do you learn about the candidates and the campaign from each of the following?

	A lot	Some	Little	Not too much	Not much at all
Watching debates live	45%	27%	13%	5%	9%
Reading newspaper stories	32%	36%	19%	4%	9%
Watching TV news stories	30%	39%	22%	4%	4%
Reading articles in magazines	21%	33%	20%	7%	19%
TV journalist analysis & commentary	18%	27%	25%	16%	13%
Watching TV debate programs	18%	19%	14%	10%	38%
Talk radio	15%	17%	17%	11%	39%
Sunday A.M. political talk shows	15%	16%	12%	12%	44%
Newspaper journalist accounts of candidate's performance	14%	30%	25%	14%	16%
Paid political ads	5%	18%	27%	28%	21%

Source: Survey by the Media Studies Center/Roper Center, September 14-18, 1996.

Figure 8
Debate Coverage Tries Too Much to Influence the Interpretation of What Happened

Question: Many news organizations that cover the presidential debates follow their debate coverage with analysis and opinions from various commentators and reporters. Do you believe the media does this to put the debates in context, or to try to influence your opinion?

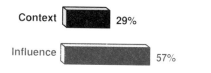

Context   29%

Influence   57%

Figure 9
We Prefer Watching Debates Without Commentary

Question: Would you prefer watching a news organization that covers the debates with opinion and analysis or without opinion and analysis?

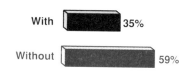

With   35%

Without   59%

Source: Survey by Fox News and Opinion Dynamics, October 4, 1996.

Figure 10
News Media Didn't Provide Unbiased
Accounts of Campaign

Question: Please tell me if you agree or disagree... News media stories about the campaign generally provide unbiased accounts of what is happening in the campaign.

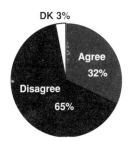

Source: Survey by the MSC/RC, September 14-18, 1996.

Figure 11
The Media Didn't Go to Great Lengths to
Ensure Fairness and Balance

Question: Do you think the television news media goes to great lengths to make sure that their coverage is fair and balanced?

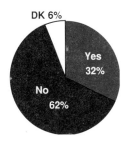

Source: Survey by Fox News and Opinion Dynamics, October 25, 1996.

Figure 12
TV Coverage Seeks to Influence
Election Outcome

Question: In general, do you think the television news media tries to influence who wins elections, or not?

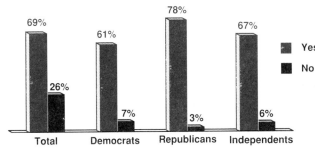

Figure 13
News Coverage Tips More to the Left

Question: In your opinion, does news coverage on television tip to the left or the right politically?

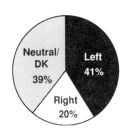

Source: Survey by Fox News and Opinion Dynamics, October 4, 1996.

Figure 14
Still, By Another Measure a Majority of Voters Say "No Bias"

Question: Do you think the news media coverage of the presidential campaign was biased?

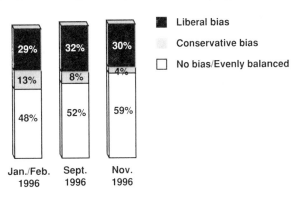

Source: Surveys by the MSC/RC.

Figure 15
Media's Treatment of Clinton and Dole

Question: Which best describes the way the media has treated (candidate)? He's been given a free ride, or he's been attacked too often?

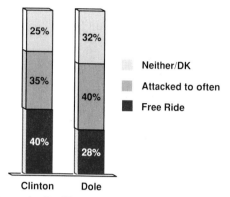

Source: Survey by Fox News and Opinion Dynamics, November 1, 1996.

Table 4
Fair to Both Dole and Clinton, But Fairer to Clinton

Question: Would you say the press has been fair or unfair in the way it has covered (candidate's) election campaign? (**Source**: The Pew Center)... Overall, how fair was news media coverage of (candidate)? (**Source**: MSC/RC)

	Fairness of Press in Covering:		
	Clinton	Dole	Perot
Pew Center Nov. 1996			
Fair	73%	65%	46%
Unfair	24%	32%	44%
MSC/RC Nov. 1996			
Very/Somewhat Fair	89%	78%	32%
Not too/ Not Fair	8%	19%	45%

On the other hand, liberal voters noting a bias were split over its direction; 11% saw a liberal bias while 9% found a conservative one. Among moderates, 25% reported a liberal bias and 5% detected a conservative leaning in campaign coverage.

Two trends in perceptions of partisan bias are also noteworthy. Opinions that media coverage favored the Democrats rose from 22% in February to 35% on November 5. Second, perceptions of a Republican bias decreased over the same time span (21% to 5%). By campaign's end, more than one-third of voters felt the news was tilting in the Democrat's favor.

Republican voters especially, and independent voters to a lesser extent, noted a political slant to the news. Among Republicans, 68% maintained that the news favored the Democratic Party. Democratic voters, however, were about as likely to feel the news favored the Republicans (7%) as the Democrats (11%).

In evaluating the performance of the news media, particularly in this era of "candidate-centered"[12] campaigns, an examination of voter perceptions of coverage of the *candidates*, apart from views of ideological or partisan bias, is important. Voters were more likely to feel that Clinton was given a free ride by the media than was Dole (40% to 28%, respectively), according to a Fox survey (see Figure 15).

Strong majorities, however, felt that both major-party candidates were treated fairly by the news media, but Pew Center and MSC/RC surveys showed that voters also felt that Bill Clinton was treated more fairly than Bob Dole by 8 and 11 percentage points respectively (Table 4). Even more

striking is the sense among voters that Ross Perot was not treated fairly. Fewer than half (46%) of Pew's respondents said that press coverage of Perot was fair, and only one-third of MSC/RC respondents assessed media coverage of Perot to be either very or somewhat fair.

Content Bias

In assessing election coverage of the 1976 campaign, Thomas Patterson noted a strong tendency for the news media to prioritize coverage of voter opinion polls, particularly the polls that focused on the horse race.[13] He concluded that horse race coverage of the election tended to dominate the news.

Since 1976, consumption of polls has increased dramatically. In 1996, there were five national daily tracking polls, numerous other organizations conducting national polls on the horse race at various points during the campaign, and statewide voter polls being conducted in 48 states. The amount of information on the horse race available to the news media was, therefore, quite extensive. Interestingly, however, an analysis of four of the five national daily tracking polls during the last month of the election found virtually no change in vote choices.[14] Despite the lack of a story in the polls (except that there was no change in vote choice), the question of whether the news media overused this vast supply of polling data emerges.

As with the question on political bias, a thorough content analysis is necessary to document the extent to which the horse race was covered in 1996. Again, however, the perception of voters is important in understanding the role of the news media in 1996 and in assessing whether

Table 5
What Voters Want and What They Get From Campaign Coverage

Question: Do you think the news media devoted too much attention, too little attention, or about the right amount of attention to stories on...

Voter Interest in Types of Stories:	% Very Interested	% saying "Too Little" and "Too Much" Attention in Media					
	Jan./Feb. 1996	Jan./Feb. 1996		Sept. 1996		Nov. 1996	
		Too little	Too much	Too little	Too much	Too little	Too much
Candidate's issue positions	77%	51%	8%	46%	8%	45%	7%
Effect of election on you	72%	51%	11%	43%	13%	38%	12%
Third party candidates	27%	49%	10%	44%	13%	58%	5%
Campaign strategies	26%	21%	33%	18%	34%	15%	34%
Who's ahead/who's behind	22%	8%	46%	7%	50%	2%	57%
Personal lives of candidates	14%	10%	68%	12%	63%	11%	50%

Source: Surveys by the Media Studies Center/Roper Center.

Figure 16
Voter Suggestions for Future Coverage
of Presidential Campaigns

Question: Four years from now when the conventions happen again, do you think the TV networks should carry the conventions live or should they carry their regular programs and only report on the conventions in their regular news programs?... There is a proposal to give the major presidential candidates free air time on network television near the end of the campaign. Do you think this would be very useful, somewhat useful, or not at all useful to you in making a decision about whom to vote for?

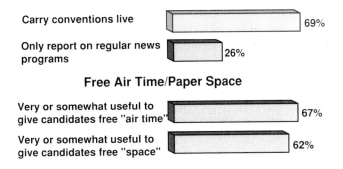

Carry conventions live — 69%
Only report on regular news programs — 26%

Free Air Time/Paper Space

Very or somewhat useful to give candidates free "air time" — 67%
Very or somewhat useful to give candidates free "space" — 62%

Source: Surveys by the MSC/RC, September 14-18, 1996.

there was a content bias to coverage.

Table 5 shows that throughout the 1996 campaign, voters consistently said "too much" news media attention was paid to stories about the horse race and to stories about the personal lives of the candidates. Additionally, as the campaign wore on, voters became increasingly critical of the media's horse race coverage, with 46% saying there was too much focus on "who's ahead and who's behind" in February, 50% noting that in September, and 57% by Election Day.

At the same time, voters consistently said that "too little" media attention was paid to candidates' stand on the issues, to third party candidates, and to how the election outcome might affect voters. Only about 1-in-10 voters said that the news media focused "too much" on these three types of stories.

Clearly, voters noticed a bias in campaign news content toward reporting on the horse race and on stories related to the personal lives of candidates. Ironically, Table 5 also shows that the types of stories that dominate the news are also the types of stories in which voters are less interested. Only 22% say they are very interested in the horse race and 14% in stories about the personal lives of the candidates. On the other hand, about three-quarters of voters reported being very interested in candidates' positions on the issues and in how the election outcome might affect them. The content bias in news, then, runs in the opposite direction of the information content needs reported by voters.

Conclusion

During the 1996 campaign, voters expressed both frustration and satisfaction with the role of the news media. A review of the survey data on

attitudes about the media's performance leaves one wondering if "the glass is half full or half empty."

On the one hand, voters claimed to have learned enough from the news to make informed choices. On the other hand, voters consistently said that the news media focused too much on information they didn't need.

Also, while voters' overall grades on the news product were good, grades given to the news gathering process and to the conduct of the media were much less favorable. Strong voter preferences for the media as a conduit of direct information (e.g., the live coverage of debates and conventions) rather than an arbiter or summarizer of campaign information (i.e. news stories written by journalists) highlights contemporary skepticism of American journalism.

The survey data on voter perceptions of political bias also provides both positive and negative feedback on the news media's performance in 1996. By Election Day a majority felt that news coverage was evenly balanced, both from a partisan and ideological perspective. Among those who sensed a bias, however, there was very strong consensus that the bias was unidirectional.

Because the media are a pervasive influence in American politics and because the news media will likely continue to be a dominant source of information for voters, identification of areas the media can improve their election coverage is vital to the life of American democracy.

Endnotes:
[1] W. Russell Neuman, *The Future of the Mass Audience* (New York: Cambridge University Press, 1991).
[2] These data are drawn from a Media Studies Center/Roper Center national voter survey (N=1,000) conducted October 17-21, 1996.
[3] The January/February sample included a sample of 2,000 voters. The September 14-18 wave included 1,000 interviews (667 panel recontact interviews and 333 new cross-sectional interviews). The 1,000 October 17-21 wave interviews included 580 panel recontact interviews and 420 new cross-sectional interviews. The November 6-11 wave included a total of 1,000 interviews (512 panel and 488 new cross-section).
[4] The Pew Center survey is based on 1,012 telephone interviews conducted November 7-10 with respondents who were recontacted on the basis of an interview first conducted in either June or October.
[5] The Harris survey, commissioned by the Center for Media and Public Affairs, is based on a national sample of 3,000 interviews conducted in November 1996.
[6] Steve and Barbara Salmore, *Candidates, Parties and Campaigns* (Washington, DC: Congressional Quarterly Press, 1989).
[7] Michael Schudson, *Discovering the News* (New York: Basic Books, 1978).
[8] John Mashek and Larry McGill, *Lethargy '96* (Washington, DC: The Freedom Forum, 1997).
[9] Elain S. Povich, *Partners and Adversaries* (Washington, DC: The Freedom Forum, 1996).
[10] A Fox News Opinion Dynamics survey of voters in October 1996 asked voters whether news coverage tipped to the left or the right, politically. In this item, respondents were not offered the option of saying coverage did not tip in either direction. The survey found that 41% felt coverage tipped to the left, 20% said it tipped to the right, and 39% volunteered that coverage was neutral (see Figure 13).
[11] The Harris survey found that 43% describe the media's politics as liberal, 19% as conservative, and 33% as middle of the road.
[12] Robert Agranoff, *The New Style in Election Campaigns* (Boston: Holbrook Press, 1976).
[13] Thomas Patterson, *The Mass Media Election* (New York: Praeger, 1980).
[14] See Kenneth Dautrich and Jennifer Dineen, "Stability in Vote Choices Characterizes the 1996 American Voter" in *Public Perspective*, Vol. 8 No.1, December/January 1997.

C hapter 9
Divided Government Defines the Era

When Dwight Eisenhower was sworn in for the second time in 1957, he was the first just-elected or re-elected president in over seventy years to face a Congress not controlled by his own party. While the opposition party had, at times, won majorities in the House and Senate in midterm elections, even those instances were rare. In the sixty-two years from 1893 through 1954, the country experienced divided government during just eight years—all in the last half of a president's term.

But when Bill Clinton took his second oath of office in 1997, he was just another in a long line of late twentieth-century chief executives to confront a Congress not of his own party. Congress and the presidency have displayed divided partisan control for much of the latter half of the 20th century. In the forty-four years from 1955 through 1998, the government will have been divided between parties for thirty years—nearly 70 percent of the time (see p. 187).

Although divided government is discussed most often in national terms, there is a striking trend toward split control in the states as well. It's development seems to follow the same pattern, with the number of states under divided control increasing quite steadily over the last several decades. The 1996 elections left over 60 percent of the states—all but 19—with at least one chamber of the legislature controlled by a party opposed to the governors (see p. 189).

The persistence of this pattern on both the national and the state level indicates that some sort of fundamental change has taken place in American politics. Analysts point to various explanations, but perhaps most often to the increasing inability of political parties in the United States to maintain a loyal following. Indeed, the divided government trend is but one indication of a much broader pattern of what one scholar calls "electoral disintegration."[1]

This disintegration manifests itself in a rise in split-ticket voting. Going into the current election cycle, a Roper Center poll found that sixty-five percent of Americans said that they typically split their ticket when voting, and well over half reported having voted for different parties in past presidential elections (see p. 190).

Further, according to the University of Michigan's National Election Study (NES), the percentage of respondents describing themselves as independents has grown from just over twenty percent in 1952 to 35 percent in 1994. This trend reflects a substantial decline in the importance of party cues.

Many scholars have decried the erosion of party ties and the subsequent rise in split party power, claiming that weak parties and divided control often lead to inefficient governing and ineffective policies. They see little beyond drift and stalemate in a divided political system.[2] But is not clear that the public shares their distaste. In fact, some analysts have suggested that voters have been engaging in a form of strategic voting and are consciously seeking divided control.[3]

Did a critical portion of the electorate deliberately vote *for* divided government in 1996? Did voters prefer continued partisan clashes to a blank-check policy for either party? Despite the recent spate of academic attention, there has been surprisingly little research on these questions.

A post-election survey by The Pew Research Center found that 53 percent of those who voted in 1996 are happy with Clinton's reelection, and 65 percent are happy with the GOP's continued control of Congress. In fact, a surprising 39 percent of Clinton voters said that they were happy that the Republicans maintained control of Congress. Of those who cast a vote for their district's Democratic House candidate, 38 percent said they were happy with the final Congressional election outcome (see p. 192). The public certainly does not appear to be unhappy with divided control, notwithstanding the scholarly chorus of laments.

Endnotes

[1] See Gary Jacobson. *The Electoral Origins of Divided Government: Competition in US House Elections, 1946-88* (Boulder: Westview Press, 1990).
[2] See especially James Sundquist, "Needed: A Political Theory for the New Era of Coalition Government in the United States," *Political Science Quarterly* 103: 613-35.
[3] See Morris Fiorina, *Divided Government* (New York: MacMillan Publishing Co., 1992).

—**Regina Dougherty**

Americans have Voted for Divided Government in Two Periods:...

Years	Party controlling presidency	Party controlling Senate	Party controlling House
1789-91	F	F	F
1791-93	F	F	F
1793-95	F	F	DR
1795-97	F	F	F
1797-99	F	F	F
1799-1801	F	F	F
1801-03	DR	DR	DR
1803-05	DR	DR	DR
1805-07	DR	DR	DR
1807-09	DR	DR	DR
1809-11	DR	DR	DR
1811-13	DR	DR	DR
1813-15	DR	DR	DR
1815-17	DR	DR	DR
1817-19	DR	DR	DR
1819-21	DR	DR	DR
1821-23	DR	DR	DR
1823-25	DR	DR	DR
1825-27	AF	AF	AF
1827-29	AF	JF	JF
1829-31	D	D	D
1831-33	D	D	D
1833-35	D	D	D
1835-37	D	D	D
1837-39	D	D	D
1839-41	D	D	D
1841-43	W	W	W

Years	Party controlling presidency	Party controlling Senate	Party controlling House
1843-45	W	W	D
1845-47	D	D	D
1847-49	D	D	W
1849-51	W	D	D
1851-53	W	D	D
1853-55	D	D	D
1855-57	D	D	D
1857-59	D	D	D
1859-61	D	D	R
1861-63	R	R	R
1863-65	R	R	R
1865-67	R/U	R/U	R/U
1867-69	R	R	R
1869-71	R	R	R
1871-73	R	R	R
1873-75	R	R	R
1875-77	R	R	D
1877-79	R	R	D
1879-81	R	D	D
1881-83	R	R	R
1883-85	R	R	D
1885-87	D	R	D
1887-89	D	R	D
1889-91	R	R	R
1891-93	R	R	D

Letter symbols for political parties

AF=Adams faction
D=Democratic
DR=Democratic-Republican
F=Federalist

JF-Jackson faction
R=Republican
U=Unionist
W=Whig

...The Latter Half of the 19th Century, and Now in the Latter Half of the 20th

	Party controlling presidency	Party controlling Senate	Party controlling House
1893-95	D	D	D
1895-97	D	R	R
1897-99	R	R	R
1899-1901	R	R	R
1901-03	R	R	R
1903-05	R	R	R
1905-07	R	R	R
1907-09	R	R	R
1909-11	R	R	R
1911-13	R	R	D
1913-15	D	D	D
1915-17	D	D	D
1917-19	D	D	D
1919-21	D	R	R
1921-23	R	R	R
1923-25	R	R	R
1925-27	R	R	R
1927-29	R	R	R
1929-31	R	R	R
1931-33	R	R	D
1933-35	D	D	D
1935-37	D	D	D
1937-39	D	D	D
1939-41	D	D	D
1941-43	D	D	D
1943-45	D	D	D
1945-47	D	D	D
1947-49	D	R	R

	Party controlling presidency	Party controlling Senate	Party controlling House
1949-51	D	D	D
1951-53	D	D	D
1953-55	R	R	R
1955-57	R	D	D
1957-59	R	D	D
1959-61	R	D	D
1961-63	D	D	D
1963-65	D	D	D
1965-67	D	D	D
1967-69	D	D	D
1969-71	R	D	D
1971-73	R	D	D
1973-75	R	D	D
1975-77	R	D	D
1977-79	D	D	D
1979-81	D	D	D
1981-83	R	R	D
1983-85	R	R	D
1985-87	R	R	D
1987-89	R	D	D
1989-91	R	D	D
1991-93	R	D	D
1993-95	D	D	D
1995-97	D	R	R
1997-99	D	R	R

Source: For 1789 to 1970 data—*Historical Statistics of the United States: Colonial Times to 1970*, Part 2 (Washington, DC: U.S. Bureau of the Census, 1975), pp. 1083-84. For 1971 to 1997—*Statistical Abstract of the United States, 1995-96* (Washington, DC: U.S. Bureau of the Census, 1995), p. 279. For 1997-1999—*Congressional Quarterly Weekly Report*, November 9, 1996, pp. 3225, 3238.

The Number of States With Divided Government Has Increased Substantially Since 1960

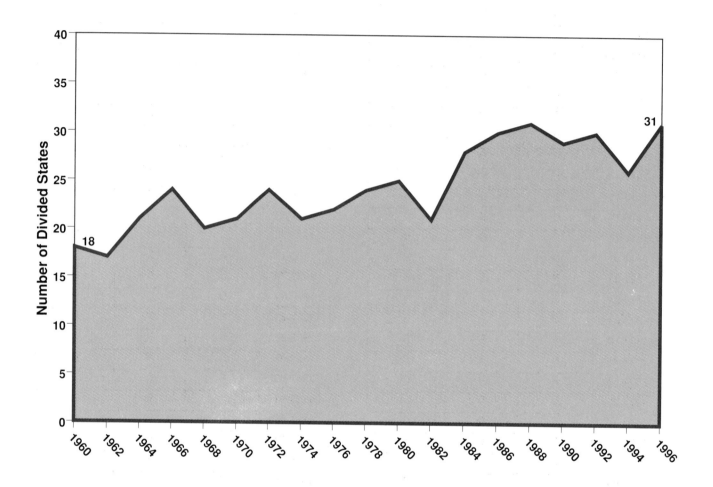

Note: A state has 'divided government' if at least one chamber of the legislature is controlled by a party different from the governor's.
Source: National Conference of State Legislatures

States With Divided Government
After the 1996 Elections

	Party controlling Governorship	Party controlling State Senate	Party controlling State House
Alabama	R	D	D
Alaska	D	R	R
Arizona	R	R	R
Arkansas	R	D	D
California	R	D	D
Colorado	D	R	R
Connecticut	R	D	D
Delaware	D	D	R
Florida	D	R	R
Georgia	D	D	D
Hawaii	D	D	D
Idaho	R	R	R
Illinois	R	R	D
Indiana	D	R	Tie
Iowa	R	R	R
Kansas	R	R	R
Kentucky	D	D	D
Louisiana	R	D	D
Maine	I	D	D
Maryland	D	D	D
Massachusetts	R	D	D
Michigan	R	R	D
Minnesota	R	D	D
Mississippi	R	D	D
Missouri	D	D	D

	Party controlling Governorship	Party controlling State Senate	Party controlling State House
Montana	R	R	R
Nebraska	D	N/A	N/A
Nevada	D	R	D
New Hampshire	D	R	R
New Jersey	R	R	R
New Mexico	R	D	D
New York	R	R	D
North Carolina	D	D	R
North Dakota	R	R	R
Ohio	R	R	R
Oklahoma	R	D	D
Oregon	D	R	R
Pennsylvania	R	R	R
Rhode Island	R	D	D
South Carolina	R	D	R
South Dakota	R	R	R
Tennessee	R	D	D
Texas	R	R	D
Utah	R	R	R
Vermont	D	D	D
Virginia	R	Tie	D
Washington	D	R	R
West Virginia	R	D	D
Wisconsin	R	D	R
Wyoming	R	R	R

Note: Nebraska has a single, bipartisan legislature.
Source: National Conference of State Legislatures

The American Electorate is Remarkably Unanchored in Partisan Terms

Questions: When voting in elections do you typically vote a straight ticket—that is for candidates of the same party, or do you typically split your ticket—that is vote for candidates from different parties?; Have you always voted for the same party for president or have you voted for different parties for president?; In 1996, how likely is it that you would vote for an independent candidate for president? Is it very likely, somewhat likely, not too likely or not at all likely?

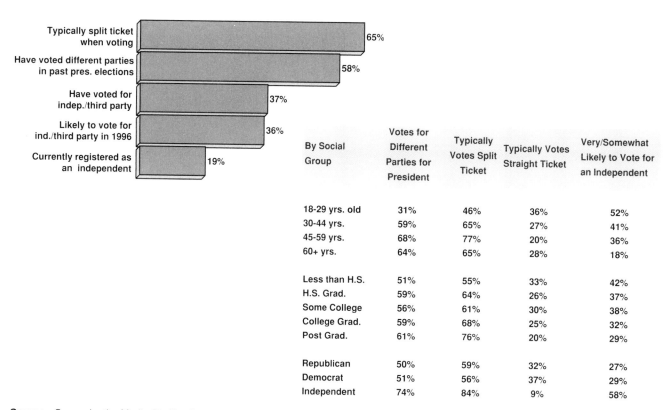

By Social Group	Votes for Different Parties for President	Typically Votes Split Ticket	Typically Votes Straight Ticket	Very/Somewhat Likely to Vote for an Independent
18-29 yrs. old	31%	46%	36%	52%
30-44 yrs.	59%	65%	27%	41%
45-59 yrs.	68%	77%	20%	36%
60+ yrs.	64%	65%	28%	18%
Less than H.S.	51%	55%	33%	42%
H.S. Grad.	59%	64%	26%	37%
Some College	56%	61%	30%	38%
College Grad.	59%	68%	25%	32%
Post Grad.	61%	76%	20%	29%
Republican	50%	59%	32%	27%
Democrat	51%	56%	37%	29%
Independent	74%	84%	9%	58%

Source: Survey by the Media Studies Center/Roper Center, February 1996.

Another Measure of Electoral Independence

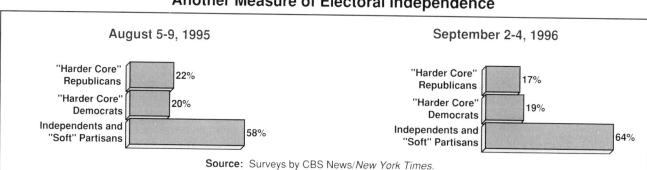

Source: Surveys by CBS News/*New York Times*.

In this exercise we redefined partisans and independents using three variables: 1. The standard party ID question; 2. A question asking respondents whether their opinion of the Republican Party is favorable or unfavorable; and 3. A question asking whether their opinion of the Democratic Party is favorable or unfavorable. A "harder core" Republican is one who is self-identified with the party, holds a favorable opinion of it and has an unfavorable opinion of the opposition. The construction of "harder core" Democrats is exactly parallel. Everyone else goes into the third category of independents and "soft" partisans. In four calculations of this measure using other survey data over 1995 and 1996, the proportion of the electorate classified as independents and soft partisans never dropped below 52%.

Many More Americans Now Say They Vote for Different Candidates for President From One Election to Another

Question: Have you always voted for the same party, or have you voted for different parties for president?

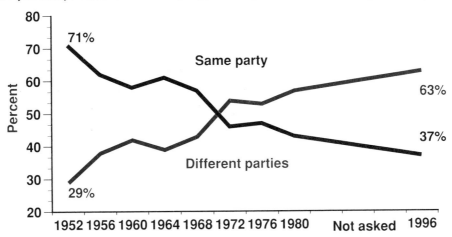

Note: Don't know/not asked/didn't vote calculated out of all questions.
Source: 1952-1980 Surveys by the Center for Political Studies, NES, University of Michigan, latest that of September 2-November 3, 1980; and 1996 by the Media Studies Center/Roper Center, February 1996.

In General, Ticket-Splitting is Up

1942

Question: Do you usually vote a straight ticket, that is vote for all the candidates of one party, or do you vote a split ticket, that is vote for some candidates of one party and some of the other?

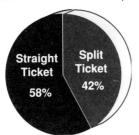

Note: For all pies on this page, don't know/not asked/didn't vote calculated out.

Source: Survey by the Gallup Organization, July 16-21, 1942.

1983

Question: ...How often would you say you vote a straight party ticket...?

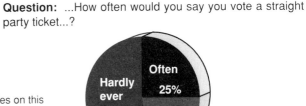

Source: Survey by ABC News/*Washington Post*, July 28-August 1, 1983.

1995

Question: ...[D]o you always vote for Democrats, mostly vote for Democrats, split your votes evenly between Democrats and Republicans, mostly vote for Republicans, or always vote for Republicans?

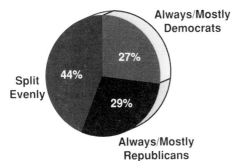

Source: Survey by NBC News/*Wall Street Journal*, March 4-7, 1995.

1996

Question: When voting in elections, do you typically vote a straight ticket—that is for candidates of the same party, or do you typically split your ticket—that is vote for candidates from different parties?

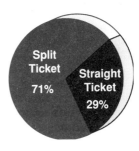

Source: Survey by the Media Studies Center/Roper Center, February 1996.

Many Voters in 1996, Including Clinton Voters, Said They Were Glad the GOP Kept Control of Congress

Question: Are you happy or unhappy that the Republican Party maintained control of the US Congress?

	Happy	Unhappy	Don't know
Everyone	65%	27%	8%
Religious Affiliation			
Total white Protestant	73	19	8
White Prot. Evangelical	77	15	8
White Prot. Non-Evanglical	67	25	8
White Catholic	59	32	9
Party ID			
Republican	95	4	1
Democrat	39	50	11
Independent	65	23	12
Lean Republican	88	6	6
Lean Democrat	42	41	17
1992 Presidential Vote			
Clinton	42	45	13
Bush	95	3	2
Perot	77	19	4
1996 Presidential Vote			
Clinton	39	49	12
Dole	97	2	1
Perot	69	19	12
1996 Congressional Vote			
Republican	89	7	4
Democrat	38	52	10

Source: Survey by the *Los Angeles Times*, November 5, 1996.

Contributors

General Editors

Regina M. Dougherty is a doctoral student in political science and research assistant, the Roper Center, University of Connecticut.

Everett C. Ladd is executive director and president, the Roper Center, and professor of political science, University of Connecticut.

David Wilber is assistant director, the Roper Center.

Lynn A. Zayachkiwsky is manager, Roper Center publications.

Editorial and Production Staff

Janice Berriault is head, design and production, Roper Center publications.

Cathy Cuneo is administrative assistant to the director, the Roper Center.

Pamela Hunter is a doctoral student in political science, and graduate assistant, the Roper Center, University of Connecticut.

Lisa Ferraro Parmelee is research librarian, the Roper Center.

Rob Persons is research librarian, the Roper Center.

Marianne Simonoff is research assistant to the director, the Roper Center.

Authors

Herbert E. Alexander is director of the Citizens' Research Foundation, and professor of political science, University of Southern California. He is co-author of *Financing the 1992 Election* (M.E. Sharpe, 1995).

Kenneth Dautrich is associate director, the Roper Center, and assistant professor of political science, University of Connecticut.

Mark DiCamillo is director, the Field Institute. Since 1978, he has worked with Mervin Field polling the opinions of Californians through the Field Poll.

Jody Newman was executive director of the National Women's Political Caucus, 1991-95 and political director of the Women's Campaign Fund, 1983-84. She is co-author of *Sex As a Political Variable: Women As Candidates and Voters in US Elections* (Lynne Rienner Publishers, 1997) .

Jim Norman is polling editor at *USA Today*, a position he has held since 1987. Before assuming this post, he contributed to the Washington section of the paper and was its original Weather Page editor.

Tom W. Smith is director of the General Social Survey, National Opinion Research Center, University of Chicago.

Michael Malbin is professor of political science at the State University of New York, Albany, and director for the Center for Legislative Studies at SUNY's Rockefeller Institute of Government. He is co-editor of *Limiting Legislative Terms* (Congressional Quarterly, 1992), and co-editor of *Vital Statistics on Congress* (Congressional Quarterly, 1996).